S0-ABD-762

American Literary Mentors

American Literary Mentors

Irene C. Goldman-Price and
Melissa McFarland Pennell, editors

University Press of Florida
Gainesville · Tallahassee · Tampa · Boca Raton
Pensacola · Orlando · Miami · Jacksonville

04 03 02 01 00 99 6 5 4 3 2 1

Library of Congress Cataloging-in-Publication Data

American literary mentors / Irene C. Goldman-Price and Melissa McFarland Pennell.
p. cm.
Includes bibliographical references and index.
ISBN 0-8130-1712-2 (alk. paper)
1. Mentoring of authors—United States. 2. American fiction—History and criticism. 3. Mentoring in literature. I. Goldman-Price, Irene C. II. Pennell, Melissa McFarland.
PS374.M47A44 1999
813.009—dc21 99-36103

The University Press of Florida is the scholarly publishing agency for the State University System of Florida, comprising Florida A&M University, Florida Atlantic University, Florida International University, Florida State University, University of Central Florida, University of Florida, University of North Florida, University of South Florida, and University of West Florida.

University Press of Florida
15 Northwest 15th Street
Gainesville, FL 32611–2079
http://www.upf.com

To Elsa Nettels, Ph.D., professor emerita of the College of William and Mary—teacher, scholar, mentor, colleague, and friend. The contributors join the editors in dedicating this collection to Dr. Nettels, a woman of great accomplishment and generosity, in honor of her recent retirement.

CONTENTS

PREFACE

This volume arose as a project to acknowledge the role that good mentoring has played in the careers of many literary scholars and academics and to honor one special mentor, Dr. Elsa Nettels, professor emerita of English at the College of William and Mary. We chose as our subject literary mentoring—how people encourage other people to produce literature—as a natural reflection of Professor Nettels's own lifelong talent. All of the contributors to the volume share an interest in American literature and have benefited in their professional lives from friendships with Elsa Nettels.

The volume should speak to literary scholars and students interested in American literature, and also to general readers who want to know more about the varying sources of inspiration and encouragement on which writers have drawn. Those interested in mentoring relationships in other fields should also find food for thought in these essays.

The editors wish to acknowledge their own mentors, in particular Dr. Elsa Nettels, to whom we dedicate this book. Over the years many literary scholars have gratefully acknowledged debts to her for professional, and sometimes personal, assistance. She has written letters for jobs, grants, awards, tenure, and promotion; she has fought adverse tenure decisions; she has shared sources, citations, and research skills generously. She has arranged numerous panels at conferences large and small, often inviting junior scholars to participate where they might not otherwise have had an opportunity to present their work. Her frequent reviews of other scholars' work are thorough, fair, and open-minded evaluations. Her warm encouragement and her criticism of new projects are always offered in the spirit of making an already good idea better. Her own scholarship, including *James and Conrad* (1977), *Language, Race, and Social Class in Howells's America* (1988), and *Language and Gender in American Fiction* (1997), as well as dozens of articles and conference presentations, sets a standard worthy of admiration and emulation.

For help with this project, we wish to acknowledge Carol Farley Kessler, Alan Price, Shirley Marchalonis, and Elizabeth Hayes for their helpful comments on the proposal and introduction to this volume, and to thank our acquisitions editor, Susan Fernandez, for picking up the project midway, and our project editor, Jacqueline Kinghorn Brown, for supporting it through to publication. Thanks to Jean Blackall for her assistance and support from the inception of the project, to Daniel Fogel for his suggestions on contributors, and to the English department of the College of William and Mary for their help in tracking down students and faculty who had worked with Elsa Nettels.

Irene Goldman-Price wishes to acknowledge Ball State University and the Pennsylvania State University—Hazleton campus for support of her research, and especially to thank Alan Price—first mentor, then friend, now husband—for his moral support and practical assistance.

Melissa McFarland Pennell wishes to acknowledge the University of Massachusetts Lowell for support of her research; she also thanks her husband, Steve Pennell, for his many kindnesses and encouragement.

Introduction

Irene C. Goldman-Price and Melissa McFarland Pennell

Whoever one's mentors are and have been, I begin to see that they take their places in the imagination like the statues of the saints above the Vatican. Or they act as the heel stone framed in the archways at Stonehenge. More likely they are the magnets in the many compasses an artist wears out over a lifetime. It is said that when human beings picture someone else, they place the person on a landscape about ten feet in front of them. Mentors cast light and shadow, complicate the foreground. Surely it is like falling in love. One needn't strain one's voice in order to speak nor cup one's ear to hear all that one's mentor has to say.

Deborah Digges (112)

"If I ever succeed in making anything of myself—as you seem to think I can—I will always count your letter as one of the principal means to that end." With these words Lizette Woodworth Reese welcomed Edmund Clarence Stedman as her mentor and guide. Over the course of their twenty-year friendship, he would praise her work, assist her in finding a publisher, advise her on preparing her manuscripts, and talk of her to his influential literary friends.

Whether it be insisting on more intellectual depth and solidity, as Edith Wharton did with Philomène de la Forest-Divonne, or undertaking the "honest, painstaking labor" of fair-minded criticism, as Marianne Moore did for Elizabeth Bishop and William Dean Howells did for so many younger writers, literary mentors in some way encourage, enable, and nurture creative expression and help an author negotiate the complicated pathway from creation to publication. Mentoring in general and as defined in the following essays takes a wide variety of forms. Mentors can give advice as to work habits, reading, and subject matter. They often introduce the protégé and his or her works to editors, publishers, critics, and other authors, using personal influence to get the work of the protégé into print. They offer truthful criticism mixed with sympathetic engagement in the lives and work of their protégés. As Diane George has described in the *Ohio Review,* her mentor "keeps on giving me permission to have feelings that I might actually write down instead of banishing them to remote islands of the unconscious . . . " (50). Mentors may provide an example, set a challenge, or lead by inspiring adulation. Some relationships are strong, intense, and exclusive, with the pair meeting frequently, while others may take the form of an occasional correspondence and rare meetings. The relationship may be rewarding or torturous to the mentor. It may continue for a lifetime, for only a brief period, or, as one of our essayists suggests, it may begin only beyond the realm of physical existence.

Metaphors abound for the ways in which one person can assist another in creative endeavor. As Deborah Digges says in the epigraph, a mentor can be seen as a magnet in the compass, the essential element that draws the arrow to true north. A mentor is a canonized saint, or perhaps author—someone whose life has been exemplary, whose worth and loyalty to the divine have been proven under duress, someone who now sits far above, offering inspiration but also, perhaps, an unreachable goal. A mentor is the heel stone, pointing to the rising sun just one day of the year, in that mysterious, mystical circle whose meaning, if we could unlock it, would explain the relation between earth and sky, between humans and the universe we inhabit, between inchoate inspiration and the words necessary to commit one's imagined world to paper. Mentors can appear to be the objects of an idealized or an eroticized love.

The term *mentor* is itself a metaphor, drawing on the role that Odysseus's friend played in bringing Telemachus into his manhood. It is worth noting that, in *The Odyssey,* Mentor is both a man and a vessel for Athene, the goddess of wisdom. As a human and an old friend of Odysseus's, Mentor can provide support for Penelope and Telemachus in keeping the suitors at bay, but it is not until Athene takes on Mentor's shape that s/he can engender the action that will send Telemachus on his journey in search of his father and thus allow his father's journey home. Mentor—man and god, male and female—gives Telemachus the courage to stand up to the suitors, to act independently of his mother, to question Nestor, to do the deeds necessary to bring his father home. When Telemachus hesitates, out of modesty and awe, to question Nestor, Mentor/Athene assures him that to question is his destiny: "For just this did you sail on the ocean to learn about your father / Where the earth has hidden him and what fate he has met" (3.15–16). Telemachus demurs, claiming that he has no experience in quick speech and that modesty becomes a young man addressing an elder. But "Then the bright-eyed goddess Athene spoke to him: / 'Telemachus, some thoughts you will have in your mind, / And a god will suggest others. For I do not think / You were born and raised without the favor of the gods'" (3.26–28). Thus Mentor/Athene affirms for the young man that his thoughts and words are divinely inspired and therefore to be trusted, and that the mission on which he has embarked is the proper one for him. When Mentor/Athene leads the way, Telemachus "[goes] along in the god's footsteps" (3.30).

This origin of the term suggests, then, that a mentor helps his or her protégé to gain access to divine guidance, serves as a vehicle through which guidance comes, and reassures the protégé that thoughts and actions will be fruitful. It might also suggest that, without such a mentor figure, the divine spark as well as the necessary guidance and advice might have no means of reaching the protégé. In that case, can a writer succeed as an entirely "self-made (wo)man"? Or will she or he languish, unproductive?

A number of recent scholarly books and one nonscholarly volume have explored the relationship between a writer and his or her teachers, patrons, and friends. Two of them are collections of essays by various scholars. Looking specifically at women writers and their male patrons, the essays in *Patrons and Protégées* (Marchalonis 1988) focus primarily on literary "friendships" of the 1840s to 1880s, examining issues of gender and hierarchy and suggesting previously unnoticed complexity in the relationships between prominent men and their (female) protégées, including Henry James and Constance Fenimore Woolson and William Dean Howells and Charlotte Perkins Gilman, among others. The essays are set in the context of gender relations and of the changing conditions of the literary marketplace. In the collection *Mothering the Mind* (Perry and Brownley 1984), various scholars raise issues concerning the ways in which "silent partners" create the conditions that "catalyze creative work" (4). Also placing their arguments in a gendered context, they explore relationships between the artist and supporting friends or relatives who perform such maternal functions as "intercepting the world, conferring unconditional approval, regulating the environment, supplying missing psychic elements, and mirroring certain aspects of the self of the artist" (6). In this metaphor of the relationship, deliberately juxtaposed with the more "insistent, judgmental, and directive exhortations" of literary fathering (14), the "mother" provides a nurturing space in which the child/artist can play in safety with benign approval.

The other two books are in-depth studies by single authors. David Laskin's *A Common Life* (1994) looks at the sometimes helpful, sometimes competitive friendships between four pairs of writers of relatively equal stature across the chronological spectrum of American literature. These relationships—Herman Melville and Nathaniel Hawthorne, Henry James and Edith Wharton, Katherine Anne Porter and Eudora Welty, and Elizabeth Bishop and Robert Lowell—while surely nurturant of creativity, are more all-encompassing than mentoring because of the quantity of nonprofessional time the writers spent together and the relative professional equality of the writers. But the complexity of the relationships makes an instructive study for those interested in how writers affect each other's careers.

Ideally, mentoring and guidance are straightforwardly helpful in nurturing an apprentice toward his or her goals. But, inevitably, as in all human interaction, emotions complicate matters. Prejudice or jealousy, the desire to dominate, the growing competence of the apprentice, or erotic attraction can skew the relationship, sometimes fueling greater productivity on the part of the apprentice, sometimes silencing the apprentice, often causing psychic damage and the breakdown of the relationship. In *Erotic Reckonings* (1994), a study of writers and their literary mentors who were also their lovers, Thomas Simmons contends that relationships of mastery and apprenticeship are inevitably erotic, modeled not after Mentor and Telemachus but rather Abelard and Héloïse. He looks at three pairs of poets and examines the complicated interactions of their personal and creative lives, finding not just support but also cruelty, theft of ideas, undermining of the other's career.

A more belle-lettristic exploration of literary mentoring came in the 1994 issue of *Ohio Review* (vol. 51), in which contemporary writers were invited to comment on their own experience of being mentored. They wrote of favorite teachers, of friends, of writers' groups, of authors whose works had inspired them or shown them the possibilities of language or subject matter. While Deborah Digges describes a constant process of taking on and then discarding mentors, David Lazar opines that "mentorship is usually a singular, if you will, monogamous, relationship. One can have many teachers, multiple and various influences, but to speak of more than one mentor . . . seems excessive, even a bit intellectually or emotionally promiscuous" (27).

It seems, then, that each protégé experiences mentorship in a distinctive and personal way; that encouragement, advice, inspiration, and other help comes in various, sometimes unexpected ways; and that the relationship has profound effects on both protégé and mentor.[1] *American Literary Mentors* seeks to extend the discussion begun in these works by exploring the mentoring relationship in the lives and works of a variety of American authors writing from the 1870s to the middle part of this century. We asked a group of scholars who we knew were interested in the subject to write for us, giving them free rein to choose the authors and works that spoke to them. The resulting essays give a rich and suggestive picture of the possibilities of the relationship and also offer a variety of approaches to the study. Some of the essays treat their subjects biographically, looking at how a particular author was or was not adequately mentored at important times in his or her development. Others look from the point of view of the literary mentor at what skills and personality traits are necessary to be a good guide for a fellow writer or artist. Some essays provide critical analyses of fictional accounts of mentoring relationships, discovering how authors have worked out imaginatively their own questions about mentors and protégés. Still others examine how encouragement and instruction can come from sources other than living human beings. The essays are representative in that they consider women and men; poets, novelists, and one diarist; editors and critics as well as creative artists; protégés and mentors. Together they present a well-rounded consideration of the origins and development of artistic ambition, craftsmanship, and productivity and of the complexities of the mentor/protégé relationship. They also suggest a variety of ways to examine these issues in the lives and works of other authors.

Although the time span covered by the essays was not deliberately chosen, changes occurred in the nature of authorship and publishing during the period from the 1870s to the 1960s in the United States, changes that made the role of mentor or guide most significant. A discussion of this period can help set a context for the essays. Authorship had just emerged as a profession in the early nineteenth century and remained in a state of flux during the post–Civil War era. Prior to the Civil War, as Shirley Marchalonis notes, "literary America was a small world of the eastern seacoast with three publishing centers: Boston, New York, and Philadelphia," and in this small world "the last great age of patronage" thrived as the literary establishment "supported itself, . . . inspected and judged new writers, and . . . perpetuated itself by letting in suitable members" (xi). For those within the establishment, personal relationships aided in the production of literary material, as printer-publishers engaged in long-term relationships with authors and provided, in some circumstances, advice and encouragement as well as remuneration. For those somewhat removed or not personally acquainted, however, a high degree of formality characterized the relationships, a pattern that lasted to the end of the century. Those outside the known circle, for instance, often received responses to inquiries and submissions in letters signed with a firm's name rather than an editor's. As Barbara Reitt explains, "The careful distance that the [editor and author] maintained could become particularly pronounced when the author was not a member of the circle of authors, scholars, publishers and other men of letters who formed the inner circle of the American literary establishment" (34). In 1860 a midwestern outsider like William Dean Howells found it necessary, as a young man of twenty-three, to seek and present letters of introduction from established New England authors to make inroads into Boston's literary marketplace.

Expansion and commercialization in the American publishing industry following the Civil War intensified the nationalization of literature. These factors also redefined relationships between authors, editors, and publishers, as the personal bonds that had characterized publishing during the prewar era began to crumble for all except the major authors. Though they had prided themselves on their status as "gentlemen" who had direct contact with the authors they published, many publishers, facing the new demands of a corporate culture and large-scale competition, became increasingly removed from the negotiations and communication with individual authors (Coultrap-McQuin 32). The greater role played by literary agents as negotiators in the publishing process by the end of the century altered the relationship between publisher and author (Tebbel 14). Though Walter Hines Page might argue that "the literary agent had no legitimate function once the author and publisher have become intimate" (Madison 161), John Tebbel suggests that "it became a question of two businessmen, agent and publisher, negotiating, while the editor-and-author relationship, with the publisher more and more removed, went on in the way now familiar in our time" (147). Thus, the old network of publisher-author relationships that once offered support and guidance was slowly giving way, declining further as the concept of "trade courtesy," which had regulated competition for authors' works at mid-century, also collapsed under the pressures of a new culture. Despite Tebbel's observation, even the editor-author relationship was not without its complexities and tensions generated by the changing practices of literary publishing. As Ellery Sedgwick indicates, editors felt increasing pressure from market forces to encourage writers to produce works that capitalized on current tastes and fashions, constraining the types of support and advice an editor might give.[2] Thus Stedman, Howells, Wharton, and Moore, as our essayists illuminate, provided truly necessary services by helping young writers to meet editors and publishers and by enticing the latter to read the work of their protégés. Moreover, they could at times offer advice and guidance less influenced by the demands of the marketplace.

Emerging authors in the late nineteenth century had to navigate a marketplace made more complex by the proliferation of magazines and the centralization of control in publishing houses.[3] Increased competition between publications that featured serious writing reflective of the values and concerns of "high culture" and those that catered to the tastes of the mass market and depended upon a steady stream of popular (but not necessarily good) writing forced writers to choose between satisfying the market, and thus earning money, or being true to their inner visions, to their authentic voices. Earlier in the century, some authors who ultimately became part of the literary establishment and whose work eventually entered the canon began their careers producing the "potboilers" that found a ready market in cheap periodicals and weekly papers. Opportunities to contribute to this market increased with the rise of the literary syndicates later in the century, tempting some authors away from "serious" but possibly less lucrative work. As Lichtenstein observes, "the advent of the literary syndicate had an immediate effect upon the relationship of the author to his work, his editor and the financial rewards of the industry" (40). Yet, by the 1880s, choosing to publish in syndicates and mass-market publications threatened one's potential for the successful placement of one's work in literary magazines and with respected publishers. Thus, novices depended on guidance from experienced authors and editors—in short, from mentors—to help them determine the appropriate career steps to take, as well as to help them develop their talents as writers and poets. The literary experiment imagined in Howells's *Hazard of New Fortunes* (1890), for instance, suggested ways for a business manager to assist both editor and contributors in producing a good literary product that would sell to the public.

The decades following the Civil War also witnessed marked changes, specifically in the experiences of women authors. Throughout the nineteenth century, women had expressed a sense of professionalism toward their work, but, in the second half, more gained entry into the publishing business through editorial work on magazines. While it made women known in the business, editorial work nevertheless posed a dual threat to a literary career, since the time it consumed could not be devoted to writing and a woman "might rise to a level of considerable responsibility within a firm without ever becoming well-known somewhere else" (Reitt 40).[4] Awareness of this threat to a promising career surely influenced Sarah Orne Jewett's 1908 remark to Willa Cather urging her to leave her position as managing editor of *McClure's:* "I cannot help saying what I think about your writing and its being hindered by such incessant, important, responsible work as you have in your hands now. I do think that it is impossible for you to work so hard and yet have your gifts mature as they should" (O'Brien 344).

Women in literary publishing still faced challenges that were influenced by gender expectations, not only at the turn of the century, but well into the modern period. To meet these challenges they depended on networks of support that included sympathetic editors as well as other women writers, often finding a significant mentor within one of these two groups. In *Doing Literary Business* (1990), Susan Coultrap-McQuin indicates that, among the women writers who did succeed, "each became confident enough of her own abilities to pass on advice to other authors, either through personal encouragement and mentoring . . . or through articles . . . on pursuing a literary career" (195). Unfortunately, those women who did not receive personal and professional support or find a mentor to guide them often struggled to fulfill their potential.

By the turn of the century, the rise of internationalism in literature (a phenomenon that affected the careers of writers like James and Wharton) added to the array of publishing outlets and professional contacts for authors, but it also increased the potential for isolation and the loss of regional literary communities. Literary work by its very nature entailed a level of isolation, and the loss of regional communities forced writers to identify with new groups forming around literary enterprises. While Howells and others acknowledged that authors' dinners and other celebratory events hosted by publishers provided advertising opportunities, these occasions also helped to reinforce a new sense of literary community centered around the publishing house rather than the regional literary center. The willingness of authors to attend these events (which began to replace the private "salons" of an earlier era) had as much to do with their need for connection to other writers as it did with the need to stay in the good graces of their publishers. For younger writers, these occasions also became opportunities to meet those with established literary reputations; the right mentor provided important avenues of contact at these galas.

Changes continued in the publishing industry throughout the modern period. Charles Madison refers to the years 1900–1945 as the era of "the commercialization of literature," though the seeds of this change had been planted in the last decades of the nineteenth century. Publishers such as Henry Holt "deplored the scrambling and scuffling to obtain best-selling authors" (Madison 161), while Frank Dodd asserted that books were selected for publication "for the credit of the house" (Tebbel 7), arguing that quality as well as salability still mattered. Many publishers began to incorporate practices from the syndicates, such as books written "on contract," and the advertising of books expanded to levels not imagined in the 1870s. In 1933 Edith Wharton wrote to Rutger B. Jewett, her editor and friend at Appleton and Co., "The fact is I am afraid that I cannot write down to the present standard of the American picture magazines. I am in as much need of money as everybody else at this moment and if I could turn out a series of potboilers for magazine consumption I should be only too glad to do so . . . " (*Letters* 572). Though there were exceptions, such as Wharton and Rutger Jewett, most publishers and editors no longer enjoyed sustained friendships with their authors, so that the depersonalization of the business of literary publishing continued.

Thus, as the publishing industry and the relationships it engendered changed profoundly over the course of a century, an author's need for guidance, supportive criticism, and encouragement remained, or even grew. As Richard Brodhead remarks, "No one appears in authorship without the prior achievement . . . of thinking him- or herself over from a person in general into that more specialized human self that is an author" (110). And no figure plays a more important role in supporting this transformation and the realization of its goals than does the literary mentor or guide.

The essays that follow concern themselves with numerous aspects of literary mentoring and comment on each other extensively. Presented chronologically, they begin with Robert J. Scholnick's investigation into a classic instance of mentoring, "'The last letter of all': Reese, Stedman, and Poetry in Late-Nineteenth-Century America," in which he contemplates Edmund Clarence Stedman's guidance of the younger, fledgling poet, Lizette Woodworth Reese. By looking at the letters between them, Scholnick chronicles the twenty-year friendship that begins with thirty-one-year-old Reese seeking reviews and help with her earliest books of poetry from the established writer and editor, to a much more secure Reese offering emotional support and loyalty to a dying widower in his seventies. The affection that grows between them, restrained by propriety, serves to inspire Reese to more and better poetry even as it assuages Stedman's sense of his own waning power as he grows older.

Two essays on William Dean Howells look more closely at the mentor than the fledgling writers—not surprisingly, perhaps, given Howells's own career as editor and "Dean" of American letters. Melissa McFarland Pennell, in "The Mentor's Charge: Literary Mentoring in Howells's Criticism and Fiction," combines biography and literary analysis as she looks at Howells's sense of the responsibilities of a mentor, both as he lived the role himself and as he depicts his character, the Reverend Mr. Sewell, in an anxiety-ridden avoidance of the role in the novel *The Minister's Charge.* Pennell finds that a crucial quality for a mentor is adequate self-confidence to give frank criticism and compassionate encouragement. In the essay that follows, "'In this particular instance I want *you*': The Booster as Mentor in *A Hazard of New Fortunes,*" Irene C. Goldman-Price explores a fictional mentor, Jonas Fulkerson, and looks at how his boosterism and business ethic provided successful guidance for publisher, editor, and contributors alike. This more modern treatment of literary endeavor takes place in New York City rather than in Boston, and although the novel is written only four years after *The Minister's Charge,* Fulkerson and his magazine seem to come from an entirely different era than the genteel Boston of Sewells's acquaintance. Thus we see the beginning of the change in publishing that affected much of the literary production in the period.

Henry and Alice James, successful brother and invalid sister, present an interesting contrast in creativity nurtured or frustrated in the same family. In "Henry James's Ghostly Mentors," Cheryl B. Torsney offers an intriguing critical/autobiographical look at ghosts in Henry James's fiction and at the ghost of Henry James who haunts her study. Examining some of the artist tales, *The Portrait of a Lady,* and her own experience as a student studying James, Torsney suggests that, for James, the best mentors are ghostly, that indeed ghosts, apparitions, and transcendent beings fill the void left behind by inadequate teachers. This idea is brought home forcibly by Esther F. Lanigan's essay on Alice James, "Negative Mentorship and the Case of Alice James," wherein she contends that Alice James's potential as a writer was thwarted by the very much living presence of her mother, Mary James. Only during Alice's trip abroad with her brother Henry, and later after her parents' deaths, did Alice achieve any kind of literary output. Comparing Lanigan's essay with the section on *The House of Mirth* in Carol Singley's essay on Edith Wharton and the section on *Lucy Gayheart* in Deborah Carlin's essay on Willa Cather reminds us of the vulnerability of women who fail to receive adequate mothering or mentoring.

On the other end of the spectrum from the sparse literary output of Alice James, Edith Wharton produced some forty-seven volumes of stories, novels, criticism, and travel writing in her life. Three of the essays here speak interestingly to each other in their explorations of Wharton as mentor and collaborator and of her fictional depictions of mentoring. They also reflect some of the insights offered by the essays on Howells and on Stedman and Reese. In "Female Models and Male Mentors in Wharton's Early Fiction," Julie Olin-Ammentorp, looking at two early stories by Wharton, finds that men's patronizing attitude toward women's intellectual efforts might be justified by the meager talent of the women, but nevertheless demonstrates an ambivalence by Wharton about the suitability of women in the literary world. Olin-Ammentorp suggests that here we have a young Wharton questioning her own vocation. Carol J. Singley examines, in a feminist context, three instances of collaboration in Wharton's life and work in her essay "Edith Wharton and Partnership: *The House of Mirth, The Decoration of Houses,* and 'Copy,'" and finds these instances rare and fraught with the possibility of betrayal or failure. She contends that Wharton exhibits a nostalgia for the possibilities of creative collaboration. But we find a much more mature, assured Wharton in Helen Killoran's "Meetings of Minds: Edith Wharton as Mentor and Guide." Killoran notes numerous instances of Wharton's helping other writers, insisting most firmly on intellectual solidity and on disciplined work habits. These essays together show Wharton's growth into self-confidence, and they create a multifaceted view of one writer's experience with mentoring.

Willa Cather wrote several novels in which young, talented artists (often singers) were befriended by professionals and helped on their way. And yet the results of the mentoring were not uniformly positive. Deborah Carlin, in her essay "'Someone young and teachable': Dimensions of Mentoring in the Fiction of Willa Cather," compares two very different kinds of mentoring in *The Song of the Lark* and *Lucy Gayheart* and speculates on why Cather never mentored anyone herself. Her analysis of the dimension of *eros* that can pervade a mentoring relationship speaks to the earlier, perhaps more innocent, relationship between Stedman and Reese. That Cather had to give up being an editor in order to be a writer and that she chose to write about artistic mentoring in terms of musical prodigies rather than literary ones may also speak to the increasingly economics-driven business of publishing.

Elizabeth Bishop was a college student writing a paper when she first contacted Marianne Moore in 1934. Margaret Wooster Freeman, in her essay "'Efforts of Affection': Mentorship and Friendship in Moore and Bishop," tells the story of the growth of this friendship and speculates about how and why it changed as Bishop became more self-assured as a poet. Like the essay on Stedman and Reese, Freeman's study offers a rich investigation into a long-term, changing relationship between two writers and, like the combined essays on Wharton, it offers a look into the maturation of a writer.

And, with the final essay on Eudora Welty, we return to the possibilities of guidance by the already dead. In "Eudora Welty: The Silent Mentors," Jean Frantz Blackall suggests that, though Welty was richly blessed with living supporters of her writing, she saw herself at times as writing in isolation. Blackall contends that the influence of Welty's reading comes out in her writing, and she makes a strong case for Welty having learned much about the possibilities of her craft by reading Jane Austen and Willa Cather. The Cather of this essay, mentoring silently through her writing, has greater presence in light of Carlin's essay on Cather's imaginative treatment of mentoring.

Thus these essays offer a variety of approaches to the subject of literary mentoring. They suggest that encouraging creativity and nurturing an artistic career can be pleasurable but also difficult activities for the mentor; sometimes people discover that they are not up to the challenges of supporting another's efforts. Mentoring can be helpful—even vital—to the apprentice writer but also possibly dangerous to the point of being fatal. The absence of mentoring can also be deadly, or it can spur creative self-nurturance. The following essays, in their variety of approaches, together create a textured conversation and suggest fruitful ways for critics and readers to explore the careers and works of writers in a continuing search for the sources of successful literary production.

Notes

1. A new book on mentoring is worth noting here for those interested in the wider subject. Necessarily idealistic, Marsha Sinetar's *The Mentor's Spirit: Life Lessons on Leadership and the Art of Encouragement* (1998) explores mentoring as a spiritual activity, a way that society transmits its sacred values. Sinetar defines the mentor's spirit as "an unseen, affirming influence and positive energy. The mentor's spirit is the heart's posture pervading healthy relationships in every family, classroom, organization, and town. . . . When the mentor's spirit is absent, we find dependency, an erosion of optimism, and impaired problem solving" (1). Because the authors—and their characters—treated in *American Literary Mentors* are profoundly human, and thus flawed, their experiences of mentoring don't often live up to this ideal. Still, as an ideal, Sinetar's thoughts on the subject are worth contemplation.

2. See his "Horace Scudder and Sarah Orne Jewett: Market Forces in Publishing in the 1890s" for a discussion of the way this effort on the part of editors could lead to either great success or dismal failure.

3. See Charvat's *Profession of Authorship in America* and Brodhead's *Culture of Letters,* especially chapter 3: "Starting Out in the 1860s: Alcott, Authorship and the Postbellum Literary Field."

4. See Reitt's description of the career of Susan Francis at Houghton Mifflin, who found herself the "eternal assistant."

Works Cited

Brodhead, Richard H. *The Culture of Letters: Scenes of Reading and Writing in Nineteenth-Century America.* Chicago: University of Chicago Press, 1993.

Charvat, William. *The Profession of Authorship in America.* Ed. Matthew Bruccoli. Columbus: Ohio State University Press, 1968.

Coultrap-McQuin, Susan. *Doing Literary Business: American Women Writers in the Nineteenth Century.* Chapel Hill: University of North Carolina Press, 1990.

Digges, Deborah. "The Waiting Room Door." *Ohio Review* 51 (1994): 112–19.

George, Diane Hume. "A Vision of My Obscured Soul." *Ohio Review* 51 (1994): 41–52.

Homer. *The Odyssey.* Trans. Albert Cook. New York: Norton, 1974.

Laskin, David. *A Common Life: Four Generations of American Literary Friendship and Influence.* New York: Simon and Schuster, 1994.

Lazar, David. "On Mentorship." *Ohio Review* 51 (1994): 25–33.

Lichtenstein, Nelson, "Authorial Professionalism and the Literary Marketplace, 1885–1900." *American Studies* (Lawrence, Kansas) 19, no.1 (spring 1978): 35–53.

Madison, Charles A. *Book Publishing in America.* New York: McGraw-Hill, 1966.

Marchalonis, Shirley, ed. *Patrons and Protégées: Gender, Friendship, and Writing in Nineteenth-Century America.* New Brunswick, New Jersey: Rutgers University Press, 1988.

O'Brien, Sharon. *Willa Cather: The Emerging Voice.* New York: Fawcett Columbine, 1988.

Perry, Ruth, and Martine Watson Brownley, eds. *Mothering the Mind: Twelve Studies of Writers and Their Silent Partners.* New York and London: Holmes and Meier, 1984.

Reitt, Barbara B. "Editorial Occupations of the American Book Trade in the 1880s and 1890s." *Book Research Quarterly* 4, no. 2 (summer 1988): 33–46.

Sedgwick, Ellery. "Horace Scudder and Sarah Orne Jewett: Market Forces in Publishing in the 1890s." *American Periodicals* 2 (1992): 79–88.

Simmons, Thomas. *Erotic Reckonings: Mastery and Apprenticeship in the Works of Poets and Lovers.* Urbana and Chicago: University of Illinois Press, 1994.

Sinetar, Marsha. *The Mentor's Spirit: Life Lessons on Leadership and the Art of Encouragement.* New York: St. Martin's, 1998.

Tebbel, John. *A History of Book Publishing in the United States.* Vol. 2. *The Expansion of an Industry, 1865–1919.* New York: Bowker, 1975.

Wharton, Edith. *The Letters of Edith Wharton.* Ed. R. W. B. and Nancy Lewis. New York: Scribner's, 1988.

"The last letter of all"

Reese, Stedman, and Poetry in Late-Nineteenth-Century America

Robert J. Scholnick

In 1887 Lizette Woodworth Reese (1856–1935), a high school English teacher in Baltimore, contracted with a local firm, Cushing and Bailey, to publish her first book of poems, *A Branch of May*. Of the run of three hundred copies, she secured commitments from one hundred subscribers, sent twenty to potential reviewers and other important "literary men and women," and sold the rest, enabling her to come out slightly ahead on expenses (*Victorian Village* 245). Commenting on the historic significance of this "obscure publication," Louise Bogan wrote in 1951 that "the first signs of feminine song from a true source were so fragile that they were easily overlooked," but Reese's book "announced the new feminine sincerity of emotion and approach. Miss Reese . . . wrote her lyrics well outside the conventional literary scene, in what were then rural and provincial surroundings. She conveyed her emotions by means of an almost weightless diction and by a syntax so natural that its art was very nearly imperceptible" (21). Reese would spend the rest of her life in Baltimore, but her decision to send the book to certain of the nation's important literary figures reflected her understanding that, if she were to sustain a career, she would need their criticism and support.

Like many other aspiring poets during these years, Reese sent a copy of her book to Edmund Clarence Stedman (1833–1908), the New York poet, anthologist, and critic, who in 1885 had published his comprehensive critical history, *Poets of America*. The leading critic and champion of poetry in his day, Stedman used his influence with editors and publishers to support younger writers. Reese recalled that he responded to her with a letter that was so "kind and sympathetic" that she wrote him that "If I ever succeed in making something of myself—as you seem to think I can—I will always count your letter as one of the principal means to that end"

(*Victorian Village* 246).[1] Stedman became Reese's literary advisor and guide; their close, intimate friendship ended only with his death in 1908. An examination of their correspondence, which has been preserved at Columbia University, sheds light on the career of this early modern poet; on the difficult situation for poetry when Reese came of age, a period that Stedman had called "the twilight of the poets"; and on the dynamics of the mentoring relationship (*Poets of America* 475). Why did that initial letter from Stedman mean so much to Reese? In what ways did his support make a difference for her career? Why did he devote so much energy to her? Why did he find the relationship with Reese so satisfying that, as he wrote her shortly before he died, he counted her among his "most beloved friends"?

Born in rural Waverly, outside Baltimore, Reese did not have the benefit of higher education. Never married, she supported herself by teaching, first in a private country school and then in the Baltimore public high schools. Not until 1921, after forty-eight years, was she able to leave the classroom. But she saw the value of having been, in her words, "a working woman for so long, for having been a part of the common lot, for reaping experiences which a thousand others were reaping alongside of me; best of all, for making and keeping a good many secure friendships" (*Victorian Village* 235).

The author of fourteen books of poetry in all, Reese was the oldest of an accomplished generation of women poets that includes Louise Guiney (1861–1920), Adelaide Crapsey (1878–1914), Sara Teasdale (1884–1933), Edna St. Vincent Millay (1892–1950), and Louise Bogan (1897–1970). Alicia Suskin Ostriker has characterized the work of these poets as "artistically self-conscious, highly crafted, and musical. Abstractions wane. . . . Clarity and irony replace the ornate fogginess of the mid-century. Much of this poetry is, of course, about love, but love now includes passion and physical sensation. The world itself now is seen as irreducibly physical, and the self is no longer identified as undefined yearning spirit." Ostriker credited these poets with having produced "the first substantial body of lyric poetry which is worth anything in the United States" (44, 46).

As Bogan recognized, Reese's mature style was evident early on, in *A Branch of May*, where she brought precision and objectivity to the study of the natural world, which she explored in both its fecundity and destructiveness, its beauty and even its terror. Eschewing sentimentality, she broke with the convention that the contemplation of nature leads directly to God. Further, she found fresh ways to speak of women's experience, as in "A Song," which uses a playful, ironic tone as a counterpoint to the treatment of disappointment in love:

The year's a little older grown;
    And fair white boughs by green ways blown
In these new days are no more known.
    (Oh, who can bring the May again?)

And we are wiser grown, we two.
Our story's told; each word was true;
And you love me, and I love you.
    (Oh, who can bring the May again?)
Was it not sweeter ere we knew?
Yet who can bring the May again?
(*A Branch of May* 6)

If, as Gilbert and Gubar have written, the challenge for the female poet at this time was to be "assertive, authoritative, radiant with powerful feelings while at the same time absorbed in her own consciousness—and hence, by definition, profoundly 'unwomanly,' even freakish," Reese met the challenge, surmounting the cultural "contradictions between her vocation and her gender" (xxii).

In sending a copy of *A Branch of May* to Stedman, Reese selected the person who was in the best position to advance her literary career. In *Poets of America,* after depicting the "dynamic insufficiency of our present metrical literature," he concluded that "the belief scarcely can be resisted that there is, if not a decadence, at least a poetic interregnum." However, Stedman encouraged younger poets, whom he urged to develop a dramatic style, one capable of exploring life's inherent conflicts. He offered particular support to women poets, whom he credited with excelling their male counterparts "in perception of the finer details of life and nature." In fact, he claimed that women poets were leading the way toward the poetic revival that yet must come: "a general advance is just as evident in their poetry as in the prose fiction for which they are held in honor throughout the English-speaking world" (457, 447–48).

Stedman received approximately one volume per week from aspiring poets eager to gain his criticism and support. Since he earned his living as a broker on Wall Street and also had undertaken a series of demanding critical and editorial projects, his time was severely constrained. Reese's first book came to him when he was editing the eleven-volume *Library of American Literature.* He responded with a form letter to most of those who sought his assistance, stating that he was unable to read the manuscript and offer criticism, but when a promising writer, such as Reese, Edwin Arlington Robinson (1869–1935), William Vaughn Moody (1869–1910), or

Josephine Preston Peabody (1874–1922), came to his attention, he could not hold back.

On Thanksgiving Day 1887, he wrote Reese:

> At last I have a spare day, & can thank you for the gift of your volume—"A Branch of May"—which I have read from first to last, without finding a poem that has not a certain exquisiteness or a line that hasn't some beauty of its own. That is something which one can very rarely say of a latter-day book of verse; and I get many & much larger books of verse, from new authors, every week in the year!
>
> Artistic, & full of thought & color, as your poems are, I do not see that they are very *American*—except a few of which the lovely "Anne" (Sudbury Lane, Old Style) is perhaps the most notable. They might have been written . . . by some choice pupil of the English art school. Now, you have the gift & taste to enable you to make what you choose of yourself. I believe in the universal franchise of the poet—he has a right to draw his themes & feeling from the world at large. But if you want to make an *impression*—to have the people everywhere listen to your song, you must discover your own new & special touch, motive, field, method. What these are, no one can indicate for you, but you must discover them—and you will not regret having done so, in the end.

Stedman unhesitatingly told her just what she most needed to hear: that she could "make" whatever she wanted of herself. Characterizing her work as not "very *American*," he challenged her to break from the British "art school," the line from Keats and Tennyson to the Pre-Raphaelites, and thereby find her own way.

As a provincial, isolated poet who learned her art on her own, Reese had apprenticed herself to an essentially British tradition—from the authors of the early ballads to Herrick, Keats, Poe, Elizabeth Barrett Browning, Dante Rossetti, and Christina Rossetti. Like others in her situation, she tended to approach the English tradition with excessive reverence. To the extent that the tradition came to Reese and her contemporaries largely through anthologies, such as Palgrave's *Golden Treasury*, there was the added danger, as David Perkins has remarked, that the "past and present of England [would come before the mind] in one dazzling, wholly intimidating, mass. England had, it seemed, cultural advantages that drab America lacked" (91).

In questioning the Americanness of her poetry, Stedman in effect suggested that Reese not listen for echoes of British poetry in her American poetic garden, as in, for instance, "Sweet Weather," but rather render her world directly, in her own voice. In her 1896 "To a Town Poet," which Stedman included in his *American Anthology* (1900), Reese counsels the young urban poet—she herself now worked and lived in the expanding city—to "Snatch the departing mood," and thereby realize that wherever one lives, "Your verse awaits you there." "Let trick of words be past," she concludes, "Strict with the thought, unfearful of the form" (611). Stedman's advice may well have reinforced the stylistic direction already evident in her poetry toward simplicity, compression, and purity of statement. In 1929 she would recall her realization that "the Victorians had a full cup and it spilled over. Their faults were over elaboration and sentimentality" (*Victorian Village* 208). Stedman had made this point in *Victorian Poets* in 1875, and reiterated it in *Poets of America* a decade later.

How, then, should Reese respond to Stedman's initial letter? What precisely did he mean in suggesting that she modify her style "to make an *impression*?" How would he define an *American* style? Should she engage him in a discussion of style? That question may have been responsible for a delay of over three months, until March 5, when she wrote him:

> A little while before Christmas I mailed you my book of poems [*A Branch of May*], and received in return a letter so brimful of encouragement and kind wishes that I must heartily thank you for it.
>
> If I ever succeed in making anything of myself—as you seem to think I can—I will always count your letter as one of the principal means to that end.
>
> Respectfully,
> Lizette Woodworth Reese.

Through that final sentence, which echoed Stedman's letter to her, Reese invited his continuing support and guidance.

Shortly thereafter, Reese took the initiative in establishing a personal relationship, requesting on April 16, 1888, that Stedman send her "one of your pictures, and when you send it, please write your name on the back of it. I want to put it into an ivory and gold frame, and stand it up in my parlor." Not put off by her directness, on April 25 Stedman offered both a photograph and an engraving. He concluded by remarking that "I was very much gratified to see you have a friendly and discriminating notice in *The Critic*," the New York literary weekly of which he was a mainstay. (The review had appeared on April 14, 1888.) Although I have no documentary evidence, it is likely that Stedman encouraged the editors, his friends Jeannette Gilder and Joseph Gilder, to review Reese's volume. Stedman himself figures in the notice. Here is an excerpt:

> There is an important distinction to be made between imitation prepense, and that scarcely conscious, though evident, imitation which is born of ardent enthusiasm. The former is sterile, is an end in itself; the latter may be a phase of artistic growth, presenting indications of the greatest promise. This seems to us the case in the slender, soberly-clad book entitled "A Branch of May." That Miss Reese has been much-influenced by the Rossettis is evidenced . . . by the exotic fragrance of such poems as "A Spinning Song" . . . and the dramatic, but crude, "Death Potion." . . . These belong distinctly to what Mr. Stedman has called "the Stained-Glass School." But what strikes one as essential is the writer's instinct for melody and unusually keen sense of beauty. These pages are all a-flush with pure color. . . . Could anything be better than "Sweet Weather" and "After the Rain"? . . . Setting aside thought of the future, we must confess our great pleasure in the present phase. A delicate aesthetic melancholy pervades the poems, but now and again a deeper tone is unmistakable. (n.s. 14: 177)

Reflecting Stedman's warning in his letter about the echoes of the "art school" in her verse, this is precisely the sort of review that is calculated to serve a young artist profitably. Stedman may also have mentioned *A Branch of May* to his friend William Dean Howells, whose perceptive notice appeared in his "Editor's Study" column in *Harper's* in September 1888. Quoting "Sunset," Howells praised Reese's "close, loving, and vivid picture(s) of nature," in which "the attitude of the poet mainly supplies the human interest" (77: 638–42).

Stedman and his wife, Laura, entertained regularly during these years, making their home something of a social center for artistic New York. At some point Reese made the first of what she would recall as "occasional" visits to the Stedmans, "first at [their] New York house in Fifty-seventh Street, and afterwards at the one on a hillside in Bronxville, which suburb had lately been developed. Everybody of consequence as artist, novelist, poet came back and forth to these unlocked, cheerful doors, raw young writers like myself, seasoned writers, and old, eager friends ready to renew past companionships. It was like one of those gay and friendly London mansions in the flashing eighteenth century" (*Victorian Village* 246–47). Another frequent visitor, the poet Harriet Monroe (1860–1933), the founder of *Poetry,* recalled the warmth of those gatherings, noting that Stedman took special pains to introduce younger writers to the veterans. Others who attended, she recalled, included Howells, as well as Richard Watson Gilder (1844–1909), editor of the *Century,* and his associate, Robert

Underwood Johnson (1853–1937). The *Century* published Reese's "Daffodils" in April 1890. Later that year Thomas Wentworth Higginson and Ella H. Bigelow included the poem in their collection, *American Sonnets* (1890), published by Houghton Mifflin (185). If one function of the mentor is to help the neophyte to associate comfortably (and profitably) with established figures, then Stedman served Reese admirably. The Stedmans' gatherings also helped her to form friendships with such contemporaries as the poet Edith Thomas (1854–1925), who, Reese recalled, pointedly warned her to avoid archaic expression (*Victorian Village* 248).

On November 12, 1889, Reese told Stedman that "A friend has given me a copy of Mr. Sharp's 'American Sonnets,' and I find—on reaching the R's—that one of mine has been included. I am very much obliged to you for remembering me and for telling Mr. Sharp about my sonnet." The British writer William Sharp had selected "Tell Me Some Way" for the collection, which he dedicated to Stedman as "the foremost American critic." The poem develops what would become a familiar theme in her work: disappointment in love. Writing on December 12, Stedman told Reese that he was not responsible for placing the sonnet, but confessed to having praised her work when Sharp had visited him. He then inquired about recent work and publishing plans:

> My Dear Sibylla,
>
> 'Tis just a month since I got your pretty note. Meantime I have been through rather deep waters, with illness of my own—& the death of a dear & beautiful mother—and am just picking up the tangled skein of life again.
>
> No: you are indebted solely to the quality of your work for the compliment paid you by my friend (& recent visitor) William Sharp. While he was our guest, I told him something about you—but his book was issued before I ever met him.
>
> I saw, somewhere, an item that you were soon to bring out another collection of your poems. If this be so, will you kindly tell me how soon it will appear? If not, can't you lend me cuttings of one or two of your lyrics, which you consider the most noteworthy, printed *since* the date of your volume?

Welcoming his involvement with her planning for her next volume, Reese, on December 14, sent him five new poems. Not coincidentally Stedman included two new poems by Reese in the final volume of *A Library of American Literature,* "In Sorrow's Hour" and "The Garden at Bemerton," as well as "Anne" from *A Branch of May* (11: 329–30). In just two years, Stedman had helped Reese establish herself as a poet with a growing national reputation.

Reese now faced the challenge of finding an established publisher who could do justice to a second volume. It was one thing for her to self-publish the first book, but it would be quite another if she were forced to do the same with the second. Most likely Stedman and Reese discussed the matter when he visited Baltimore in June 1890, possibly to make arrangements for the Turnbull Lectureship in Poetry at Johns Hopkins, which he inaugurated the next year. When Stedman returned to Baltimore for the lectures, the two had somewhat more time to consider her publishing plans. Would she include *A Branch of May* in the new volume? What could Stedman do? On March 22, 1891, Reese wrote accepting Stedman's offer to act as her literary agent:

> I enclose my Ms. with this. C. Y. Turner, the artist, is anxious to illustrate the poems for me. However, the publishers generally do what they please in the matter. I have promised to mention Mr. Turner, and so I keep my promise. Mr. Stedman, I have done my best in writing these verses; I feel sore whenever I think about them. I feel sore because I wish they were so much better.
>
> But I am very, very slow; it takes me a year to absorb an idea that other people only take an hour to absorb. Some day I may do better.
>
> You see I enclose my old book. I am glad you are so kind to me.
>
> Sincerely,
> Lizette Woodworth Reese.
>
> Perhaps they would rather publish the new verse in a separate edition. The title for new or for old and new together, is "A Handful of Lavender."

On March 24, in seeking to clarify the question of whether Reese had sent the book to publishing houses, Stedman used yet another name in addressing her:

> Dear Gemina,
>
> I don't know whether they teach Latin in schools like yours, but, if you *do*, you will know why I call you *Gemina*! I give a select few of my lady correspondents pet-names: for example, I have among them Hypatia, Parthenia, Titania, & Egeria. But you are Gemina, by your own confession.
>
> Your *Mss.* reached me, with your letter, & I have read some of the poems. They are *all* remarkably and daintily finished, and where

> you get your quaint atmosphere and thoughts is more than I know. I see you have a noteworthy care for, & choice of, *words*. A fine & unusual trait. But I write to know if I misunderstand you. I thought you said these poems were *now* at the Harpers, and I told you that you might entrust them to me if they should send them back. Did they do so? I ask, because I do not wish, of course, to offer them *there* if they already have examined & declined them. In short, has *any* house as yet considered them? If so, what firm or firms?

Since Reese was a twin, Gemina was not an inappropriate nickname; yet one winces at Stedman's habit of giving pet names only to his female correspondents. He had addressed her as Sibylla, and though it may seem that he was placing her in the traditional female role of muse or Sibyl, inspirer of others, that is unlikely, since he had committed himself to promoting her poetic development. His use of the term *Sibylla* may have been a way to acknowledge that Reese had become her own muse. Still, there is a gendered response in his reference to her work as "daintily finished"—not a remark that he would apply to work by a male poet. Reese did not accept such limitations, writing approvingly of strong, subversive women, such as "Nina":

> She was a woman like a candle-flame—
> This stranger dead a score of years ago—
> Tall, clearly dark. We loved, but said not so,
> The slowness and the music of her name.
> A widow. She was kind, the women knew,
> And lent them patterns of her violet frocks;
> And she had lovers. Past her high, crabbed box,
> Went the sour judge, the rosy doctor, too.
> Once, twice, a black word pricked the country-side.
> She heard, and held a flower up to her lips,
> Spoke brightly of our town, its small, close life:
> On a wild morning of a sudden she died.
> The next, a loud man, with the air of ships,
> Stood at her coffin head: she was his wife.
> (*White April* 45)

In the introduction to *An American Anthology,* which generously represents works by women, Stedman reflects the somewhat contradictory contemporary expectations for women's poetry—speaking of their work as "exquisite, some of it as strong as sweet; indeed, a notable portion of our treasure-trove would be missing if their space in the present volume were otherwise filled" (xxvii).

Apologizing to Stedman on March 27 for not informing him about her efforts to find a publisher, Reese spoke of the difficult situation for poetry:

> I am sorry that I was so stupid as not to tell you about Harper's. They returned it with these words—"Although our readers have spoken in some respects favorably of 'A Handful of Lavender,' we do not feel encouraged to undertake its publication." And also—"We have for several years published but little in the way of poetry—in fact our publishing a poetical work has been a rare exception and the trade has come to look to other houses for new issues in that department of literature. In view of this fact," etc. etc. Also, they advised me to try Houghton Mifflin & Co.
>
> I have tried *only* Harper's.
>
> I am very glad that you are pleased with the verses. I enclose a sonnet written within the last two days to be put amongst the rest. All of the verse (apart from about eight) have been published in various magazines etc.
>
> Thank you for all the kind words you have to say. I am not sure if my English is good—where I got it except out of my prayer-book. It seems to me that people—as a rule—brought up upon a liturgical form of worship use better language than those brought up without it.

Stedman told Reese that he would try his own publisher, Houghton Mifflin, but warned that "I am in grave doubt as to success with that firm. Some months ago they declined to take a volume of poetry by a long-time favorite, although acknowledging that the standard was high & a moderately good sale would be sure. They said that their list of authors & books was so unwieldy that they could make no *additions* to it except in the case of *exceptionally* important works. . . . I suppose the real trouble is that the big houses wish to compete for British authors, under the new copyright law."

As far as I know, this is the first indication that the passage of international copyright not long before worked *against* American authors.

In sending Reese a publisher's letter acknowledging the receipt of the manuscript on April 1, Stedman again cautioned her: "I have little hope of getting you on their list at this time, as their list is very large already. However, I am trying, you see, the best house *first*." His contact at the firm was Horace Scudder (1838–1902), also editor of the *Atlantic Monthly*, to whom Stedman praised Reese's work in the strongest terms. Two days later Reese saw the power of Stedman's advocacy when she received through him a letter from the firm expressing its willingness to consider the volume. She acknowledged to him that a poet in her situation would be powerless without such an advocate:

> I got a kind little note from you on Tuesday, and started to answer it; but I was too stupid (I have not been well all this week), to say in it just what I wished, and so put it by for a while. . . . This morning another note (inclosing one from Houghton & Co.), reached me, and I shall try to thank you as you deserve . . . .
>
> No, I don't suppose Houghton & Co will put me on their list. I am quite sure, too, that if *I* had mailed them the Ms, they would have returned it unopened. I am afraid I owe you so much I will never be able to pay you.
>
> I hope you are not giving yourself too much trouble over those verses of mine.

On April 26, Scudder asked Stedman if Reese was "a poet who can afford the luxury of paying for publication? . . . *Entre nous* I have a pretty hard time of it usually getting a volume of verse through. This is an evil and adulterous generation that seeketh after a sign other than the existence of the spirit of poetry in a book." But such was Stedman's authority and such was Scudder's persuasiveness that, along with Laura Stedman's timely intervention of replying in her husband's absence that no, Reese could not afford a subvention, the Boston firm accepted the book without one—as Stedman explained in a letter to Reese on May 3. Assuming other functions of the mentor, in that letter Stedman attempts to instruct her on the mysteries of negotiating with the publisher; taking care of the niceties of literary politics; and the importance of not becoming identified as Stedman's protégée. In a moment of exuberance, he predicts that she will now have a place on Houghton Mifflin's list "for life," a prediction that did not come about. The firm declined her fourth book, *A Wayside Lute,* which Thomas Mosher of Portland, Maine, published in 1909. Stedman also urges her to write "fewer sonnets if you wish continued success—a career."

Perhaps Stedman counseled Reese not to write sonnets because the form had become all too familiar. William Sharp, in the introduction of *American Sonnets,* remarked that the sonnet "has flourished in America mightily in the last three decades. It is now, probably, the favourite form of at least two-thirds of the younger poets and versifiers overseas" (xxii). The almost simultaneous appearance of his *American Sonnets* and

Higginson and Bigelow's identically titled volume reflects a sonnet mania. In thanking Stedman on May 4, Reese told him of her decision not to write more sonnets, a promise, which, fortunately, she did not keep:

> God bless you. I have just written Houghton Mifflin & Co. my acceptance of their kind offer, and also a little note to the kind Mr. Scudder.
>
> It is *you*, however, who deserve all the thanks. I feel quite sure my good luck is due entirely to you. If you had not written that "strenuous" letter, and done so much in other ways to encourage and help me, I feel that everybody else and everything else would have been nought. I am not going to write any more sonnets unless I can help it, and I thank you for telling me about it. I do so *love* a lyric, that I intend to see whether my Muse won't always inspire me to write *that* and nothing else. No, I will say nothing about your helping me with the book; I understand how you feel about it. It shall be one of my secrets to remember how good and kind you are.
>
> I have told the publishers about my re-copied Ms., paging, etc. (You suggested my doing so.) . . .
>
> And now, goodbye, my dear Mr. Stedman. Remember me to Mrs. Stedman, and thank her for me for writing what she did to the publishers. I enclose Mr. Scudder's letter. I am glad you let me read it. God bless you.

Stedman had every reason to be pleased with *A Handful of Lavender,* which, in addition to the thirty-three poems from *A Branch of May,* included forty-three new poems. He told Reese on October 4 that "I like your verse better than ever, now it is all together between covers. The *tone* of the collection is unbroken throughout, & very individual. I am sure it will attract and charm. You have done wisely to alternate the Sudbury lyrics, throughout the book, with the sonnets. It is well adjusted. And now you are on tiptoe to see what the critics will say? So am I. But I think you will find favor & readers. I am glad to receive the 'first of all' copy, & to be your friend, & by and by you shall come on & cement the friendship *chez nous*?" In a postscript, he requested that she "*Please*" send him "a photograph, to go with your book."

Since *A Branch of May* was no longer available, the decision to include it as part of *A Handful of Lavender* proved wise. Reviewers treated the new book as a debut volume. In December 1891, the *Atlantic,* which would publish seven of her poems over the next decade, noted that the volume is "full of fine thought and an elevated spirit" (68: 845). And, in its review of December 12, 1891, the *Critic* asserted that Reese's poems "are sure to captivate every reader who loves verse that is full of fancy and sentiment expressed in a simple and natural manner" ("Miss Reese" 330).

Despite the critical success of *A Handful of Lavender,* Reese's material situation did not change. Her verse could not support her, and few, if any, career options were open to poets as poets, male or female. She had no choice but to keep her teaching position, despite its heavy demands and poor pay. Stedman continued to promote her work, but there was little that he could do that would fundamentally change her situation. Still, their friendship deepened. She looked to both Stedmans—each in different ways—for emotional support and affection, and developed the habit of writing to each separately.

Telling Stedman on October 26, 1891, that she would soon send him a photograph, Reese flirted: "I shall be very careful in wrapping it so that it won't reach you with a mark across the eyes, or the impress of a United States stamp on some other part of the body." Responding on November 15, 1891, Stedman saw in her picture a woman who had achieved a remarkable victory over the pain of rejection in love: "Yes, my minstrel lass of Sudbury, I *did* indeed receive your bright new photograph, & am grateful thereof—though methinks 'tis somewhat graver than your wont, & as of a maiden who has thought & suffered—and so of more account, & of truer beauty, than of one who has found life all roses and candy. (I do not know who he was, but he was not worthy of you, & his chief use in life was to be the poor means of raising you quite above him.)"

On November 12, Reese told Stedman of her pleasure at the "very, very favorable" reviews of *A Handful of Lavender,* writing that "the *un*favorable ones have done me a great deal of good, and I feel in very good humor with all the universe." However, less than a month later she confessed that a recent illness was enough "to make me dread a return of an old enemy of mine—nervous prostration." Reflecting their developing closeness, she sent him a sprig of lavender, perhaps in response to the heliotrope that he had sent her in October. She promised to visit "the 'dear and good' Stedmans (if they be settled or not), and . . . bid them a Merry and Happy New Year."

In thanking Stedman the next November for the gift of *The Nature and Elements of Poetry,* his Johns Hopkins lectures, Reese told him that she would "keep it in my own room and for Sunday afternoons; and I know it is going to help and comfort me." Taking exception to his reference in the inscription to himself as a "gray beard," she wrote that "neither you nor Mrs. Stedman will ever be *old.*" Several weeks later she reported that she was reading his "noble book" while sitting at the bedside of her fatally ill brother. There would be no need for Stedman to respond: "Just imagine I have met you on the street and told you all these things." She learned his size from his secretary and, as she wrote shortly before Christmas 1892, she knitted a shawl "for your pretty shoulders," enabling her to embrace him. He gave her a "beautiful memorandum book" for which she thanked him with the comment that "I hardly ever buy myself pretty things, so this is one of them I would forever [have] done without only that you were sweet enough to send it to me." Providing the space in which to do her work, the gift symbolized Stedman's confidence in her creative powers—despite a recent fallow period.

A visit to the Stedmans the next spring gave Reese a sense of artistic renewal: "I really believe I am about to take up my writing again," she wrote on April 13, 1893. "I feel so much better and stronger in body and spirit. I am 'honing' to get hold of my little memorandum book, and write something that will be worth keeping therein. I have already set about copying a story that I have had in my mind two years and more." After an apparent break in their correspondence, on April 25, 1895, Reese sent the Stedmans' younger son, Arthur, one or more short stories, apparently with the request that he serve as her agent in placing them. Two stories appeared in the *Outlook* during next few years: "Adam" on January 30, 1897, and "Old Mis' Rich" on February 5, 1898. She never collected her stories, but in December 1895 she shared with Stedman her plans to "get out a new book by the title of 'A Quiet Road.'" The next September she wrote Laura Stedman that Houghton Mifflin would publish the collection in the fall, and promised to send the Stedmans the first copy. The new collection solidified Reese's reputation. *The Critic* asserted in January 1887 that "her voice has acquired depth and richness without losing any of its sweetness. . . . The absolute simplicity of her language, the freshness and fitness of her imagery and, above all, the genuineness of her singing make one hope for more poems from the same source" (n.s. 27: 406). Apparently "sweetness" remained a quality that reviewers expected of women poets.

Congratulating Reese in October 1896, Stedman wrote of his own difficulties: "The year has been a sad one for me. . . . I am far from well, a[m] very weary, & books and letters lie unacknowledged. But I seldom hear from one of my own, like you, & you see I *am* writing you forthwith." He urged her to visit in Bronxville, where she "would see no enemy—not even Winter and rough weather—before our hickory fire. There is a nice room expressly for you, & you know I never shall see much of you unless we confabulate for more than a single evening under my own roof." What had begun as a relationship in which a newcomer looked to an important literary critic for help had developed into a friendship based on absolute trust and growing intimacy.

On Thanksgiving Eve 1896 Reese, after describing her pleasure in the new book, told Stedman of the collapse of her family's finances and his importance to her:

> I count your friendship one of the loveliest things I have to be thankful for. I cannot tell you what a comfort your letter was to me; it almost brought tears to my eyes. The book has received a good deal of favorable comment; and I believe it is selling well.
>
> How fine you and Mrs. Stedman must feel in your new house. I can see it plainly every time I think of it (which is often), and more plainly than any other part of it that little room which you kindly think of in connection with me. Alas, I am not coming North this year, or next, and perhaps never at all! My time is just now taken up with trying to keep out of debt, and keep things straightened out, and it is very hard to a woman who is a spendthrift by nature to count every cent that comes here and strive to make it go farther than it is natural for a cent to go. However, everything comes right, and I *can't* believe I am worse-treated than anyone else.
>
> Dear Mr. Stedman, you are the best-loved man of the century. Whenever you feel tired or out of heart with the times . . . just think of that, and warm yourself at it.

The very act of describing her difficulties to Stedman helped Reese to muster the strength to face them. He and Laura remained secure islands of love and acceptance in a difficult world.

Reflecting the growing intimacy between them, Stedman told Reese on December 20, 1896, how strongly he was drawn to her:

> I was much touched and upheld by your recent words to me. Of course you evolved the epithet which was so medicinal from your own loyal "subjectivity"—but that made it all the more effective. For, between ourselves, if you felt moved to make it even in the "positive" instead of the "superlative" degree, and I were a quarter-century younger and not blessed as now with a mate, it would go hard but that the children of Baltimore School District No. ? should be deprived of their present educational advantages over all other school children!
>
> I am so gratified to find again, as in your case, how surely the true poet come[s] to his own. Several notices like Mr. Stoddard's have met my eye.

Reese developed similar feelings of love for Stedman, her most passionate letter coming on April 7, 1899, after a visit to the Stedmans:

> We are so dull here in Baltimore. We know so little about Art, and we think we know so much. Still, it is a great deal for me to feel that I have stood by my guns. Yes, it pays [?].
>
> Dear Poet, I really believe I am going to write some more verse. Something I thought I had lost has come back again. It began to blossom while I was at your house, (the heavenly time I had there quickened it), and now it has blown out, and I am the happiest creature in the world. I tell you because you understand.
>
> This is the last letter of all. I have kept my best [wine?] for the end. Dear, dear Poet, I send you my love, and you are not to answer this.

This was not Reese's "last letter"—that would come in December 1907, a month before Stedman's death—but Reese could go no further in expressing her love for him.

On October 15, 1900, Reese thanked Stedman for the gift of *An American Anthology,* which included twelve of her poems. In the biographical entry Stedman wrote that "Miss Reese's poetry is of a rare quality—artistic, natural, beautiful with the old-time atmosphere and associations, and at times rising to a noble classicism, of which the lines 'To a Town Poet' . . . afford a fine example" (818). A note in the Reese collection of the Clifton Waller Barrett Collection at the University of Virginia asserts that the publication of "Tears" in Stedman's *American Anthology* "first attracted universal attention to this sonnet," her most famous poem. David Perkins has written that "Tears" "deserves its fame, if only because of its fine, elegiac cadence and swift accumulation of suggestive metaphors," but that it is "slightly sentimental" and therefore "not quite characteristic" (110).

At the end of December 1901, Reese told Stedman of her plans for a trip to England: "But I have at last decided to cut loose and have seven or eight weeks of liberty and fun. I hardly dare think about it, it is so entrancing. (Is this the Puritan in me? God forbid!)." Stedman helped by providing letters of introduction. On April 23, 1902, he wrote, "You poor little caged lark! Years ago you should have visited the scenes so dear to *us.* . . . There is no sensation like that of an American's *first* footfall upon England's soil. . . . My dear child, let me confess to you that for 19 years *I* have been a prisoner here. All my old comrades have aged, & have ceased to write me. But I give you notes to those who are still near to me." Part way across the Atlantic that next year, Reese's ship became disabled. She had to wait until the next summer to take the trip, which brought her "days of unalloyed delights," as she told the Stedmans, who had seen her off at the dock—the last time, as best one can tell, that Reese and Stedman would see each other.

In January 1903 Reese thanked Stedman for the gift of a new picture: "It is very, very like, the same kind, spirited face, the keen eyes, the beautiful brows—the best of the Puritans with, a dash of the Cavalier. I shall hang it over my bookcase, in a gilt and white frame." She also reported that "I have written a story for Harper's and am at work on two others. But art is long—and School Boards (mostly composed of fools) are getting more little-minded everyday. The best of my time is spent correcting compositions! Two hundred of them!" On April 10, 1902, she complained that the "school board treats us like serfs, and I may have extra duties assigned." But she told him on June 28, 1903, that "they say I am writing better than ever. Also, I am trying stories. *Harper's* published one ["Cornelia's Birthday"] in June, and one has been accepted by another editor. The latter writes me it is a genuine piece of art and he is proud of me."

Aware of Stedman's failing health but unable to visit, Reese regularly told him and Laura how important they remained to her. After the sudden death of Laura Stedman in August 1905, Reese asked Stedman for a keepsake from her possessions. He told her on August 15 that "You *know* that she loved you—and her loves were chosen well, and, when fastened, held to the last." With health and financial resources failing, in 1907 Stedman moved from Bronxville to an apartment at 2643 Broadway. He told her of his concern that she had not published a volume of poetry since 1896: "I often wonder if you are writing more poetry. It is not that we don't have poets—but that the press & public don't read poetry, & they scarcely know what it is." Reese replied that "Soon I expect to have a book ready for the publisher. I am now revising it for the last time. When it is finished, I shall try Houghton for the third time, but do not know if he will agree to print it or not." But Stedman now lacked the authority to intervene and Reese had no other patron to place the book with a prominent firm.

On December 12, 1907, a month before his death, Stedman said farewell:

> I cannot for the moment find the letter, which I *temporarily* answered, in which you wish to have some relic of my wife [and] that went to my heart. She liked none of her younger friends better than you, & knew that you loved her. I can't find that letter today, having now no regular secretary and being rather unequal to my distressing piled-up mails; but I have never for a moment forgotten my promise, and at last have been able to open up the stored-trunk of what things are left that were my wife's.

> Perhaps this rather old-fashioned, but pretty, breast-pin is the thing which . . . you may care to wear now and then in remembrance of L.H.S. I think the blue pendant, with its blossoms and its Psyche alluding Love, befit your ladyship in more ways than one.
>
> I have been trying to write, & edit my poems,—the former for means of living, the latter against the chances of one's 75th year. . . . So I must say Yea-Yea & Nay-nay (& even say farewell) to my most loved friends. But you are always dear to me, & I am so glad you wrote that you are to bring out another book of your beautiful poems.

Through his gift of the love pin, Stedman recognized Reese's passional nature, which, he saw, figures importantly in her work.

After she learned of Stedman's death, Reese wrote his granddaughter, Laura: "I felt as if a heavy hand had been laid upon my heart. I shall never know anyone like him again. He was so chivalrous, so kind, so many-sided, so fond of beauty and art—one of the best beloved men of his day. It is hard to think of him dead. How we shall all miss him! Dear soul!" She dedicated *A Wayside Lute* to his memory with the following prefatory poem:

> House, how still you are;
> Hearth, how cold!
> He was vital as a star,
> As the April mold.
> Friend and singer, lad and knight,
> Very dear;—
> Hearts, how bare the dark, the light,
> Since he is not here!

The Reese-Stedman correspondence demonstrates the many ways that Stedman served Reese and she him. In addition to that crucially important initial letter of recognition, he offered her stylistic advice, secured the best possible publisher for her second book, promoted her work with influential friends, and made it possible for her to meet major and minor writers. She knew when to accept and when to reject his advice. The friendship and affection of both Stedmans filled an important place in her life even as she figured significantly in theirs. Reese and Stedman developed a relationship of particular intimacy. He took pride in her achievements as one of a new generation of poets who would make good his prediction of a renaissance of poetry in America.

Note

1. Reese's letters to Stedman and his to her are housed in the Edmund Clarence Stedman Papers, Rare Book and Manuscript Library, Columbia University. The letters are owned by Columbia University and are quoted with the permission of the university. I have also consulted the Lizette Woodworth Reese Collection, Clifton Barret Library, University of Virginia, which is the major repository of Reese material.

I dealt briefly with the Stedman-Reese relationship in my *Edmund Clarence Stedman* (1997). My profile of Reese appeared in *Legacy: A Journal of American Women Writers* in 1998. A useful source for both biographical and bibliographical information about Reese is Robert J. Jones, *In Praise of Common Things* (1992). Jones reprints approximately two hundred poems by Reese. Useful critical discussions are to be found in Horace Gregory and Marya Zaturenska, *A History of American Poetry, 1900–1940,* Emily Stipes Watts, *The Poetry of American Women, 1632 to 1945,* and Cheryl Walker, *The Nightingale's Burden.*

Works Cited

Review of *A Branch of May. The Critic,* n.s. 14 (April 14, 1888): 177.

Review of *A Handful of Lavender. Atlantic Monthly* 68 (December 1891): 845.

Review of *A Quiet Road. The Critic,* 30 (n.s. 27) (January 1897): 406.

Bennett, Paula. "Late-Nineteenth-Century American Women's Nature Poetry and the Evolution of the Imagist Poem." *Legacy* 9 (1992): 89–103.

———. "Not Just Filler and Not Just Sentimental: Women's Poetry in American Victorian Periodicals, 1860–1900." *Periodical Literature in Nineteenth-Century America.* Ed. Kenneth M. Price and Susan Belasco Smith. Charlottesville: University Press of Virginia, 1995: 202–19.

Bogan, Louise. *Achievement in American Poetry.* Chicago: Henry Regency, 1951.

Frank, Elisabeth. *Louise Bogan.* New York: Knopf, 1985.

Gilbert, Sandra, and Susan Gubar, eds. *Shakespeare's Sisters: Feminist Essays on Women Poets.* Bloomington: Indiana University Press, 1979.

Gregory, Horace, and Marya Zaturenska. *A History of American Poetry, 1900–1940.* New York: Harcourt, Brace, 1946.

Higginson, T. W., and E. H. Bigelow, eds. *American Sonnets.* Boston: Houghton Mifflin, 1890.

Howells, William Dean. "Editor's Study." *Harper's New Monthly Magazine* 77 (September 1888): 638–42.

Jones, Robert J. *In Praise of Common Things: Lizette Woodworth Reese Revisited.* Westport, Connecticut: Greenwood Press, 1992.

"Miss Reese's 'Handful of Lavender.'" *The Critic* 19 (n.s. 16) (December 12, 1891): 330.

Monroe, Harriet. *A Poet's Life.* New York: Macmillan, 1938.

Ostriker, Alicia Suskin. *Stealing the Language.* Boston: Beacon Press, 1986.

Perkins, David. *A History of Modern Poetry.* Cambridge: Harvard University Press, 1976.

Reese, Lizette Woodworth. *A Branch of May*. Baltimore: Cushing and Bailey, 1887.
———. "Adam." *Outlook* 55 (January 30, 1897): 352–56.
———. "Cornelia's Birthday." *Harper's Monthly* 107 (June 1903): 25–30.
———. *A Handful of Lavender*. Boston: Houghton Mifflin, 1891.
———. *Little Henrietta*. New York: George H. Doran, 1927.
———. *The Old House in the Country*. New York: Farrar and Rinehart, 1936.
———. "Old Mis' Rich." *Outlook* 58 (February 5, 1898): 343–47.
———. *Pastures*. New York: Farrar and Rinehart, 1933.
———. *A Quiet Road*. Boston: Houghton Mifflin, 1896.
———. *The Selected Poems*. New York: George H. Doran, 1926.
———. *Spicewood*. Baltimore: Norman Remington, 1920.
———. *A Victorian Village*. New York: Farrar and Rinehart, 1929.
———. *A Wayside Lute*. Portland, Maine: Thomas B. Mosher, 1909.
———. *White April*. New York: Farrar and Rinehart, 1930.
———. *Wild Cherry*. Baltimore: Norman Remington, 1923.
———. *Worleys*. New York: Farrar and Rinehart, 1936.
———. *The York Road*. New York: Farrar and Rinehart, 1931.
Scholnick, Robert J. *Edmund Clarence Stedman*. Twayne United States Authors Series 286. Boston: Twayne, 1977.
———. "Lizette Woodword Reese." *Legacy* 15 (1998): 213–22.
Sharp, William, ed. *American Sonnets*. London: Walter Scott, 1889.
Stedman, Edmund Clarence, ed. *An American Anthology, 1787–1900*. Boston: Houghton Mifflin, 1900.
———, ed. *A Library of American Literature* (with Ellen Mackay Hutchinson). 11 vols. New York: C. L. Webster, 1888–90.
———. *The Nature and Elements of Poetry*. Boston: Houghton Mifflin, 1892.
———. *Poets of America*. Boston: Houghton Mifflin, 1885.
Walker, Cheryl. *The Nightingale's Burden*. Bloomington: Indiana University Press, 1982.
Watts, Emily Stipes. *The Poetry of American Women, from 1632 to 1945*. Austin: University of Texas Press, 1977.

The Mentor's Charge

Literary Mentoring in Howells's Criticism and Fiction

MELISSA MCFARLAND PENNELL

Even in early writings, William Dean Howells expressed the commitment to literature and to literary criticism that defined his career as author, editor, reader, and correspondent. He observed that "true" criticism "consists of a calm, just and fearless handling of its subject, and in pointing out in all honesty whatever is hitherto undiscovered of merit, and in equal honesty, whatever there has been concealed of defect" (*Literary Criticism* 60). He admitted that it is much easier to "beherald every new book with eulogistic bravado," but asserted that the "honest, painstaking labor" of fair criticism was "infinitely more valuable to the cause of American literature" (*Literary Criticism* 62). Such scrutiny was not always easy for an author to bear, especially one just beginning a career. Yet Howells believed that this was the most opportune time for critical review, claiming "we deal attentively with the work of those young writers, because if criticism is to affect literature at all, it must be through the writers who have newly left the starting point, and are reasonably uncertain of the race"(*Editor's Study* 32).

His concern for the professional development of writers and their continued efforts toward mastery of the genres in which they wrote shaped the content of both his public writings and private correspondence. A prolific writer of reviews, prefaces, and editorials, Howells brought numerous writers to the attention of the American public. As Kenneth Lynn notes, he "created an audience for their work where none had existed before" (285). He also wrote letters of encouragement, advice, and guidance to peers and to writers of a younger generation who sought his counsel. Though he never held a formal teaching position, Howells instructed many on fine points of style and composition, hoping that such attention might enable them to produce works that would distinguish American literature in the international market.

Attaining the influential position of editor at the *Atlantic Monthly* did not rob Howells of his compassion for novice writers. His own experiences as a beginner too heavily influenced by his literary models and as an outsider to the Eastern literary establishment seemed instead to widen his sympathy. He felt the young writer's impatience and anxiety over attempts to publish his poems, evident in an 1859 letter to John J. Piatt. Howells wrote, "Those confounded Atlantic people haven't printed my verses in their October number. O, if they only knew how agonizing it is to wait" (*Letters* 1: 44). As a Midwestern contributor whose contact with editors of influential Eastern magazines came primarily through the mails, Howells invested those individuals with a degree of power and authority that at times intensified his insecurities (see Lynn 72–73). Having exercised his own authority as editor of the *Atlantic,* Howells commented (half in jest) to the new editor Thomas Bailey Aldrich, "I have become so abjectly a contributor that I am getting doubtful about points in my work, and feel like asking you to bolster me up" (*Letters* 2: 294). Expressing once again his own need for affirmative goodwill, Howells kept in mind authorial insecurities when dealing with those who sent work to him.

Howells also recognized the importance of connections to the literary networks of Boston and New York in furthering one's career. He reminded his friend Piatt that although he was "known and popular throughout the West," he must submit selections to Eastern magazines to become better known to editors and publishers there (*Letters* 1: 42–44). After his pilgrimage to New England in 1860, however, Howells more fully grasped the challenge of establishing professional and personal ties to the Boston network, given the reserve of Brahmin Boston and his own shyness. Fortunately, he made a positive impression on James Russell Lowell, who became his advocate and friend. Lowell urged Howells to read more extensively, to avoid rushing work into publication, to gain distance from his early literary passions. Their relationship involved complexities that Howells acknowledged later in life, but he valued Lowell's insights and understanding. Even as an established man of letters, he sought Lowell's counsel in 1882 when he was offered a professorship at Johns Hopkins.

One might assume that his willingness to mentor others and to guide their literary development grew out of Howells's experiences with benefactors like Lowell, but he felt inclined to help much earlier. Responding to his sister Victoria's frustrations with her life in Jefferson and the family cares that were increasingly hers, Howells remarked, "Why don't you write, dear Vic? If you will write a little story or sketch of any kind, I will engage to sell it for you" (*Letters* 1: 24–25). His sister Anne did pursue a career in writing, and Howells offered advice, though it was not always welcomed or received objectively. But it was those outside his family to whom Howells devoted his literary attention and commentary, given publicly in reviews and privately in letters.

His efforts began in earnest when he assumed the assistant editorship of the *Atlantic;* those with whom he corresponded and whose work he critiqued included novelists, poets, short story writers, and playwrights. In his reviews, he praised what was worthy of note, finding Jewett's characters in *Deephaven* "all touched with a hand that holds itself far from every trick of exaggeration, and that subtly delights in the very tint and form of reality" (*Literary Criticism* 275), and condemned those elements that undermined effect, such as Eggleston's tendency in *The Circuit Rider* to interrupt his narrative "to make the reader an ironical or defiant apology for treating of such unrefined matters. . . . This is bad art, as Mr. Eggleston must himself feel, and he ought not indulge it" (*Literary Criticism* 235). Likewise in letters he directed writers toward the improvement of their work, telling H. H. Boyesen "this is the best poem you've ever written, though it stands at the same time such an imperfect one that I cannot use it as it stands. There are very beautiful passages in it, and more beautiful lines than in any poem of yours that I know; but it ends weakly. . . . I think you need greatly to study brevity and simplicity of style. One mustn't overdress" (*Letters* 1: 408).

Howells's efforts on behalf of writers whose reputations have remained secure or whose work has once again merited attention present interesting (and well-known) case studies in literary history. More remarkable is Howells's willingness to respond to those who did not achieve even minor success with their literary endeavors. This may reflect Howells's editorial and business acumen in not wanting to alienate potential contributors, but the level of personal attention he invested in his responses suggests a genuine interest. In the many letters he addressed to these hopefuls, Howells makes reference to his own experiences, attempting to maintain a balance between honest appraisal and encouragement. To Benjamin Parker he promises, "I will serve you in any way I can," then goes on to explain, "Any book house will undertake the publication of your poems, if you pay the expense; but otherwise I think you will find it hard to get a publisher. . . . It is well to consider a little about printing a book of poetry—it hardly ever pays. You will do better to try to make a magazine reputation first" (*Letters* 1: 252). Another aspiring poet, Don Wyman, is cautioned "till you feel quite sure that you have not imitated [Heine] you ought not to publish. I am quite frank with you, and I wish I had not been tardily frank with myself" (*Letters* 1: 275). Shortly after sending this letter, Howells recommended that his father try to find a place for Wyman at the *Ashtabula Sentinel.* For some writers he recommended a change in subject matter, as he did to Will Carleton, stating that he hoped to "pave the way . . . to our future relations as editor and contributor" by encouraging Carleton to avoid the temptation to let his poems "slop over" by taking "some subject of the life about you" to present with restraint (*Letters* 1: 368). As John K. Reeves notes, "through his correspondence Howells learned the art of rejecting a piece of writing without impairing a personal friendship" (*Letters* 1: 246).

This desire to maintain personal friendships led Howells to shepherd some aspiring poets toward other genres. In an 1877 letter to Belton O. Townsend, Howells wrote, "You must forgive me for letting your letter go so long unanswered: it was not an easy letter to answer, especially when I must return your lines. They express, or rather intimate a deep and true feeling, but they are not poetry. That is final with me, against them; . . . I have no doubt that your destiny is literature, but that it is poetry I am not at all sure; in fact I do doubt that. Why not try something in the way of a very realistic short story of South Carolinian life?" (*Letters* 2: 171). In 1884 Townsend sent him a volume of poems recently published, to which Howells responded with uncharacteristic sharpness: "It was extremely pleasant to see your handwriting again, and to know that you still valued our old relation. But I cannot mar the recollection of that by praising your volume of verse, which is wholly bad as a thing of the kind can be. . . . I should have been less than your friend if I had foreborne" (*Letters* 3: 99). Howells later regretted the stinging tone of his letter and apologized to Townsend, but he could not be dishonest: "I should be wronging you very cruelly to praise them; but I like you so much—you seem to me so true and good and brave a spirit—that I wish with all my heart I could praise them" (*Letters* 3: 99).

These excerpts suggest the level of personal responsibility that Howells felt toward those whom he counseled; they also reflect the complexity of the mentoring relationship that requires striking a balance between personal regard and honesty. The exchanges with Townsend in particular also reveal the difficulties a mentor has in responding when a protégé's choices differ from the mentor's recommendations. For Howells, the difficulties intensify when complicated by gender expectations, as Joanne Karpinski demonstrates in her study of Howells's relationship with Charlotte Perkins Gilman.

While he conducted the exchange with Townsend and shortly before he began writing "The Editor's Study" for *Harper's,* Howells was drafting *The Minister's Charge,* a novel that opens with an aspiring poet's desire to achieve success and become part of the literary world of Boston. Of his central character, Lemuel Barker, Howells claims, "I meant to make a simple, earnest, and often very pathetic figure of my country boy, whose adventures and qualities should win him the reader's entire sympathy and respect" (*Letters* 3: 98). Kenneth Eble suggests that Howells was "eminently qualified to write [the story] . . . of the young provincial person of talent trying to make his way in a more sophisticated society" (101), aligning Howells with his central character. Others have treated *The Minister's Charge* as one of Howells's economic novels, emphasizing the subtitle *The Apprenticeship of Lemuel Barker* and examining issues of class conflict and Barker's attempts to succeed despite the obstacles that hinder him. In light of Howells's contemporaneous letters to Townsend and his efforts on behalf of other aspirants, the novel's main title, however, invites closer examination of the relationship between the minister and Barker. Throughout the novel the Reverend David Sewell claims concern for Barker, but seems incapable of affording him genuine help. Given his own generous assistance to writers, not only those who became literary successes but also those who never achieved literary significance, why does Howells focus upon a failed relationship in this novel? In what ways does he draw upon his own experiences as a mentor to depict what goes wrong between Sewell and Barker?

In the opening chapter of *The Minister's Charge,* Howells introduces both the young rustic Lemuel Barker and the Reverend David Sewell, whose opinion Barker values. Sewell, a summer visitor to the farming community of Willoughby Pastures, depends upon his own ability to use language in his profession, especially in the writing of sermons and counseling of his congregation. He embodies for Barker a figure marked by what Cady has called "the prestige of the minister-scholar" (129), associated in the minds of New Englanders with the significance of ideas and letters. He also carries the cultural responsibility of maintaining standards of taste and correct usage, a role charged to teachers and ministers by the nineteenth-century editors of *Harper's* (Nettels 12). Ministerial influence as a social and political force, however, is on the wane by the late nineteenth century, especially from within the mainline churches (Douglas 19–23). Sewell, conscious of his own precarious position in the influence hierarchy of Boston, attempts to avoid offense in his personal and public interactions with members of his congregation, who are predominantly members of Boston's elite. Sensitive to criticism from his wife and others, Sewell hesitates to espouse strong convictions or give voice to opinions that he feels are not generally accepted. Thus, he proves a poor choice as mentor, for he lacks sufficient belief in the value of his own work and ideas to appreciate the meaning with which another might invest such endeavors.

Dishonesty during the first encounter with Barker sets in motion a problematic relationship between Sewell and the young poet. Sewell's wife cautions him that praising Barker's poetry has been a mistake, that it will further false hopes in the young man. Sewell does not agree. When Barker sends him additional verses, seeking his approval and encouragement, Sewell is perturbed. Having given false praise at the beginning, he cannot envision how he might now give constructive criticism, and he attempts to avoid the issue by conveniently misplacing Barker's letter. When Barker shows up on his doorstep, Sewell reacts with dismay and attempts to protect his own fragile ego by being unduly harsh with him. He informs Mrs. Sewell, "'I see that I shall inflict twice the pain that I should have done if I had spoken to him frankly at first; and of course there will be the added disappointment, and the expense of his coming to Boston. . . . I'm going to take him around to a publisher and let him convince himself that there's no hope for him in a literary way'"(13). She recognizes what he is about to do and confronts him: "'Why should you expose the poor fellow to the mortification of a perfectly needless refusal? Do you want to shirk the responsibility—to put it on someone else?'"(13). Indeed, Sewell hopes to escape responsibility and to sever his ties to Barker, regardless of the pain he may inflict. These early contacts reflect the pattern of avoidance that shapes Sewell's approach to Barker.

Sewell assumes that in calling on the authority of the nameless editor, he will also dissociate himself from his earlier praise of Barker's work, not wanting his literate, urbane colleagues and congregation to think he values the amateurish verse of a rustic poet. The very name Barker, a term that Sewell and the reader associate more closely with the popular culture of the carnival than the genteel tastes of literary Boston, emphasizes in Sewell's mind the distance that separates him from his "protégé." Barker apparently lacks sufficient talent to succeed in the literary market (the reader never sees any of Barker's poetry to make an assessment), but Sewell's failure as a mentor occurs because he hesitates in his commitment to the young man, personally as well as professionally. In his response to Barker's literary hopes, Sewell is less concerned with Barker's development than he is with preserving his own reputation as a man of refined taste and good judgment. Sewell cannot relate to Barker as an individual with feelings. He also fails to perceive that Barker has put him on a pedestal, regarding him and valuing his opinions more highly than do most members of Sewell's church.

Sewell does everything he can to make Barker an object to be disposed of quickly. During their meeting at Sewell's house, Sewell refers to New England men of arts and sciences—Emerson and Agassiz—invoking their authority to disguise his own sense of inadequacy. Uncomfortable in the silences that punctuate his early remarks, Sewell chatters away, attempting to shield himself behind a wall of words. His awkwardness in asking about Barker's life in Willoughby Pastures reveals that Sewell's only comfort comes when posing questions to which he already knows the answers. He fears losing control of the situation with Barker and "followed him, and helped him find his hat, and made him shake hands. He went with him to the door" (23) and all but gave him the bum's rush in hopes of sending him back home. When he claims that "'do what I would, I couldn't find any common ground where we could stand together'" (27), he deceives himself about the implications of his behavior, implications that Barker understands perfectly well.

As Barker leaves the minister's house he reflects on what has occurred and admits to himself that he would not "have left home if there had been anything for him to do there" (28). His hopes to make his way in Boston are less tied to a literary career than to a desire to find gainful employment, something about which Sewell never inquires. Had Sewell even told him what Miss Vane observes (echoing Howells's observations), that poetry "'doesn't pay, even in extreme cases of genius'" (24), Barker would have sought other directions. What pains Barker is not the realization that his poetry is a failure, but the personal rejection he experiences: "At the bottom of all was a simple grief that he should have lost the friend whom he thought he had in the minister; the friend he had talked of and dreamed of ever since he had seen and heard him speak those cordial words; the friend he had trusted through all, and had come down to Boston counting upon so much" (28–29). After his encounters with con men, the police, and the courts leave him destitute and alone, Barker considers approaching Sewell for assistance, but "the thought of going to Mr. Sewell was, even in the secret which it would remain between him and the minister, a pang so cruel to his pride he recoiled from it instantly" (60). Barker acknowledges the sting of rejection and resolves to make his own way despite circumstances.

In *The Social Construction of American Realism*, Amy Kaplan observes that "although Howells tries to construct a community based on character, on mutual recognition, his narratives depend upon the media to bring together characters in spite of their diverse worlds" (43). No better example of this occurs than in *The Minister's Charge*. Since he has not heard from Barker, Sewell believes that his burden has been lifted, and he begins to assert his superior sensibility with regard to the reading matter he and his wife peruse at breakfast. Thinking to illustrate for her the inferiority of a publication called the *Sunrise* when compared to his preferred *Advertiser,* Sewell reads aloud the police report, only to discover there the details of Barker's appearance in court. Sewell assumes that Barker has been convicted and resolves to see him. Finding Barker at the Wayfarer's Lodge, Sewell hesitates and his authority again fails him. He lacks "the smooth superiority of address" (83) that characterizes his usual manner.

When he sees Barker, Sewell casts him in imagined scenarios of failure, into "the dire life of idleness and dependence," and speaks to him with "the asperity of anticipated censure" (88). Sewell equates the insufficiency of Barker's poetry with Barker himself, unable to separate the person from the work. During their encounter, Sewell attempts to achieve paternal control over Barker, but Barker asserts his independence, against which Sewell "felt himself helpless" and moved to heave "a sigh of hopeless perplexity" (84). To regain the upper hand, Sewell resorts to making an issue of Barker's poetic failure, thereby justifying his rejection of Barker. Though he preaches a sermon that urges his congregation to "strive most of all to do good to those you have done harm to" (91), Sewell cannot recover his relationship with Barker. He does not consider Barker his equal in ability with words or in understanding of life, and contrary to his own preaching, sees no possibility for Barker to improve or develop.

Ironically, Sewell cannot separate himself from Barker. He must see his initial judgment confirmed. He refers to Barker as a "burden," (136) and imagines a "course of calamity" (167) for Barker that will drive him back to Willoughby Pastures. When Barker approaches him for advice, Sewell again speaks to him with a "cold didacticism" (202) in an attempt to remain distant, but, as their conversation continues, Sewell experiences a rare moment of honest and sincere feeling. Barker admits to him, "'I couldn't explain very well that I hadn't come to the city just to be in the city, but because I had to do something to help along at home. You didn't seem to understand that there wasn't anything there for me to take hold of'" (206). Sewell confesses, "'No, I'm afraid I didn't or wouldn't quite understand that; I was talking and acting, I'm afraid, from a preconceived notion'" (207). Having said this, Sewell ignores his own words and returns to preconceived notions when he gives Barker advice. Rather than let Barker explain, Sewell assumes that he knows what counsel Barker seeks, that he is involved in "some ridiculous love affair" (209).

To highlight the problematic nature of Sewell's behavior toward Barker and to establish foils to his character, Howells creates scenarios in which three other characters interact with Barker and see him in different lights. Though none can be called a mentor in the traditional sense, Miss

Vane, Evans, and Bromfield Corey contribute to Barker's development in ways that Sewell never contemplates. All three are figures secure in their social place who do not doubt the validity or value of their opinions. They are honest with Barker, making plain their expectations. Each expresses a warmth of feeling toward him as each discovers aspects of his character to which Sewell remains blind.

Aware of Barker's literary aspirations and his current hardship, Miss Vane agrees to hire him to tend her furnace and serve as a general handyman. Sensitive to his situation, "she treated him at once, not like a servant, but like a young person, and yet she used a sort of respect for his independence which was soothing to his rustic pride. She put it on the money basis at once" (89). Though she verbally tweaks Sewell with a comment about whether this is appropriate "work for a literary man" (90), the barb is directed at Sewell, not Barker. She also observes that Sewell preaches his "self-denying sermons" at Barker every Sunday, hinting that Sewell can only communicate with Barker from an official position of safety—while Sewell is in the pulpit, Barker cannot talk back. When a misunderstanding occurs over an encounter between her niece Sybil and Barker, Miss Vane fires him, but quickly regrets her action. She discovers that she misses his presence in the household and attempts to work through Sewell to apologize.

Like Miss Vane, Evans, the editor of *Saturday Afternoon*, treats Barker as an individual who has the potential to develop. He and Barker discuss the books Barker has been reading, and Evans lends him others to widen his exposure. He cultivates Barker's desire to learn and genuinely enjoys conversing with him. Evans jokes with Sewell that since Barker does not seem to be writing more verse, it is safe to remain friendly (164), but Evans lends Barker books of poetry, not discouraging his literary interests. Busy at his job in the residential hotel where Evans lives, Barker "would have liked better to read, to go to lectures, to hear sermons; with the knowledge of Mr. Evans's life as an editor and the incentive of a writer near him, he would have liked to try again if he could not write something, though the shame of his failure in Mr. Sewell's eyes had burned so deep" (214).

Evans also cultivates a relationship with Barker, finding him a refreshing companion as they explore Boston together: "they became friends after a fashion, and were in each other's confidence as regarded their opinions and ideas, rather than their history" (214–15). Because Evans listens to him, Barker feels comfortable confessing his anxieties over the presence of the ex-con Williams. Evans comforts him, advising that "'we must live things down, not lie them down'" and putting "his arm caressingly across the boy's shoulder" tries to buoy his spirits (233). This moment marks the first sympathetic connection that Barker experiences with a member of the Boston literary establishment. He informs Sewell later that "'I shan't forget [Evans's words]. . . . They've been in my head ever since. If it hadn't been for them, I don't know what I would have done'" (242). Impelled by his bond with Evans, Barker searches out Evans and his wife when the hotel catches fire, guiding them to safety. Slow to recover from the trauma of the fire, Evans accompanies his wife on a journey abroad. His departure leaves Barker once again without a friend and guide, throwing him back upon Sewell's lukewarm benevolence.

Another member of Sewell's congregation, Bromfield Corey, becomes the third figure to contribute to Barker's development and to see in him attributes that Sewell cannot discern. Like Miss Vane, Corey enjoys the comfortable status that wealth provides, and in this novel his character develops more sympathetically than in *Silas Lapham*. Sewell serves as the agent by which Corey and Barker become acquainted, referring to Barker as his "client" (251) to define their relationship. While he attempts to secure a place for Barker in the Corey household, Sewell reflects, "It seemed to him, as he began, that he was always telling [Barker's] story, and that his part in the affair was always becoming less and less respectable" (250). Like Evans (whose son died in an accident), Corey suffers the absence of his son Tom (business interests have taken him from Boston) and finds in Barker a potential substitute.

Corey takes an immediate liking to Barker and begins to have an influence upon him. "He corrected Lemuel's pronunciation where he found it faulty, and amused himself with Lemuel's struggles to conceal his hurt vanity, and his final good sense in profiting by the correction" (257). He also takes a personal interest in Barker, much as Evans did, finding that "he liked to hear Lemuel talk, and he used the art of getting at the boy's life by being frank with his own experience" (257). This expression of personal concern and the exposure to a variety of literary works under Corey's direction rekindle in Barker "the ambition to write, stunned by the first disastrous adventures in Boston, and dormant ever since, except as it had stirred under the promptings of Evans's kindly interest" (260). Though Barker does not complete any of the works he begins, now in prose rather than verse, the effort suggests the return of self-confidence that had been undermined by his encounters with Sewell. Unfortunately, Barker abruptly resigns his position with Corey to fulfill what he believes is his duty toward Statira, a young woman with whom he has had an ambiguous romance. When this occurs, Corey expresses a sense of loss at his departure, having discovered in Barker's company a youthful honesty that reinvigorates him.

Though others see attributes in Barker that make him an attractive and engaging figure, Sewell remains oblivious to Barker's potential. Faced with another moral dilemma, Barker seeks Sewell's counsel, only to be treated as he had been on his first visit to Sewell's house. Sewell greets Barker "with a cordiality which he did not keep free from reluctance," using his need to write a sermon as an excuse. He allows Barker to say next to nothing, wrings Barker's "hand again, this time in perfect sincerity, and eagerly shut him out into the night" (275). Having experienced this rejection before, Barker ponders, "But whom to turn to for counsel now? The one friend in whom he had trusted, to whom he had just gone ready to fling down his whole heart before him, had failed him, failed him unwittingly, unwillingly, as he had failed him once before, but this time in infinitely greater stress" (276).

Since he perceives Sewell as his last resort, Barker approaches him one last time for help. On this occasion, because he asks for money, a loan to buy a horse-car conductor's uniform, Sewell responds "with eager cordiality" (295). As long as Barker asks for something that is not a personal commitment, Sewell is only too happy to respond. Even with this gesture, however, he does not tax his own resources, for the money comes from funds donated by Miss Vane and Corey. Throughout the novel, Sewell has speculated on the nature of one's duty to others, but his ability to respond to Barker perennially falls short. When Barker breaks his leg in a horse-car accident, Sewell goes "often to see him" (300), a duty he does not hesitate to perform because it is clearly spelled out in the New Testament directive "I was sick and you visited me" (Matt. 25:36). Though as a minister he professes progressive religious sentiments, Sewell falls back upon the letter of the law, unable to embody its spirit.

Inspired by his encounters with Barker, Sewell preaches a sermon that articulates the doctrine of complicity, that each individual is linked to others and responsible for their well-being. This sermon explores a concept that Howells had embraced, but Sewell is an ironic spokesman. He has attempted throughout to shield himself not only from pain but from inconvenience by distancing himself from those who threaten to become obligations. In a contemporary review of the novel, Anna Dawes remarks on the "mixed nature" of Sewell, composed of "all the brave words of inspiration and helpfulness he could and did speak to people as their minister, all his weakness as a man when duty laid off the gown and came down out of the pulpit and confronted him" (96). She comments further that he "fails of his possibilities, loses his chance, and the reason for failure we are made to see is the unwillingness on his part—the unreadiness is a better word—to put himself into the mental sympathy with the man who asks his help" (96). In the end, Sewell admits that he had missed an opportunity with Barker, that he had been "recreant to [his] charge" (310).

Howells suggests that this missed opportunity results not only from Sewell's lack of feeling for Barker, but from his lack of faith in himself; his own insecurities, apparent in conversations with his wife and parishioners like Miss Vane, cause him to shield himself from the risk of embarrassment. To avoid this risk, Sewell hesitates to accept Evans's invitation to write for *Saturday Afternoon*. Though he seeks opportunities to display his own insights and talents, the offer ignites anxieties for Sewell over his ability to succeed with words. Rather than providing a means to relate to Barker, these anxieties further inhibit his willingness to identify with a writer he fears is a failure. Because he cannot accept his own vulnerability, Sewell cannot act with compassion or sympathy; because he cannot separate his own identity from the writing he produces, he cannot distinguish between Barker and his poems.

Drawing upon his experience as an editor and mentor, Howells examines this failed mentoring relationship to highlight what is necessary for one to succeed. In exploring Sewell's vulnerability to criticism, stated or implied, Howells begins to probe the need for self-confidence in a mentor. Howells suggests that a mentor must have confidence in himself or herself before he or she can inspire confidence in another. Coming off the success of *The Rise of Silas Lapham*, Howells may have felt himself to be in a better position to confront this issue. In his treatment of Sewell, Howells also explores the mentor's need to be honest from the beginning, both with the individual who seeks guidance and with the self. Having grappled with the pain inflicted by his own honesty in response to Belton Townsend, Howells places this question of honesty at the center of the novel. He demonstrates how destructive dishonesty can be, by raising false hopes and cutting off avenues for constructive criticism. Further, he suggests that such dishonesty inhibits the expression of genuine compassion and supportive encouragement, both of which a writer needs. While he may not always have lived up to his own ideals, Howells went on in the years following publication of *The Minister's Charge* to contribute to the development and support the careers of many of the major voices in American literature.

Works Cited

Cady, Edwin H. *The Road to Realism: The Early Years, 1837–1885, of William Dean Howells.* Syracuse, New York: Syracuse University Press, 1956.

Dawes, Anna Laurens. "The Moral Purpose in Howells's Novels." Reprinted in *Critical Essays on W. D. Howells, 1866–1920.* Ed. Edwin H. Cady and Norma W. Cady. Boston: G. K. Hall, 1983.

Douglas, Ann. *The Feminization of American Culture.* New York: Avon, 1978.

Eble, Kenneth E. *William Dean Howells.* 2nd ed. Boston: Twayne, 1982.

Howells, William Dean. *Editor's Study.* Ed. James W. Simpson. Troy, New York: Whitson Publishing, 1983.

———. *Literary Friends and Acquaintance.* 1901. Bloomington: Indiana University Press, 1968.

———. *The Minister's Charge: The Apprenticeship of Lemuel Barker.* 1886. New York: Library of America, 1989.

———. *Selected Letters.* Ed. George Arms et al. 6 vols. Boston: Twayne, 1979–1983.

———. *Selected Literary Criticism.* Ed. Ulrich Halfmann et al. Vol. 1. Bloomington: Indiana University Press, 1993. 3 vols.

Kaplan, Amy. *The Social Construction of American Realism.* Chicago: University of Chicago Press, 1988.

Karpinski, Joanne B. "When the Marriage of True Minds Admits Impediments: Charlotte Perkins Gilman and William Dean Howells." *Patrons and Protégées.* Ed. Shirley Marchalonis. New Brunswick, New Jersey: Rutgers University Press, 1988. 212–34.

Lynn, Kenneth S. *William Dean Howells: An American Life.* New York: Harcourt Brace Jovanovich, 1971.

Nettels, Elsa. *Language, Race and Social Class in Howells's America.* Lexington: University of Kentucky Press, 1988.

"In this particular instance I want *you*"

The Booster As Mentor in *A Hazard of New Fortunes*

IRENE C. GOLDMAN-PRICE

In 1890 a reviewer for *The Nation* had this to say about *A Hazard of New Fortunes:* "The action of the novel centres about the office of the magazine *Every Other Week*. . . . There is, first of all, Fulkerson the 'organizer,' the life and soul of the enterprise, and the life, though not the soul, of the story. Comment upon him could only wrong him."[1]

At the risk of wronging that likable character, I suggest that comment on Jonas Fulkerson is overdue. Henry James overlooked him entirely in his long letter of praise of the novel to Howells, and critics ever since have largely been ignoring him or treating him lightly. And yet, as *The Nation* reviewer notes, Fulkerson is, at the least, the life of the story. Without Fulkerson, there would never have been new fortunes for the other characters in the book to hazard. And he gives the others, and the novel, their spark. By means of tall talk, good-natured cajoling, and relentless boosting, Fulkerson brings his cohorts together, helps them to develop their separate talents, and guides them into the new, modern world of enterprise. In doing so, he also models a new way of mentoring for a new age of publishing.

Most critics assume without question that Basil March is the protagonist of the novel, as he is of several other Howells novels. And surely March's experience and thought processes are of great interest to the reader. But I think Howells made a distinction between hero—arguably March—and protagonist. In 1909 he wrote an introduction, called "Bibliographical," to what would be the 1911 library edition of the novel, and he also left us with a draft manuscript of that introduction called "Autobiographical." In "Bibliographical," Howells dubbed March his "suppositious literary adventurer" (3), whom he had invited to join him in his study of New York. But in the much longer draft of the introduction,

Howells spoke of the Marches as "subsidiary persons of the drama, exteriorated at times into a chorus, and sometimes frankly conducted to places in the audience" ("Autob." 502–3). He had in mind another protagonist:

> The protagonist, if Fulkerson is indeed anything so formidable, took his name from a boy in the Southwestern Ohio village where my own boyhood was mostly past, and his nature from a friend, long and tragically dead, whose story should have been a sweet comedy, and whom I have learned to love more and more as the years have gone by. It was perhaps by an impulse of this affection that I was moved to commemorate Ralph Keeler in a character for which I could wish the reader to feel a measure of my own kindness; and if he should read into his keeping the circumstances of another friend of mine, still potently and usefully alive, it could not be to the disadvantage of the mainly imaginary Fulkerson.[2]

Ralph Keeler, the friend Howells remembered with such fondness and sought to memorialize in Fulkerson, was a writer who died tragically in the early 1870s on his way to Cuba, where he had agreed to report for a newspaper on the growing war for independence. He had a background similar to that of Sam Clemens, who is, presumably, the other unnamed friend on whom Fulkerson is modeled, the one still "prodigiously and usefully alive." An orphan, Keeler had at first aspired to being "a clog-dancer in a troupe of Negro minstrels," but once attaining that profession, he found he preferred being on the steamboat as a worker rather than a performer. So, like Clemens, he spent several years of his life riding up and down the Mississippi, though not as a pilot. He went briefly to a Jesuit college in Missouri, then to Europe, then California, from whence he traveled to Boston with the manuscript of a novel in hand that he wanted Howells to publish. Though Howells recommended against it, Keeler published it at his own expense. Howells recalled that it "failed instantly and decisively" (*Friends* 232). Howells recalled Keeler in *Literary Friends and Acquaintance:*

> If I am to meet somewhere else the friends who are no longer here, I should like to meet Ralph Keeler, and I would take some chances of meeting in a happy place a soul which had by no means kept itself unspotted, but which in all its consciousness of error, cheerfully trusted that "the Almighty was not going to scoop any of us." The faith worded so grotesquely could not have been more simply or humbly affirmed, and no man I think could have been more help-

> lessly sincere. . . . He had always an essential gayety not to be damped by any discipline. . . . (233)

In a letter to M. M. Hurd shortly after Keeler's death, Howells eulogized him: "He was a man who had ever so much kindness in him . . ." (January 9, 1874, in M. Howells).

Keeler must have been delightful to be around, sharing Clemens's and Howells's midwestern tall talk and sense of fun. Though poor, he was host of at least one memorable literary lunch at Lock Obers, at which Howells, James T. Fields, Thomas Bailey Aldrich, Bret Harte, and Sam Clemens were the guests. Unlike the dinner Fulkerson throws at Dryfoos's house, it was evidently an occasion of much hilarity as well as literary conversation, for Howells wrote of it in *My Mark Twain* and recalled some thirty years later, in a letter to Aldrich, "that lurid lunch which the divine Keeler gave us out of his poverty at Obers . . . " (May 7, 1907, in M. Howells). Keeler was included in many of the literary meals put on by the editors of the *Atlantic* about which Howells writes so fondly in *My Mark Twain*. "Of course," said Howells about these meals, "the subtle fiend of advertising . . . lurked under the covers at these banquets . . . but they were really very simple-hearted and honestly meant hospitalities, and they prospered as they ought, and gave great pleasure and no pain" (*Mark* 49).

Thus we see that the model for Jonas Fulkerson was a risk-taker; generous, kind, and, if a little rough around the edges, nevertheless charming. But in what way can Fulkerson be seen as the protagonist for the novel? If the protagonist is the leader of the agon, or contest, then cannot the adventures anatomized in *Hazard* be seen as a contest of humanity against the "whole massive Hercules" of New York City? ("Bibliog." 5). Or perhaps of artists against the newly encroaching changes in publishing from a cultural activity to a business activity? March, the artist Angus Beaton, and the others follow Fulkerson into the fray as surely as the soldiers did King John in the play from which Howells drew his title. But instead of a political leader or a warrior, Fulkerson is the type of the new, modern American businessman, and his relationship with his contributors is a model for a new kind of literary mentorship in a new literary marketplace.

Fulkerson epitomizes American modernity in a number of ways. He is democratic and egalitarian, socializing as easily with the rather formal southern gentleman, Colonel Woodburn, as with the socially helpless Mrs. Dryfoos, and recognizing the worth of two such opposite beings as the genteel Mrs. Mandel and the socialist Berthold Lindau. He is informal, as relaxed in his body movements (notice how often he puts his feet up on chairs or sits on them backwards, astride) as in his speech, prone to call on people at odd hours and to say anything in front of anybody. And, most important, he is an entrepreneur with an excellent head for business.

Prior to starting *Every Other Week,* Fulkerson was a syndicate man, which in itself suggests he was modern, opportunistic, and forward-looking. In 1889, when Howells wrote the novel, syndication was new, the first syndicate of any size having been started by Irving Bacheller in 1883. Bacheller handled short stories, household departments, news, and gossip letters, and soon other syndicates developed, including one by Samuel S. McClure (later to start *McClure's* magazine) that carried, among other things, works by Howells himself (Mott 482). According to Howells, syndicates supplied the need for cheap and abundant material to fill Sunday editions of newspapers. They carried mostly "interviews, personal adventure, popular science, useful information, travel, sketches, and short stories" ("Man" 441), but they might never rival magazines for fiction because women didn't read the Sunday papers much. Consequently, the fiction in them was "mainly of the inferior sort with which boys and men beguile their leisure" ("Man" 441).

At the same time, the magazine trade was undergoing a profound change in business practices and in content. Instead of being financed primarily by readers (by means of the cost of subscription), magazines in the 1880s began to be the willing recipients of advertising from all kinds of companies that had discovered the power of national brand names and national advertising. While publishers were happy to be able to reduce subscription prices substantially, perhaps inadvertently they were opening the way for the content of their magazines to be radically changed, even controlled, by the advertisers.[3] Howells was deeply concerned by the several problems he foresaw for the future of literary magazines, and part of the mission of *A Hazard of New Fortunes* was to explore the possibilities of a new kind of literary venture. Fulkerson, of course, was the engine running the venture.

A newspaperman who had jumped on the new bandwagon of syndication, Fulkerson was astute enough to recognize the poor quality of syndicated stories and wanted to provide an even better product—as he puts it, a "princely present" to the American public (*Hazard* 138). That he could look at the stories and illustrations of a magazine as a "product" while simultaneously appreciating their aesthetic value and honoring the workmanship of the contributors who produced the product was a part of his genius.

Leaving the syndicate business just a half dozen years after it began, Fulkerson again goes for something original, new, and modern. He locates several weaknesses in the literary market and seeks to capitalize on remedying them. One was the limited amount of actual literary material being published in magazines; another was the related difficulty for new writers to find a market for their work. Howells himself lamented that only about a third of the material that appeared in magazines at the time was what he called "belles lettres," the rest being popular science, politics, economics, and other nonliterary subjects. And of the literary material, according to Howells, most of it was contributed by agreement between author and editor; even the greatest magazine used fewer than fifty unsolicited manuscripts in a year ("Man"). Fulkerson's idea for *Every Other Week* was to use only new writers and artists and to have contributors share in the profits, a plan that alleviated some of the financial risk of using untried authors and illustrators. It also worked to address the even more vexing problem for Howells of how to value objectively a subjective item. Howells was vehemently opposed to valuing a written piece by the word, which he likened to valuing a picture by the square inch, rather than by its intrinsic qualities. The experiment of profit sharing, which Howells has Fulkerson suggest, was one possible solution. Within the novel, Fulkerson's idea—which he ascribes to March—to start a literary magazine that would take mainly unsolicited work to the benefit of the contributors is self-serving to some degree, but it is also innovative in important ways. It moves Fulkerson from working on a third-rate product to a first-rate one; but it also provides a new, purely literary magazine for the public, an opportunity for new writers and artists to break into print, and a model for a fairer compensation for works of art. Howells uses Fulkerson's character to set in motion the experimental enterprise.

In doing so, Howells draws an early portrait of that purely American figure, the tall-talking booster. Fulkerson is an entrepreneur—one might almost call him the impresario of the *Every Other Week* show—a booster but with none of the stupid hypocrisy of a Babbitt, to whom he has been compared. First he finds the financial "angel," Mr. Dryfoos, offering him an outlet for his money and a genteel job for his sensitive son, Conrad. Then, having staffed the magazine and seen to the production of the first issue, he offers to do almost anything to promote it, from throwing a dinner for a hundred of the top literary men in the country at Delmonico's to walking up and down Broadway with a sandwich board advertising it. (Interestingly, he does not suggest selling advertising space.) His innovation and enterprise is typical of what historian Sally Griffith has labeled the "booster ethos." To Griffith, boosterism went beyond mere bluster—in fact, newspapermen and businessmen who promoted their towns helped in "the transformation of boosterism into an instrument of nationalism" (*Home Town News* 245n). Boosters preached and organized on behalf of their towns:

> Briefly put, the booster ethos addressed the need in American communities for both economic growth and social order. It fused economic and moral values in the belief that a town's prosperity depended upon its collective spiritual condition, particularly upon its citizens' unity and public-spiritedness. Moreover, the booster ethos offered a vision of the community as a self-contained entity in which all interests were identical and interdependent. Consequently, the fortune of each individual, whether businessman, farmer, or laborer, rested upon the health of the community as a whole, and each was expected to return a portion to the community through voluntary public service and contributions to community institutions or enterprises. ("Order" 132–33)

To historian Daniel Boorstin, the emerging businessman of the midwest "thrived on growth and expansion. His loyalties were intense, naive, optimistic, and quickly transferable. . . . Versatility was his hallmark. . . . Rewards went to the organizer, the persuader, the discoverer of new opportunities, the projector, the risk-taker . . ." (123). The businessman-booster talked "tall talk" that "blurred the edges of fact and fiction" (290). Booster talk was "the language of anticipation," "a new linguistic confusion of present and future, fact and hope" (296). These exaggerations were not misrepresentations so much as "optimistic descriptions": "Freed to name as they pleased, Americans often cast their nomenclature in the mold of their hopes," hopes of "prosperity, wealth, culture, or glory" (297).

Jonas Fulkerson is a booster in the sense that Boorstin and Griffith describe. From the outset, he tells March, "This is the greatest idea that has been struck since . . . since the creation of man" (*Hazard* 7). And he continues to urge his plan forward with that mixture of fact and hope, exaggeration and optimism. By promoting his enterprise, *Every Other Week,* he secures his own economic well-being and that of the men and women of the *Every Other Week* community, a community he himself creates. He also brings a measure of social harmony by creating this community, though ultimately harmony is achieved as much by the deus ex machina tragedy of Conrad's and Lindau's deaths at the street car strike (a reflection, perhaps, of Howells's own sense that the extremes of society must be smoothed out for it to function well). And he helps to nurture the talents of his cohorts.

Fulkerson's guidance affects almost all the working artists and writers around him. He assists Colonel Woodburn in making a living by suggesting that he submit his manuscript on slavery to *Every Other Week,* then convincing March, as editor, to accept it. He helps the young artist Alma Leighton and her mother to make it in New York by advocating women's work. It is Fulkerson who asks Wetmore's art class to work up illustrations for the magazine, and he argues, against Wetmore and Beaton, that a woman's artistic output can be mature and worthy of publication. When he visits the Leightons, which soon becomes daily, he makes a point of encouraging Alma's work and taking an active interest in her choice of subjects. He suggests to both Beaton and March that they should develop what he calls "schools" of illustrators and story writers, a goal that would benefit the arts and the careers of the individuals involved as well as *Every Other Week.*

While Alma Leighton and Colonel Woodburn benefit from Fulkerson's encouragement, they are already productive artists before they meet the entrepreneur. Not so with Basil March. More than any of the others, March benefits from the guidance and encouragement of Fulkerson. It is Fulkerson who gives March the courage to make a midlife transition from a position of dull comfort to a job and life that present a new challenge and rejuvenate him and his family. March has lacked the courage to make a change from his settled routine working in insurance, despite his sense that the firm is about to demote, or even fire, him. Fulkerson comes in to March's office and breathes new life into him. He literally defines March to himself: "You're a natural-born literary man" (7). "What I want is an editor who has taste, and you've got it; and conscience, and you've got it; and horse sense, and you've got that" (9). He tells March that he is broad in his sympathies, that he has the western style of fun with a good knowledge of Boston, and that he is the man to "make this thing go" (10). He even tells March what March himself wants and needs: "What you want to do is to get out of the insurance business. . . . You never liked it and now it makes you sick" (7). By his heartily expressed faith in March's talent, he gives March the necessary boost to discuss the opportunity with Mrs. March, and the courage to pursue it. When Mrs. March secretly expresses her doubts about her husband's abilities to handle the job, again Fulkerson paints a picture that the two of them can believe in:

> He [Fulkerson] explained how the enterprise differed from others and how he needed for its direction a man who combined general

> business experience and business ideas with a love for the thing and a natural aptness for it. He did not want a young man, and yet he wanted youth—its freshness, its zest—such as March would feel in a thing he could put his whole heart into. He would not run in ruts, like an old fellow who had got hackneyed; he would not have any hobbies; he would not have any friends nor any enemies. . . . March was a man that people took to; she [Mrs. March] knew that herself; he had a kind of charm. (35)

Thus Fulkerson helps the Marches to see in Basil what he wants them to see.

Once March is committed, Fulkerson helps him to become a better editor by suggesting stories, contributors, and ideas. He encourages March again and again to do some writing of his own, though we have no indication that March ever actually pens a line. But it is Fulkerson who brings in Colonel Woodburn as a contributor and Lindau as a translator, and who generates ideas for stories about New York and the strike. And when the magazine is a success, Fulkerson liberally and generously hands out credit to March and Beaton rather than taking it for himself.

By the end of the novel, March has arguably developed in his understanding of the world; his acquaintance has been broadened and democratized, he has meaningful work, and he is now the part owner of a successful magazine. If his sympathies have been widened—and I think they have been—this, too, is a result of the opportunities brought to him by Fulkerson. Perhaps March has it in him to be a better man than Fulkerson; Fulkerson himself senses this and encourages his friend to use his full potential. He pulls March and his family through a difficult time so that in the end March can live successfully in a changing, challenging world. Surely March's hazard would not have been as fortunate if he had not been cajoled along by Fulkerson's optimistic talk and constant encouragement.

The other artist successfully mentored by Fulkerson is Angus Beaton, a twenty-seven-year-old man with an ego as large as his considerable talent. As Fulkerson says, Beaton could be "as many kinds of an ass as he was kinds of an artist" (102). But Fulkerson sees in him the talented artist, the gifted critic and teacher, and the man who is able to get along well with other young artists. Surely Beaton would be in danger of self-destruction if Fulkerson didn't keep him steady enough to earn a living. When we first see them together, Fulkerson is insisting that Beaton finish his letter for the syndicate. He asks Beaton to be art editor of *Every Other*

Week, he "punches him up," and, as he had for March, he defines for Beaton his own niche:

> We'll get up a School of Illustration. . . . You can read the things and explain 'em, and your pupils can make their sketches under your eye. . . . You might select from what comes in and make up a sort of pictorial variations to the literature without any particular reference to it. Well, I understand you to accept?" (123–24)

When Beaton says no, Fulkerson nevertheless leaves him money as an advance and drops the hint that the new syndicate owner, who has replaced Fulkerson, will be paying him less.

Once Beaton comes on the magazine, Fulkerson praises him lavishly and seeks his advice frequently. He smoothes his feathers again and again over perceived slights and insults. By doing so, Fulkerson coerces Beaton into using his talents in a way that not only helps the magazine but also brings the artist money and public notice. And Beaton's personal development takes a lesson from Fulkerson, too; by Fulkerson's example of successful courtship, Beaton is at last brought to recognize, if not to rectify, his own failed relations with women.

Fulkerson's example of courtship is interesting in itself, for in this respect his intended, Miss Woodburn, shows herself as modern and as astute an entrepreneur as her chosen partner. When Beaton suggests to Miss Woodburn that southerners despise business, Miss Woodburn rejoins, "*Despahse* it? Mah goodness! We want to get *into* it, and 'work it fo' all it's wo'th,' as Mr. Fulkerson says" (238). Miss Woodburn here is artfully interrogating Beaton about Fulkerson and the magazine, looking after her father's business—and perhaps her own personal—interests. She is no shrinking violet about business or love; later on it will be Miss Woodburn who transforms a business conversation into a proposal of marriage from the surprised, but delighted, Fulkerson. She makes a fit wife for a New York businessman. Appropriately, they begin married life in the rooms above the office of *Every Other Week.*

As Howells suggests, the role of protagonist in this novel is not very formidable. And yet we should not take Fulkerson too lightly. He initiates the contest and sees it through. Entrepreneur and booster, Jonas Fulkerson is the modern man, the one who can negotiate all social classes in a way that neither March, on the one hand, nor Dryfoos, on the other, could have managed. By bringing together elements of different social classes, seeing them through the inevitable period of clash, and bringing them out smoothly to the end, he has, as it were, tamed and populated a little section of New York, created a community, and contributed to nation building, just as Sally Griffith argues about boosters in general. In a newly complicated literary market, he forges from them and for them a comfortably established business that, if we can believe Howells's later novel, *An Open-Eyed Conspiracy,* lasts for many years. By developing an innovative enterprise, he creates something from nothing, giving the public a new magazine and the artists an opportunity to showcase their work. He serves as mentor to the others, a guide through the new and complicated Herculean world of money making and social democratization that is New York at the turn of the century.

Notes

1. "Mr. Howells's Latest Novel," *The Nation,* 454. Everett Carter attributes this review to Annie R. M. Logan.

2. William Dean Howells, "Autobiographical," 505. I have omitted crossed-out words and words written above the line by Howells. For a more exact rendering of the manuscript, see Carter.

3. For an interesting and full discussion of this, see Ohmann, *Selling Culture,* Garvey, *The Adman in the Parlor,* and Kaestle et. al., *Literacy in the United States.* Interestingly, although Howells treated the financial situation and opportunities of writers quite thoroughly in "The Man of Letters As a Man of Business" in 1893, he made no mention of advertising as a force changing the magazine or literary landscape.

Works Cited

Boorstin, Daniel. *The Americans: The National Experience.* London: Weidenfeld and Nicolson, 1966.

Garvey, Ellen. *The Adman in the Parlor.* New York and Oxford: Oxford University Press, 1996.

Griffith, Sally Foreman. *Home Town News.* New York and Oxford: Oxford University Press, 1989.

———. "'Order, Discipline, and a Few Cannon': Benjamin Franklin, the Association, and the Rhetoric and Practice of Boosterism." *Pennsylvania Magazine* 116 (1992): 131–55.

Howells, Mildred. *Life in Letters of William Dean Howells.* Garden City, New York: Doubleday Doran, 1928.

Howells, William Dean. "Autobiographical." *A Hazard of New Fortunes.* Ed. Everett Carter. Bloomington: Indiana University Press, 1976. 501–10.

———. "Bibliographical." *A Hazard of New Fortunes.* Ed. Everett Carter. Bloomington: Indiana University Press, 1976. 3–6.

———. *A Hazard of New Fortunes.* 1890. Bloomington: Indiana University Press, 1976. Introduction by Everett Carter.

———. *Literary Friends and Acquaintance.* New York and London: Harper, 1901.

———. "The Man of Letters As a Man of Business." *Scribner's* 14 (1893): 429–45.

———. *My Mark Twain*. 1910. Baton Rouge: Louisiana State University Press, 1967.

Kaestle, Carl F., et. al. *Literacy in the United States*. New Haven: Yale University Press, 1991.

"Mr. Howells's Latest Novel." *The Nation* (June 5, 1890): 454–55.

Mott, Frank Luther. *American Journalism*. New York: Macmillan, 1941.

Ohmann, Richard. *Selling Culture*. New York and London: Verso, 1996.

Henry James's Ghostly Mentors

Cheryl B. Torsney

Miss Brodie, Mr. Chips, Samuel Pickering (or at least his fictionalized self as played by Robin Williams in *Dead Poets' Society*): these are teachers the world has come to recognize as the right inheritors of Socrates. Among Jamesians, other names arise, some familiar—Frank Kermode, Richard A. Hocks, Elsa Nettels (teachers who are thanked in acknowledgments, essays, and Festschriften)—and some not so familiar (our mothers, our high school teachers, internet acquaintances from discussion lists).[1] Learning is found in the activities of editing as well as teaching and researching, as so engagingly represented by the essays Susan Griffin includes in the "Teaching James Forum" of the *Henry James Review*. But the teachers, ever the teachers, are the focus of our own personal histories with James. It is the truly exceptional one of us who found his or her way to James without a strong and patient guide, without a teacher whom we trusted and admired.

Are these teachers the authors of our academic beings, the creators of our James-o-centric universe? Or are they, like Barthes's and Foucault's authors, "dead" (even if they're still actually in the classroom and the world)? Instead of envisioning these teachers as either writers themselves (and us as their products) or as already-written constructs of their texts, we can reread them as inhabiting some sort of nether world in which they function as mediums, channeling their own teachers, the ghosts of their own written worlds. Boundary crossers par excellence, they are our own ghostly mentors responding to the ghosts in their past, who respond to *their* own ghosts, and so on: a spectral model of *mise-en-abîme* and intertextuality. In this essay I will show how ghosts—in James's life, in his fiction, and in the apparitions they inspire in our own lives—may well be the best teachers of all.

To understand the relationship between teaching and haunting in James's narratives, we must first turn to what we know of his own teachers and then to the teachers he creates in his fiction. It is in this way that we can understand how ghosts—be they memories, true supernatural visitations, or, as James says, communications with "sources"—permeate James's life and works and our own experiences with James and, through the ghost of the Master, with our teachers as well.

Henry James's own education was a rather haphazard affair. Henry Sr. experimented with educational methods, moving his children from school to school and from continent to continent, all the while believing that his sons, save William, were simply not bright enough to benefit from a formal education. Pierre Walker and Alfred Habegger conclude that "the father's instability, his belief in Henry's incapacity, and his quest for a school suitable to his talents were probably more influential factors in determining the future novelist's disorganized scholastic career than some hopeful theory that the boy would find his own feet under Divine Guidance" (110). James's own memories of this chaotic school history run to quirky details describing his earliest teachers, who were women, much to his chagrin. His eye focuses on the cut of these women's skirts, the tints of their hair and skin, their personal eccentricities. As he notes in his autobiography:

> A bevy of these educative ladies passed before me, I still possess their names; as for instance that of Mrs. Daly and that of Miss Rogers (previously of the "Chelsea Female Institute" . . .), whose benches indeed my brother didn't *haunt,* but who handled us literally with gloves. . . . Mrs. Daly, clearly the immediate successor to the nebulous Miss Bayou, remains quite substantial—perhaps because the sphere of her small influence has succeeded in not passing away. . . . Of pure unimported strain, however, were Miss Sedgwick and Mrs. Wright (Lavinia D.), the next figures in the procession—the procession that was to wind up indeed with two foreign recruits, small brown snappy Mademoiselle Delavignie . . . and a large Russian lady in an extraordinarily short cape . . . and Merovingian side-braids that seemed to require the royal crown of Frédégonde or Brunéhaut to complete their effect. (11–12, emphasis added)

James thus describes his memories of his teachers in ghostly terms: they are female figures alternately nebulous and substantial. At least one haunts him in literal terms, her "small influence [having] succeeded in not passing away." These teachers float in and out of the procession that the mature James imagines as he contemplates his youth.

In fact, James gives over a good chunk of *A Small Boy and Others* to an apparitional narrative of his irregular education, in which various teachers briefly surface only to sink back into the texture of memory. Chapter 15 discusses the Institution Vergnès, which, in the early fifties, was situated in the middle of Broadway. M. Vergnès himself is characterized as "quite 'old,' very old indeed . . . and highly irritated and markedly bristling" (114). When this placement didn't work out, the James brothers transferred to the establishment of Mr. Richard Pulling Jenks, where they encountered Mr. Coe, the drawing master, and Mr. Dolmidge, the writing master, who are then described as "old-world images, figures of an antique stamp" (116). Dolmidge is "a pure pen-holder of a man, melancholy and mild," while Coe is "bristling with the question of the 'hard,' but somehow too with the revelation of the soft, the deeply attaching" (117). Then it was on to the Messrs. Forest and Quackenboss. James writes: "I make out with clearness that Mr. Forest was awful and arid, and yet that somehow, by the same stroke, we didn't under his sway, go in terror, only went exceedingly in want" (122). This was 1854.

When the James family decamped to France, James was enrolled at the Institution Fezandié in Paris for four or five months during 1857. Despite Henry Sr.'s memoirs, which characterized it as a Fourierist institution, it was really just an expensive language school for foreign children. That summer, young Henry attended Boulogne's Collège Communal, which employed a M. Ansieaux, who may well have been among the faculty William criticized as "inflated, pompous, pedantic literary Professors in their magisterial robes" (Walker, "France in James" 3).

Later the James children had quite a string of governesses whose "*ghostly* names, again, so far as I recall them, I like piously to preserve, Augustine Danse, Amélie Fortin, Marie Guyard, Marie Bonningue, Félicie Bonningue, Clarisse Bader." James continues, "I can no more imagine why, sociable and charitable, we so often changed governesses than I had contemporaneously grasped the principle of our succession of schools" (173, emphasis added). Again, the names of the teachers achieve apparitional status as they cross from the realm of deep memory into autobiographical consciousness.

These women were followed by a succession of male tutors: "good Robert Thompson was followed by *fin* M. Lerambert" (183). And so the James children's education, such as it was, progressed. James reasons that he and William were finally educated in spite of themselves:

> Method certainly never quite raged among us; but it was our fortune nevertheless that everything had its turn, and that such indifferences were no more pedantic than certain rigours might perhaps have been. . . . That definite reflection is that if we had not had in us to some degree the root of the matter no method, however confess-

> edly or aggressively "pedantic," would much have availed for us; and that since we apparently did have it, deep down and inert in our small patches of virgin soil, the fashion after which it struggled forth was an experience as intense as any other and a record of as great a dignity. (124)

Mysteriously, then, the James brothers were educated almost by their own efforts, owing little to those ghosts represented in James's autobiography.

It is as though James wants us to believe that, although he is haunted by his teachers' names, he has paradoxically managed to escape possession by their memories. In this way, the very paradox of ghostliness is both replicated and screwed about a quarter turn further into the grain of the autobiographical text. For, as Terry Castle explains, a ghost is a spirit who nonetheless haunts, that is, visits, "reappears continually." Thus, the ghost is itself a paradox: "Though nonexistent, it nonetheless *appears.* Indeed, so vividly does it appear—if only in the 'mind's eye'—one feels unable to get away from it" (46). James can hardly escape the memories of these teachers, however; they have possessed him so completely that he has written a large part of *A Small Boy and Others* in order to exorcise them.

In James's fiction, too, those entrusted to educating a child or those who certain supplicants hope will offer lessons—tutors, governesses, mentors of various sorts—are instead figures who impede the growth of knowledge or who are outstripped by their "charges'" perception. These various educators fail—as they'd failed Henry—in the artist-mentor tales of the mid-1880s to the late 1890s (collected in *The Figure in the Carpet and Other Stories*), in "The Pupil" (1891), and in James's most famous tale of education, *The Turn of the Screw* (1898). In failing, however, they become specters who are more able to achieve their educational goals.

The mentoring performed by the established writers of the artist-mentor tales comes to naught time and time again. The narrator of "The Author of Beltraffio," for instance, idolizes Mark Ambient, keeping his photograph "enshrined" on his mantle shelf (*Figure* 59), believing that Ambient and he share a voice (61), and describing himself as having "sat in the school in which he was master" (78). Yet, when he visits Ambient and his family at their home, he becomes embroiled in the events that lead to Ambient's son's death. In "The Lesson of the Master," Paul Overt notes his "own immense debt" to Henry St. George (*Figure* 117), who tells the younger novelist that marriage is to be avoided, that children are a curse, and that a real artist can have neither. St. George becomes, by the end, a "mocking fiend" (187) by marrying Overt's own lover. In "The Middle

Years," Dencombe, the author of the book of the same title, meets an admirer, Dr. Hugh, at a seaside resort. Dr. Hugh tells the writer that he wants to be like him, "to learn by [his] mistakes" (*Figure* 250). Dencombe believes that Dr. Hugh is "an apparition" who is "above the law"; in an odd twist, Dr. Hugh, who is young and healthy, haunts the famous author, who is soon to be a ghost himself. Despite his devotion, however, the young supplicant does not understand what Dencombe is trying to teach in his novel. At the end, as Dencombe is dying, the lesson of this master—that there are no second chances, that frustration is all—remains misunderstood.

We learn in James's preface to the New York Edition volume containing "The Middle Years" and "The Author of Beltraffio" that the "air-blown" particle and grain—the famous Jamesian germ—of both these tales are ghosts: the first concerns "a young artist long dead, and whom [James] had yet briefly seen and was to remember with kindness"; and the second is "of an eminent author, these several years dead and on some of the embarrassments of whose life and character a common friend was enlarging" (*Figure* 49–50). Apparitional memories, then, lie at the heart of both these tales, connecting for us ghosts and teacher/mentors.

"The Pupil" (1891) and *The Turn of the Screw* treat the teacher-student relationship in the most obvious manner. In the former, the tutor, Pemberton, has charge of the "supernaturally clever" Morgan Moreen (*Complete Tales* 418), who becomes less his student than his sidekick. The Moreens keep Pemberton off-balance by refusing to pay him regularly, leaving him wondering about his "footing" with the family.

Morgan, however, knows the game his parents are playing, for he has seen the pattern before, with his nurse, Zénobie. A type of teacher, Zénobie shrewdly recognizes the Moreens' plan and informs Morgan before she leaves his family's employ "in a fearful rage one night" (435). A tender ghost in Morgan's memory, he substantiates her for Pemberton through recalling the circumstances of her departure. But Pemberton refuses to learn from Morgan, who acts as the medium. As Morgan comments, Zénobie was part of his experience and now he is part of Pemberton's. Pemberton, however, will not be instructed, either by Morgan or, through him, by his ghostly nurse; thus, Pemberton abdicates his own teacherly responsibility not only to teach but also to learn. He and Morgan become playmates, talking of their escape from the eccentric Moreen family "as if they were making up a 'boy's book' together" (454). When Morgan's parents finally give him up to his tutor, Morgan dies with Pemberton still clueless.

In James's other famous story of death and pedagogy, Miles, another preternaturally intelligent child who performs "the dizziest feats of arithmetic, soaring quite out of *my* feeble range, and perpetrated, in higher spirits than ever, geographical and historical jokes" (*Turn* 92), dies. The governess, a female Pemberton, attributes this knowledge to Miles's acquaintance with "the imagination of all evil" (92). Critics manage to agree on a few issues connected with James's writing of the tale: that James heard the germ of the tale at tea at the home of the Archbishop of Canterbury, only five days after the disastrous opening night of *Guy Domville,* an event that signaled the death of James's hopes for a career as a playwright; that spectral phenomena were subject of serious scholarly study during the last half of the nineteenth century; that James himself attended at least one meeting of the Society for Psychical Research as William's representative (see Beidler, "Introduction," 12–17).

What no one can agree upon is where precisely the evil lies in what James calls "this perfectly independent and irresponsible little fiction." Perhaps it is in the demonic children; maybe in the governess: Miss Jessel, the past governess who haunts the children and the present governess, may be the locus of evil—or of knowledge, which amounts to much the same thing. At any rate, the schoolroom is not a site of instruction, and no matter how we read *The Turn of the Screw,* we would not want to rely on this governess for the education of our children.

One of the more provocative recent readings of this tale is that offered by Terry Castle, who argues that lesbians, because of the unspeakability of their identities, become spectral metaphors in literature ranging from Balzac and Dickens to Lillian Hellman: "And just as lesbians get turned 'into' ghosts in such literature, ghosts—to their discredit—also get turned into lesbians. To the extent, for example, that the mysterious Miss Jessel in Henry James's *The Turn of the Screw* manifests herself as an apparition hungering 'infamously' after little Flora, it is tempting also to read her as a cryptolesbian: in the sinister metaphorical dynamic of James's story the two identities, ghost and girl-lover, seem indeed to be endlessly and horrifyingly interchangeable" (45–46). Indeed, whether we buy the queer reading of the novel or not, it is the interchangeability of identity—between ghost and living character—that so compels us to horror.

These ghosts among us trump the "real" teachers for insight and instruction. In *The Turn of the Screw,* the apparitional Miss Jessel makes knowledge visible, but the governess disapproves of what she's teaching Flora, and she teaches the governess herself by negative example. These ghosts become us, *are* us. In her enduringly important *Henry James and the Occult* (1972), Martha Banta asserts that, in James, "Supernatural, occult, psychical, and transcendent" refer to the human mind and its operations rather than "demons, nature spirits, gods, or the stars or the planets" (3). In other words, if there are any ghosts to be busted in James, they reside in the minds of his characters. More recently, T. J. Lustig has extended Banta's discussion by insisting that James himself is a ghost haunting his works. Ghosts are go-betweens, boundary leapers; they obscure origins, represent the unrepresentable (97). In seeing an apparition, the ghost-seer indulges a transcendent, border-crossing consciousness, and becomes a type of ghost himself or herself (189).

For many characters in James, seeing a ghost is *the* supreme learning experience, the revelation of self-knowledge, the way in which one transcends. In the most famous of these scenes, Isabel Archer finally sees the ghost Ralph had promised her would be revealed after she had suffered sufficiently. He had told her that "the privilege isn't given to every one; it's not enviable. It has never been seen by a young, happy, innocent person like you. You must have suffered first, have suffered greatly, have gained some miserable knowledge" (*Portrait* 52). That miserable knowledge is specifically self-knowledge. To recall Terry Castle's reading of the ghost in *The Turn of the Screw*, it is the interchangeability between ghost and living representative that yields the terror, or here, the terrible, sad knowledge of what one has become. Through the vehicle of the Gardencourt ghost, Isabel can claim her own suffering and experience its transcendence. According to Banta, Isabel's seeing the Gardencourt ghost upon Ralph's death "measures [her] deepest point of awareness," recognizes her new knowledge of emotional pain. She has entered into self-knowledge, seen herself as a ghost of her "young, happy, innocent" past, for the ghost is Isabel herself.

Spencer Brydon, in "The Jolly Corner," is similarly haunted, but by the very person he might have been had he stayed in this country to fight the Civil War instead of decamping to England. And James himself is self-haunted, which might well be the most succinct definition we have of autobiography—self-haunting—in the three volumes of his life story. He is certainly haunted by the ghost of Constance Fenimore Woolson, whom Leon Edel believes to be James's model for May Bartram in "The Beast in the Jungle" (Edel 377).

There's an even more intriguing story of Woolson's haunting of Henry James. When Woolson died from a suicidal fall from a second-story window of a Venetian palace in 1894, James refused to attend the funeral of his dear friend. When, however, her sister and niece asked James to come to help them to organize her affairs—James spoke Italian, and they didn't—he traveled to Venice. Speculation abounds regarding what, if anything, James found and probably destroyed among Woolson's papers—letters, perhaps, revealing the truth of their relationship. What he most certainly did do, however, was to collect her black silk dresses, hire a gondolier, and dump the gowns into the canal. As the story goes, "he threw them in the water and they came up like balloons all around him, and the more he tried to throw them down, the more they came up and he was surrounded by these horrible black balloons" (54–55).[2] Dresses like black balloons. Or, like dead bodies bloated with gases and serving as a floating reproach. Here is an apparition of Constance Woolson that haunts anyone who imagines it—and that must have haunted James for the rest of his life. It's a ghost that he, like Isabel Archer, would have seen: one signifying personal knowledge of suffering.

For James believed in ghosts, though not in the more literal ways William did. In "Is There a Life After Death?", James's chapter in William Dean Howells's *In After Days: Thoughts on the Future Life,* James writes that, as an artist, he finds himself "in communication with *sources;* sources to which I owe the apprehension of far more and far other combinations than observation and experience, in their originary sense, have given me the pattern of" (224). Complete disconnection of this consciousness with the world is, he implies, unlikely. What, then, does the world beyond do but teach—in ways that teachers of this world don't and can't? The young Henry James's governesses didn't teach him much; but recalling them from their world beyond—he terms their names *ghostly* in *A Small Boy and Others*—reveals something worth knowing.

Like James, we are all, I suspect, haunted by "sources." Sometimes these sources are genuine ghosts; sometimes they are this altered consciousness that Banta suggests resides in our minds. They are voices our education in pain teaches us to hear; their voices are interchangeable with our own.

Still in my teens, I believed, as Isabel Archer does early in *The Portrait of a Lady:* "Nothing that belongs to me is any measure of me; everything's on the contrary a limit, a barrier, and a perfectly arbitrary one. Certainly the clothes which, as you say, I choose to wear, don't express me; and heaven forbid they should" (175). When I first read the novel, I resembled Isabel at the beginning of the novel: I was still too naive to grasp the sad truth of the requisite nature of forms understood by Madame Merle, the former lover of Isabel's husband, Gilbert Osmond. At Louisiana State University, where I completed my master's degree, where New Critical power and politics were played out in the forties, where James was nearly ingrained in the woodwork, I was to experience my own transformation from naive schoolgirl to a woman who could recognize ghosts.

Late one routine afternoon, hardly prepared for melodrama, I was pacing the hallway in the garret where many of the graduate students' and instructors' offices were located, grumbling about what I perceived as the departmental obsession with James, complaining about the interminable sentences, the labyrinthine relationships, the huge doorstoppers of books with thin pages and small type in which nothing seemed to happen, my already nearsighted vision, which reading James was putting at further risk. At some point in what had devolved into a harangue, one of the instructors, John Finlay, a poet who saw bourbon-induced visions of the Virgin, invited me into his office and sat me down.

I knew that John was devoted to Yvor Winters and to his orthodox brand of Catholicism. John wrote of Winters's thought in "To the Holy Spirit" as though it were his own: "His commitment to the intellect made him suspicious of God, and yet without God that intellect and the objects of its perception would not even exist. And how can the creator of a thing reasonably be viewed as a threat to its existence?" This schismatic view of the world was expressed more poetically in John's poem "Audubon at Oakley," wherein he wrote that the legends underneath the drawings of the birds, "defining them, combined: / The clean abstraction of their Latin names, / The salty richness of the Saxon slang." The language that John found so compelling—from Winters and from Audubon—was the language associated with ghosts: of the Holy Spirit, of the spirits of dead birds, both of them metaphors, both of them soaring to eternity.

What I didn't know was that John was devoted to another ghost, one I envisioned as my bitterest enemy. In the dark office lit only by a low-wattage incandescent bulb in a goosenecked lamp, John squinted at me over the top of his wire-rimmed glasses, asked my age in that slow, soft Alabama accent of his, and then explained that I just needed to be older to understand James. As I peered over his shoulder, I noted a framed postcard of the John Singer Sargent portrait of the Master hanging on the wall nearest his desk. Behind me burned some candles and, though I can't swear to it, some incense on the university-issue bookshelf. I realized that I was in a shrine and that John of the Madonna Visions was its high priest. At the time, it seemed odd that an Alabama boy, as wiry as James was portly, would serve the Master in such a capacity. It's hard to reconcile the image of the devoted acolyte with one of my last memories of him, in a car full of beery academics driving home to Baton Rouge on the River Road from a crawfish restaurant in Convent, Louisiana. And harder still to realize that John has now been dead for over a decade.

John was right. At my first communion in his office, he had promised that mysteries would be revealed, that desire for the Master would be confirmed. It wasn't long after that meeting that, while reading *The Golden Bowl* in a seminar devoted to James, Lawrence, and Conrad, the once-innocent Isabel recognized that she had grown, almost imperceptibly but most surely, into the experienced Charlotte Stant.

Charlotte is first the best friend and later the stepmother of Maggie Verver, the heroine of *The Golden Bowl* (1904), James's last great novel. Early in the narrative, Maggie, the daughter of millionaire businessman and art collector Adam Verver, to whom she has been exceedingly devoted, marries Prince Amerigo, a charming but poor Italian nobleman. Because her marriage leaves her father alone, Maggie and her husband successfully plot to marry Charlotte to Adam. Throughout the narrative, then, the foursome is rather naturally thrown together, the father and the beautiful stepmother, the daughter and her Prince. What Maggie discovers in the course of the novel is what the reader knows from the opening chapters: that the Prince and Charlotte are lovers who did not marry only for lack of financial means. The most memorable scenes, those with a distinct erotic charge, are devoted to a description of Charlotte and the Prince's moments alone during a shopping trip for a wedding gift for Maggie on the eve of the marriage.

Although Maggie becomes the supremely intelligent consciousness that organizes the narrative in Part Two of the novel, James never gives her a corporeal incarnation. Her body is nearly as elusive (though not as ill) as that of Milly Theale, the heroic dove of *The Wings of the Dove* (1902). Charlotte, however, is given to us in physical terms. She embodies desire, need, dark beauty, and is the subject of some of James's most erotic description. We learn about Charlotte from the perspective of her former lover:

> He saw again that her thick hair was, vulgarly speaking, brown, but that there was a shade of tawny autumn leaf in it for 'appreciation'—a colour indescribable and of which he had known no other case, something that gave her at moments the sylvan head of a huntress. He saw the sleeves of her jacket drawn to her wrist, but he again made out the free arms within them to be of the completely rounded, and polished slimness that Florentine sculptors, in the great time, had loved, and of which the apparent firmness is expressed in their old silver and old bronze. He knew her narrow hands, he knew her long fingers and the shape and colour of her finger-nails, he knew her special beauty of movement and line when she turned her back. . . . He knew above all the extraordinary fineness of her flexible waist, the stem of an expanded flower which gave her a likeness also

> to some long, loose silk purse, well filled with gold pieces, but having been passed, empty, through a finger-ring that held it together. (59)

Experience told me that I could now see the Gardencourt ghost myself, experience borne of using the excuse of having been, like Charlotte and the Prince, "arranged together" to rationalize a relationship with a colleague that violated Jamesian propriety. My logic was Charlotte's. In seminar meetings during which the class discussed *The Golden Bowl,* I didn't dare offer why James spoke so clearly to me in the novel that my classmates believed to be his most opaque, why I always felt a kinship with James's "bad girls," those who flouted convention.

I couldn't talk about how Charlotte's excruciating anguish at the end of the novel—a pain precipitated by Maggie Verver's recognition that Charlotte and her husband have been engaged in an unconscionable ménage and by Maggie's subtle reorchestration of her life with the Prince—figured my own suffering. Charlotte's quavering high voice sounds to Maggie "like the shriek of a soul in pain," but no one of such fine consciousness heard mine. Though maybe John intuited it. As he had promised, James's great delicacy and immense capacity for truth, however one defines it, was at last exposed to me. Such revelation had its tragic prerequisites, however: my innocent former self was now a ghost, and age and experience had to initiate new narratives. John Finlay had envisioned it, I am convinced—truly foreseen it. Maybe Mary had told him. Although I didn't know then, I discovered later that John was dying at this time, preparing to become a ghost himself.

Once an Isabel protesting limitation in all embodiments—from behavior to clothing—I was now a Charlotte, a respecter of shape, a devotee of form. I had suffered, and I had learned. Now, each time I gaze up at the Katherine MacClelland photograph of James on the Library of America poster hanging in my study, I see not only James but also the ghost of John Finlay—and my own ghostly self as well as Isabel Archer's—gazing back over the same pair of wire-rimmed glasses.

I have been lucky. My teachers of James have been brilliant readers and writers and encouraging, supportive people. James's own teachers, however, generally ineffectual and mercenary, did not contribute effectively to young Henry's education, though James liked several of them well enough, I suppose. His fictional teachers, like Pemberton and the governess, are variously read as queer, mad, or vicious from one perspective or another. They are not exemplary citizens and neither mentor nor teach effectively. Those figures who do genuinely instruct are more often ghosts, specters who, freed from their earthly bonds, may educate and advocate in ways they could not while living. Like the ghost of John Finlay. Or they are apparitional representatives of an expanded consciousness. Like the Gardencourt ghost. They may not even be dead: just existing on another plane, often a retrospective one. They may be our own teachers, or our earlier selves, still thriving, whose thoughts and deeds haunt us years later.

Teaching is haunting; haunting is teaching. James knew; John Finlay knew; and now we know. In these twin transcendent activities we are able to discover our greatest terror—or our greatest enlightenment.

Notes

1. See especially Walker, "Frank Kermode as a Teacher of Henry James."

2. According to Lyndall Gordon's source notes, the story comes to us through a rather circuitous route:

> In 1956, Mercede Huntington of the Villa Mercede (once called the Villa Castellani), Bellosguardo, Florence [once one of Woolson's residences], recalled a "strange tale" told to her by Henry James. The record appears in an unedited transcript of interviews recorded on tape for the BBC (Third Programme), "Recollections of Henry James in His Later Years," transmitted on June 14, 1956. Originally owned by HJ's amanuensis, Theodora Bosanquet. Now in Houghton: bMS Eng 1213.4(20). Details published by Alide Cagidimetrio (Gordon 377).

Works Cited

Banta, Martha. *Henry James and the Occult: The Great Extension.* Bloomington: Indiana University Press, 1972.

Beidler, Peter G., ed. "Introduction: Biographical and Historical Contexts." Introduction to *The Turn of the Screw,* by Henry James. Boston: Bedford, 1995. 3–19.

Castle, Terry. *The Apparitional Lesbian: Female Homosexuality and Modern Culture.* New York: Columbia University Press, 1993.

Edel, Leon. *The Middle Years: 1882–1895.* Vol. 3 of *The Life of Henry James.* Philadelphia: Lippincott, 1962. Reprint, New York: Avon, 1978.

Finlay, John. "Audubon at Oakley." *The Southern Review* 18 (1982): 357.

———. "The Unfleshed Eye: A Reading of Yvor Winters' 'To the Holy Spirit.'" *The Southern Review* 17 (1981): 873–86.

Gordon, Lyndall. *A Private Life of Henry James.* New York: Norton, 1999.

Griffin, Susan M., ed. "Teaching James Forum." *The Henry James Review* 17 (fall 1996): 211–99.

James, Henry. *The Figure in the Carpet and Other Stories.* Ed. Frank Kermode. Harmondsworth, England: Penguin, 1986.

———. "Is There a Life After Death?" In *After Days: Thoughts on the Future Life.* Ed. William Dean Howells. New York: Harper, 1910. 199–233.

———. *The Jolly Corner and Other Tales.* Ed. Frank Kermode. Harmondsworth: Penguin, 1986.

———. *The Portrait of a Lady.* New York: Norton, 1984.

———. "The Pupil." *The Complete Tales of Henry James.* Vol. 7. New York: Lippincott, 1963. 409–62.

———. *A Small Boy and Others.* Vol. 1 of *Autobiography.* Ed. Frederick W. Dupee. Princeton, New Jersey: Princeton University Press, 1983.

———. *The Turn of the Screw.* Ed. Peter G. Beidler. Boston: Bedford, 1995.

Lustig, T. J. *Henry James and the Ghostly.* Cambridge, England: Cambridge University Press, 1994.

Walker, Pierre A. "Frank Kermode as a Teacher of James." *The Henry James Review* 17 (fall 1996): 281–87.

———. "From France in James to James in France." Paper given at the 1996 meeting of the Modern Language Association in Washington, D.C.

Walker, Pierre A., and Alfred Habegger. "Young Henry James and the *Institution Fezandié.*" *The Henry James Review* 15 (spring 1994): 107–20.

Negative Mentorship and the Case of Alice James

Esther F. Lanigan

The woman activist or artist born of a family-centered mother may in any case feel that her mother cannot understand or sympathize with the imperatives of her life; or that her mother may have preferred or valued a more conventional daughter, or a son.

Adrienne Rich (229)

Alice James, sister of the brilliant Henry and William, and diarist of little note until Jean Strouse wrote a much-acclaimed biography of her, has received scant scholarly attention when one considers the virtual scholarly industry focused on her famous brothers. The Strouse biography reveals a brilliant woman, stunted by her personality, a woman who made invalidism a career until her death of cancer in 1892 at age forty-four. Inexplicable and chronic nervous illnesses stalked her and shaped her life into that of a reclusive, bedridden woman.[1] Reading the biography, the letters, and the biographical and autobiographical accounts that explore Alice James's family, one is struck by the effect of Alice's mother, Mary Walsh James, on her daughter's life and negative literary career as contrasted to the careers of her notable brothers.

Since Alice left so small a written legacy compared to that of either William or Henry, one might wonder why the lack of mentoring matters. From the letters and the diary, however, emerges evidence that Alice James cared deeply about writing. She also cared about the record of her own life and hoped to leave a written account that might reveal aspects of a self not defined by illness or by her family. In a letter to Annie Ashburner, Alice pleads that her "pen is unequal to the task" of doing justice to an amusing figure (Yeazell 57), but this remark highlights her self-awareness as a writer, a writer highly conscious of the effect and power of words. Long before she begins her diary, Alice's letters reveal a concern for the dramatic moment and an eye for detail that rivaled the observant powers of her brother Henry. In an 1867 letter to brother William, she narrates an amusing family moment, but before doing so inserts a line that echoes stage directions for a play: "The scene is laid in the dining room, time, dinner" (Yeazell 52). Letter after letter includes scenes, characters, and incidents that reflect her wit, wry humor, and eye for the dramatic moment. Before her death, she asked that the manuscript of her diary be typewritten; Katharine Loring assumed that she intended it for publication (Yeazell 5). Given her abilities and the desire she expressed even late in her life to "have a career somewhere" (Yeazell 144), Alice James's inability to break through the social and familial barriers that prevented a public, literary life invites exploration.

My purpose here is to ask some questions and to offer a few notes on the problematic absence or presence of the mother figure in Alice's life. How much did Mary Walsh James have to do with the psychosomatic illnesses visited on all James children? Why did Mary Walsh James never seem to be afflicted herself with illness while it flourished all around her? Why did Alice choose to make a conscious cult of illness? What did the plethora of absent or unpleasant mothers in Henry James's fiction have to do with Mary James and with daughter Alice, especially when the evidence contained in letters and diaries indicates that as a mother Mary was beloved by her family?[2] Why does Alice seem so relieved following her mother's death? How might Mary James have been a symbol of negative achievement to her daughter? What defines a mother's role in a family where the father "wanted to be everything to his children—father, mother, teacher, fellow pupil, intimate friend" (Strouse 17–18)? Where is the mother in the James family—because the father is so clearly there—especially in the life of Alice? To whom did Alice look as substitute mother figures?

These are only matters for speculation. Some patterns emerge, however, that spark the imagination, especially when one considers what Alice's career might have been like if Mary Walsh James had been a different sort of person—more of an intellectual, say, or perhaps if she had died early as Virginia Woolf's mother, Julia Stephen, did. As it happened Mary James lived a long life, and her presence kept the home fires burning, even if it did not ignite the intellectual flames within the James family household. Mary James, as we find her, is a more interesting figure for what was not said about her in the massive accumulation of James family evidence than those engaged in James family biography had thought to explore until recent years.

Although she never writes a fictive version of her experience, the problems inherent in Alice James's life and in her relationship to her mother bear striking resemblance to the difficulties posed for nineteenth-century heroines of fiction as described by Marianne Hirsch. In *The Mother/Daughter Plot,* Hirsch suggests that "the fantasy that controls the female family romance is the desire for the heroine's singularity based on a disidentification from the fate of other women, especially mothers" (10). Further, she explains that "motherhood in Victorian ideology . . . represents a confinement and potential destruction impossible to combine with the freedom and expansiveness seen as necessary to artistic creativity" (Hirsch 45). Thus, the woman "who wants to write, or who wants in anyway to be productive and creative, . . . must break from her mother, so as not to be identified with the mother's silence" (Hirsch 45). Analyzing her own attempts to become like the neutral and silent figure her mother embodied within the family circle, Alice likened it to "killing" herself (Yeazell 13).

Alice's position in the family circle, at the sidelines of the central action, appears in William's early letters from Europe. From Bonn, where Henry and William were enrolled in school in 1860, William wrote to the family in Paris: "We wondered what our beloved parents were doing at that moment (half-past eleven), and thought you must all have been in the parlor, Alice, the widow, with her eyes fixed on her novel, eating some rich fruit which Father has just brought in for her from the Palais Royal, and lovely Mother and Aunt Kate in arm-chairs with their hands crossed in front of them, listening to Father, who is walking up and down speaking of the superiority of America to these countries" (Matthiessen 91). Although William comments that he wishes he could be there to "join in the conversation," he evokes in his letter a world where girls and mothers watch passively while men engage in intellectual activity, where daughters idly page through novels while Father lectures to Mother and Aunt, who listen attentively but uncritically to his ideas. This arrangement of the family circle, in which Alice appears "a figure at the edge of the frame" (Yeazell 7), recurs when the family returns to America. Recalling a James family dinner in 1861, Edward Emerson described the heated exchanges between brothers, moderated by their father, while "the quiet little sister ate her dinner, close to the combatants" (Strouse 66).

The line of demarcation between Alice and her brothers was accentuated through her education. Protofeminists of the time, Mary L. Booth, historian and editor of *Harper's Bazaar* among them, were writing strong articles protesting the "degree of distinction made by mothers between male and female children not warranted by sex" (Leach 65). It seems unlikely that Henry James Sr. and, more particularly, Mary Walsh James were prepared to grapple with such an article advocating feminist child-rearing practices. The ground had been laid early on in the James marriage for Mary to listen to and live for "Father's Ideas," never her own, if she had any beyond the domestic realm. These gender arrangements were accepted in the James household as the natural order of things and were reinforced through the choices the James parents made for their children. While younger sons Garth Wilkinson and Robertson were sent to Frank Sanborn's coeducational school in Concord, Massachusetts, where their classmates included Emerson daughters, Alice was kept at home. Surely the discrimination practiced by her parents was made more evident to Alice through the presence of young women at her brothers' school.

Alice, the child who stayed closest to her mother for thirty years, the only daughter and the youngest in a family of five children, seems to be the most distant child spiritually from the mother's heart. Henry James was to remember, in looking back at his mother's life, her unflagging devotion to her husband and to Alice: "Summer after summer she never left Cambridge—it was impossible that father should leave his own house. The country, the sea, the change of air and scene, were an exquisite enjoyment to her; but she bore with deepest gentleness and patience the constant loss of such opportunities. She passed her nights and her days in that dry, flat, hot, stale and odious Boston, and had never a thought while she did so but for father and Alice. It was a perfect mother's life—the life of a perfect wife" (*Notebooks* 40). Alice neither adds to nor subtracts from Henry's benediction of Mother, but one might speculate that her reaction to such self-sacrifice was guilt in realizing that she could never measure up to this standard of faultless "devotion," and perhaps a measure of relief when her mother died, thus ending a competition engendered by the principles of "the cult of domesticity."

If Alice admired wife and motherhood in the abstract, she makes it clear in the diary that these are pleasures she can cheerfully forego in her own life. Her references to fears of the physicality of childbearing are notable for their frequency. Typical is a letter she wrote to Aunt Kate before New Year's 1888, in which she describes "the groans of the woman in labour in the room above, where the mystery of Life & Death was acting itself out. How my heart burned within me at the cruelty of men! I have been haunted by the thought of Alice [Gibbens James, William's wife] and all the childbearing women ever since" (Yeazell 156). Since her mother's major accomplishment, selfless wifehood and maternity, maps onto one of Alice's greatest fears (the physicality and intimacy of childbearing), how can we take Alice at face value when she recalls the splendor of Mary James's maternal and conjugal career?

We do know that Alice proclaimed of her closest female friend, Katharine Loring, at the outset of their friendship, admiration for "a woman free of enslavements to husband, children and country" (Strouse 219). At the same time we know from reading Strouse that Katharine's maternal devotion to Alice was extraordinary. Katharine seems to fascinate Alice because she had escaped the confines that Alice perceived constrained her own mother. "There is nothing [Katharine] cannot do from hewing wood & drawing water to driving run-away horses & educating all the women in North America," Alice wrote to her friend, Sara Sedgwick Darwin in 1879 (Yeazell 82). Katharine's ministrations to Alice were sometimes interrupted to address the needs of her own invalid sister, a situation that caused Alice much jealousy and grief. In contrast to Alice's mother, however, Katharine's maternal availability, coupled with her own professional and intellectual accomplishments (Loring was a professor of history at the Society to Encourage Studies at Home), must have held out the best of all possible physical and spiritual worlds to Alice James.

Before Katharine Loring encountered Alice James, Alice and her mother were charting the mysterious territory of debilitating illness, of fainting spells, paralysis, headaches, and stomach gout, which Alice was to travel for twenty years. This was a territory Mary Walsh James knew well, for hadn't she and her sister Kate been pillars of strength in the Walsh family for those afflicted with bouts of "depression" and "nerves," of melancholy and backaches, offering continuous consolation and advice as needed?

In reading the Strouse biography of Alice James, it is impossible to refrain from asking—where is Mary James when daughter Alice first begins to suffer from "violent turns of hysteria"? Her presence for and her influence over Alice seem to be negligible except for brief letters validating her daughter's illness when she is away from home, mainly advice about coping with or understanding an illness that would not go away except when Alice went away from home. From 1866 to 1867, Mary James did not accompany Alice to New York for her "motorpathy" treatment under Dr. Taylor. Rather, she sent her lieutenant, Aunt Kate, for this mission. Mother's letters are cheery missives of encouragement, but also of reinforcement of Alice's "condition." In January of 1867, for example, Mother notes that she has heard "such fine accounts of your blooming appearance that I shall expect to hear that the good work of restoration is almost completed" (Strouse 109).[3] Mary James seems never to have questioned Alice's need of "restoration" nor what underlay the cause of her "illness." Understandably, given the period, neither in Dr. Taylor's treatment protocol nor in Mary James's letters appears a linking of nervous disorders in the daughter to her family's patterns of interaction. Alice becomes the only sibling unable to and incapable of permanently distancing herself from a household that appears to have made her sick.

The prescribed cures, whether at Dr. Taylor's or a dozen other retreats for female nervous ailments, were informed by the principle that women must empty their minds and uncritically conform to the regimen outlined by physicians so that they might return to their families rather than be released from them. To Alice the family identity bestowed on her was that of "invalid," an accepted niche for women in the late nineteenth century. Psychiatric intervention in the late nineteenth century, fixed as it was on rest cures, exercise, clinics, regular routines, and sensory deprivation, did not consider that the patient might actually hate the family who had admitted her to care (or why Alice in 1868 thought of killing herself and her father). Rather, medical treatment of women's psychological symptoms intervened to convert the young woman into a cooperative "invalid" and, in so doing, to avoid confrontation of those persons most responsible for her feelings of powerlessness. For Alice, the need to empty her mind must have recalled the struggles first felt early in adolescence, the neutralizing of herself that seemed a "killing." Interestingly, brother William's nervous disorder during the same decade resulted in his taking a leave from Harvard Medical School to join Dr. Jean Agassiz's expedition to South America—a rigorous adventure thought to be beneficial for his full recovery. How might Alice have fared had she, too, been encouraged to make an adventurous journey to assist her recovery from illness?

Instead, in Alice's case invalidism seems to have worked itself into a vicious circle of rage and breakdown. It appears that next to her brilliant older brothers, she perceived herself as nothing less than "idiotoid," as she signed herself in a letter to William in August of 1867. Her father, overprotective and overprotected by Mother and Aunt Kate, failed to take Alice's intellect seriously; her mother, apparently content with a life of domestic detail, seems not to have understood her daughter's "nervous diseases" for what they were: a rebellion against her assigned family role and its constraints. Neither content to commit herself to domestic detail nor seriously able to compete as a player in the intellectual life of the males of the James family, Alice's only real option was to "languish and loll about the house," a choice that made contact with her mother inevitable (Strouse 69). Mother Mary and Aunt Kate, both bustling figures, provided no model as far as we can see for Alice's lassitude. Instead, we hear of Mother being ill, "which she bears like an angel, doing any amount of work at the same time, putting up cornices and raking out the garret-room like a little buffalo," a memory from William's youth (Matthiessen 103). And we also know of Mary James's comparison between Alice's weakness and her own vigor: "Alice I am sorry to say, from a little over-exertion has had one of her old attacks; and a very bad one," she writes to William. "She will have to live with the *extremest* care. . . . The poor old mater wears well I am happy to say; strong in the back, strong in the nerves, and strong in the eyes so far, and equal to her day" (Strouse 113, emphasis added). In another letter of the same period, this to son Garth Wilkinson James in May 1868, Mother writes, "We are as well as usual except Alice who is very miserable." Continuing in this strain she goes on to her son, "Poor dear child she bears her confinement patiently. She is obliged to give up all out of door exercise, and lies upon the bed or sofa pretty much all day with the windows open as much as possible" (Strouse 122), an ironic parallel to a woman's "confinement" for pregnancy.

This is not to ignore the confining rituals of illness and convalescence that were accepted practices of the day, nor to suggest that Alice violently resisted them. Rather, it is to suggest how the patterns of chronic invalidism worked inside the James household to restrict and control Alice's movement so that her life was lived proximately to her mother, who solicitously monitored its tone and tempo. The implied comparisons between the mother's efficiency and the daughter's enforced idleness, since mentioned so often in the correspondence, must not have been lost on Alice herself. The choice for Alice, apparently, was to remain convalescent and excused from household duties in which she seemed not to have taken the least interest, or to be well and involved in her mother's concerns of sending the laundry home from Maine and seeing that the wisteria was trimmed correctly (see Strouse 143). Possibly Mary James preferred to attend to these duties herself and to gather single-handedly the garlands of family praise for her efficiency; little evidence exists that Mary desired Alice to do more than "improve." When we consider Alice in this way, she becomes a pathetically liminal personality with no real niche in life save to be sick, to improve, and to relapse.

In 1872, after four years of suffering at home from neurasthenia, nervous exhaustion, hypochondria, and hysteria—all foreign to her mother's nature—Alice escaped to Europe accompanied by brother Henry and Aunt Kate. Strouse gives us the telling information that although Alice's letters from Europe "were enthusiastically received and lavishly praised

. . . not one of the letters she wrote two or three times a week to Quincy Street during her six months abroad has survived from the period when brother Will compares her to an emerging Madame de Sévigné (Strouse 145).

Alice, as did all the Jameses, had a complex set of relationships with various members of her family congruent with contemporary psychiatry's recognition of the "characteristics of the family as a dynamic set of relationships to significant others in the family."[4] As daughter and sister, Alice's relationships were constantly in flux depending upon the presence or absence of one or another family member. The difficult problem of documenting Alice's relationship with her parents, particularly her mother, surfaces here. We know the historical record to be blurred. Scholars have conjectured that Alice destroyed her own letters to her parents after they died; and we know for a certainty that Aunt Kate burned correspondence she thought the children (middle aged at the time) should not be permitted to see after her sister's death. Did Mary simply feel that Alice's letters were of no account since Alice's "career" was of no importance in the eyes of the James family? Did Mary resent Alice's glowing descriptions of her life abroad, a study in contrast to her life at home?

We do have Henry's description of Alice during her European trip. Alice is "like a rejuvenated creature," writes her brother. She "displayed more gaiety, more elasticity, more genuine youthful animal spirits than I have ever seen in her" (Strouse 149). In Europe the Boston parental dyad is replaced with the more congenial team of Aunt Kate and Henry acting the parts of her permissive mother and father. Although Mary James reports her delight with her daughter's exploits in Europe to the network of family correspondents, certain implied dissimilarities between Alice at home and Alice at liberty abroad are too blatant to have been missed by Mother: most crudely, Alice abroad appears happier than she has ever been, while at home in Quincy Street, she is sick and miserable. Strangely, the letters to Alice from her mother during the 1872 trip to Europe are filled with news about marriages taking place among Alice's friends in Cambridge during her absence and are sprinkled with caution for Alice not to overdo. Surely her unconscious reading of these letters might have been that daughters who stay at home with their mothers eventually marry and replicate the life of the mother, while freedom from the mother suggests an escape from what Alice might have considered a passive, unrewarding future.[5] In 1872, when she is still in her early twenties, it seems fair to speculate that her family expected Alice to eventually marry, though her own remarks upon marriage, including the experiences of her friends, suggest that Alice had her reservations.

We look in vain at the rest of Alice's life for an experience to rival the idyllic European vacation spent with Henry Jr. and Aunt Kate. "Everything had been arranged for her pleasure," writes her biographer. "She had Henry and Kate all to herself—two experienced travelers and sensitive companions who encouraged her independence" (Strouse 159). After her return from this journey, however, following a period of basking in the glow of memories from her exhilarating trip away from home, life settled into its routine on Quincy Street. An interesting surviving comment about Alice occurs in a letter from Mary James to her son Henry in April 1873: "Alice is full of the most vivid memories of all your love and care last summer, and is so eloquent on the subject, that she brings *wrath* upon Will's countenance while she brings *tears into my eyes*." The letter continues, "I think she enjoys her journey more in thinking it over, and her greatest delight would be *to go again and stay longer. This is not be thought of now, but nor will it ever be possible during Father's lifetime—still is a great source of pleasure to her both in the past and in the future*" (Strouse 160, emphasis added).

Mother's letter to Henry is rich in its implications, for Mary James more than suggests Alice's enjoyment of her time away from Quincy Street with her brother and Aunt Kate. Brother William fumes, while Mary tears (with delight or because Alice so enjoys being away?). Despite Alice's obvious pleasure in travel, her mother will deny her another such adventurous trip. Indeed, Alice can only journey abroad if her father dies, a rather cruel condition upon which to hinge such possibilities. Eleven years after this more than prophetic letter, following the deaths of both her mother and father, Alice was again on her way to Europe, this time as a permanent resident and permanent invalid. If Alice knew that release from the family circle could come again only with the death of both parents, that her freedom hinged upon the cost of her parents' lives, one could surmise that the only life choice open to her caused her guilt that she cloaked in permanent invalidism. That her brilliant and creatively productive brothers refused to openly refer to these motives certainly cannot have been from lack of recognition of the symptoms. A more likely theory seems that Henry and William needed to preserve their own delicate sense of "family" and refused to see the destructive relationship between their sister and their mother as anything other than a wholesome, loving one, because the idea of a cohesive family in which "a native in the James family . . . has no other country," in William's phrase (Mathiessen 69), must be preserved at all costs. Pervasive notions of gender allowed the brothers to move away from Quincy Street, albeit painfully, to lives of their own. Their backward glances toward the family as they remembered life at Quincy Street, saturated as it was with nostalgia for the past, reflected what they could psychologically manage.

The intense female friendship that Alice maintained with Katharine Loring from 1873 until her own death of cancer in 1892 fulfilled for Alice the many needs that went unmet in her relationship with her mother. It was a one-sided relationship, insofar as it was Katharine's life to serve and stimulate Alice intellectually with no expectation of reciprocity in kind. This relationship, however, gave Alice James the freedom to write her diaries, her oeuvre. As Kathie Carlson explains, in order to escape the confines of patriarchy and the limitations on thought and concepts of self that it imposes, women "define themselves and the world from a woman-centered position" (156). Alice James's relationship with Katharine Loring, unlike her stunting relationship with Mother Mary, provided the space for the daughter to take her own writing and the life of the mind seriously—the most productive period of self-assertion she was ever to know before her premature death. Tragically, she wrote toward the end of her life that she was glad that finally her physicians had discovered that she suffered from cancer to account for her chronic invalidism. "When I am gone, pray don't think of me simply as a creature who might have been something else," she states. For, she continues, "I have always had significance for myself . . . and what more can a human soul ask for?" (Yeazell 104–5)

A similar domestic situation was played out in another intellectual family, that of Leslie Stephen, eminent Victorian editor of the *Dictionary of National Biography*, only a few years later. Quentin Bell writes vividly of Julia Stephen's (Virginia's mother) devotion to home and family: "Essentially the happiness of the Stephen home derived from the fact that the children knew their parents to be deeply and happily in love. . . . Despite her charities and her maternal commitment, Julia lived chiefly for her husband; everyone needed her [in their family of five children] but he needed her most" (Bell 38). In contrast, when one reads the biography, diaries, and letters of Virginia Woolf (1882–1941), whose young adulthood through the end of the nineteenth century was similarly governed by the stern Victorian mores and choices that constrained Alice, one sees immediately that much of Virginia Woolf's independence and freedom to create (like her sister Vanessa's) derived from the deaths of her parents in her early adolescence and young womanhood. Her gifted and beloved brother, Thoby, also died during her young womanhood. Although mental illness and melancholia plagued Virginia Woolf's life, she was able, unlike Alice James, to "convert" experience into art. Hence, she refigures the image of the domestic, nonintellectual mother figure and the artist-daughter figure to shape out of her familial experience an important modernist novel, *To the Lighthouse*, published in 1927.[6]

When Woolf's parents died, she (Virginia Stephen) and her talented sister and brothers lived unchaperoned in a house in London's Gordon Square. They enjoyed many liberties and opportunities to break with convention denied Alice James during most of her youth. Where Alice felt strained and humiliated with the social intercourse between men and women as it occurred at Quincy Street, Virginia and Vanessa Stephen conversed freely and unselfconsciously with Clive Bell, Lytton Strachey, Leonard Woolf, and other Cambridge wits and friends of their brothers' at the Stephens's notorious Thursday evenings. Woolf rankled that as a woman she was not afforded the education that her brothers enjoyed, but she seems not to have let that stunt her career in letters. Virginia Woolf did not feel, as did Alice James, that in Jean Strouse's words, "To be a James and a girl, then, was a contradiction in terms" (Strouse xiii). Quentin Bell writes that the Stephens sisters did not consider their Bloomsbury gatherings as rituals to meet husbands; rather, "the purpose of a party in Bloomsbury was to exchange ideas" (Bell 98–99).

In Quincy Street's stifling atmosphere Alice did not enjoy this untrammeled cerebral liberty as she apparently sat passively by mother and aunt while the James males vigorously sparred with one another in their arguments and discussions. We might contrast Alice James's demeanor with that of the rather free and easy Gordon Square life when Virginia and Adrian Stephen reportedly used butter pats "as missiles when other arguments failed, so that the walls were starred with flattened projectiles" (Bell 117), a scene unimaginable at Quincy Street between Alice and her brothers. Even when they emerged into their own adult intellectual circles, neither William nor Henry invited Alice to join them. They were willing to chaperon her travels, to conduct business transactions for her, but they did not recognize her as an intellectual or creative equal who might have benefited from interaction with those they knew. Like their father, Alice's brothers wished to see her as a replica of their mother, not a competitor in their own professional lives.[7]

In sum, Alice James had no spiritual mother as existed for Virginia Woolf, who converted her own dead mother into a spiritual presence that fueled her art. Rather, Alice, without a sister and possessed of brothers anxious to realize the promise of genius that had been projected onto them at home, faced the daily, all-too-real presence of a practical mother, whose exemplary maternal character was worshipped by Henry and William James, a figure Alice rejected as a model for her own mature life. When it became manifestly clear that the role of wife and mother had passed Alice by, the family seized on her identity as a permanent invalid—to explain the surface nothingness of their only sister's life. Alice James, by force of circumstance and habit, came to see no alternative identity for herself.

Notes

1. Alice James (1848–1892) was the fifth child and only daughter of Mary Robertson Walsh and Henry James Sr. Like her brothers and other family members, she spent the majority of her youth in Newport, Rhode Island, and in Europe, where the James family traveled among the major European capitals. From the age of nineteen on, Alice James suffered extended bouts of what was known at the time as hysteria or "neurasthenia," eventually dying of breast cancer in England, where her companion Katharine Loring and her brother Henry attended her.

2. A problematic mother-daughter relationship appears in Henry's early *Daisy Miller* (1878), in which Mrs. Miller, herself a product of early nineteenth-century Albany, cannot guide her daughter through the intricacies of the European social scene nor command her daughter's attention and respect. Only when Daisy falls ill does Mrs. Miller regain her sense of usefulness and purpose.

3. Note that the years 1866–1868 mark the first major breakdown of AJ according to the chronology in Yeazell. See Charlotte Perkins Gilman, *The Yellow Wall-Paper* (1892), for a gothic feminist fiction with the theme of women and hysteria in the nineteenth century. The model for the doctor in the novella is S. Weir Mitchell, the famous nineteenth-century "rest cure" doctor.

4. See R. D. Laing, *Sanity, Madness, and the Family,* in which the psychiatrist locates the site of madness within the modern family.

5. See Nancy Chodorow, *The Reproduction of Mothering,* 133–40. In her controversial study, Chodorow suggests that in the so-called Oedipal and post–Oedipal periods, a girl recognizes the similarity of her own body to her mother's. She may learn to identify the gender disempowerment that accompanies her bodily sameness to the mother and difference from the father as the primary cause of her inability to seize what she deems the more powerful world of male hegemony—in the Jamesian sense, the world of ideas operating outside the realm of the mother.

6. Two reflections on Woolf's parents in *To the Lighthouse* seem relevant here. In a letter to Vanessa Bell, May 25, 1927, Woolf writes: "I'm in a terrible state of pleasure that you should think Mrs. Ramsey so much like mother. At the same time, it is a psychological mystery what she should be: how a child could know about her; except that it haunted me, partly, I suppose her beauty; and then dying at that moment, I suppose she cut a great figure on one's mind when it was just awake, and had not any experience of life" (Woolf, *Letters* 383). An entry in Woolf's diary (November 28, 1929) corroborates the importance of the dead parent figures for her creative imagination. "Father's birthday. He would have been . . . 96, like other people one has known; but mercifully was not. His life would have ended mine. What would have happened? No writing, no books—inconceivable. I used to think of him & mother daily; but writing The Lighthouse laid them in my

mind. And now he comes back sometimes, but differently. (I believe this to be true—that I may be obsessed by them both, unhealthily; & writing of them was a necessary act)" (Woolf, *Diary* 208).

7. The contrast between Henry James's treatment of Alice compared to Howells's treatment of his sister Victoria poses a striking contrast. While Henry was sympathetic to Alice's sufferings through her illness, he does not encourage her to write for publication as Howells did his sister, offering to help her place her work.

Works Cited

Bell, Quentin. *Virginia Woolf: A Biography.* Vol. 1. New York: Harcourt, 1972.

Carlson, Kathie. *Life's Daughter/Death's Bride: Inner Transformations through the Goddess Demeter/Persephone.* Boston: Shambhala, 1997.

Chodorow, Nancy. *The Reproduction of Mothering: Psychoanalysis and the Sociology of Gender.* Berkeley: University of California Press, 1978.

Hirsch, Marianne. *The Mother/Daughter Plot: Narrative, Psychoanalysis, Feminism.* Bloomington: Indiana University Press, 1989.

James, Alice. *The Diary of Alice James.* Ed. Leon Edel. New York: Dodd, Mead, 1964.

James, Henry. *The Notebooks of Henry James.* Ed. F. O. Matthiessen and Kenneth B. Murdock. Chicago: University of Chicago Press, 1981.

Laing, R. D. *Sanity, Madness, and the Family.* New York: Basic Books, 1964.

Leach, William. *True Love and Perfect Union.* New York: Basic Books, 1980.

Matthiessen, F. O. *The James Family.* New York: Knopf, 1947.

Rich, Adrienne. *Of Woman Born.* New York: Norton, 1976.

Strouse, Jean. *Alice James: A Biography.* Boston: Houghton Mifflin, 1980.

Woolf, Virginia. *The Diary of Virginia Woolf.* Vol. 3. Ed. Anne Olivier Bell. London: Hogarth, 1980.

———. *The Letters of Virginia Woolf.* Vol. 3. Ed. Nigel Nicholson and Joanne Trautmann. New York: Harcourt, 1977.

Yeazell, Ruth, ed. *The Death and Letters of Alice James.* Berkeley: University of California Press, 1981.

Female Models and Male Mentors in Wharton's Early Fiction

Julie Olin-Ammentorp

In 1907 Edith Wharton wrote to her friend and fellow novelist Robert Grant: "I am beginning to see exactly where my weakest point is.—I conceive my subjects like a man—that is, rather more architectonically & dramatically than most women—& then execute them like a woman; or rather, I sacrifice, to my desire for construction & breadth, the small incidental effects that women have always excelled in, the episodical characterisation, I mean" (*Letters* 124).

Although she never fully articulated her sense of the difference between men's and women's writing, Wharton here implies much about that difference: that men's writing is structured "architectonically and dramatically," while women's depends on "small incidental effects" for "episodical characterisation." In this passage, Wharton suggests a tension between the two approaches; while they may not be mutually exclusive, they are not easily combined. Yet she deprecates neither approach. She does not want to give up the larger structures, but also regrets her "sacrifice" of those "small incidental effects" that lead to well-developed characterization.

The tension between masculine and feminine modes of writing—and of thinking—is particularly acute in the period of Wharton's "apprenticeship" as it has been defined by R. W. B. and Nancy Lewis (*Letters* 27–29)—the years before the 1902 publication of her first novel, *The Valley of Decision*. Works from this period suggest that, in these early years, Wharton was not as approving as she would be in 1907 of the "small incidental effects that women have always excelled in." On the contrary, two early stories, "The Pelican" (1898) and "April Showers" (1900), suggest that Wharton believed that, for aspiring women intellectuals, other women provided attractive but ultimately unreliable role models, while men, though their advice might be unpleasant and their view biased, provided a necessary intellectual standard against which women's accomplishments could be measured. Nevertheless, the men in these stories fail to become true mentors: they discourage women from pursuing intellectual goals rather than providing them with encouragement or worthwhile advice.

"The Pelican" is narrated by an unnamed male who, judging from his sense of his own knowledge and his contacts at "Western universities" (*Collected Stories* 96), is either a university professor himself or an established gentleman scholar. The story spans about thirty years, with the narrator observing and analyzing the lecture-circuit career of one Mrs. Amyot. Though Wharton does much to indicate that her narrator's judgment is far from infallible, she also constructs her story to suggest that, regardless of his foibles, his criticisms of Mrs. Amyot are largely legitimate.

It is clear from the story's opening that the narrator's interest in Mrs. Amyot is not purely professional. "She was very pretty when I first knew her," the first paragraph begins; and the second, as if establishing a corollary axiom, "I don't think nature had meant her to be 'intellectual'" (88). The narrator's attitude indicates his inability to take Mrs. Amyot seriously. He seems to believe that women who are pretty can't be intellectual; women who are intellectual can't be pretty—hence, not worth a man's attention. Mrs. Amyot gains the narrator's attention because she is pretty, but fails to win his approval for her fledgling intellectual career.

In fact, the narrator is biased against Mrs. Amyot not because she lacks an intellectual heritage, but because she *has* one. As far as he is concerned, Mrs. Amyot's descent from a family of women intellectuals—women on whom she models herself—is ludicrous, having only the effect of pushing her into a mistaken line of work. As the narrator describes them, Mrs. Amyot's female predecessors do not come off with much dignity: "Her mother, the celebrated Irene Astarte Pratt, had written a poem in blank verse on 'The Fall of Man'; one of her aunts was dean of a girls' college; another had translated Euripides—with such a family, the poor child's fate was sealed in advance. The only way of paying her [deceased] husband's debts and keeping the baby clothed was to be intellectual" (88). Though readers are never given "The Fall of Man" or the translations to judge their quality for themselves, the narrator strongly implies that they are worthless. In his view, a family tradition of women's intellectual accomplishment creates a disastrous "fate" for a young woman who is now reduced to the stature of a "poor child."

He further discredits Mrs. Amyot's intellect by paying her compliments that turn into insults. He relates that she "had two fatal gifts: a capacious but inaccurate memory, and an extraordinary fluency of speech. There was nothing she did not remember—wrongly[.]" Her occasional use of Greek phrases, though it "str[ikes] awe to the hearts of ladies," only results, the male narrator asserts from his position of authority, in Mrs. Amyot's "indulgently mistranslating the phrase" (89). All of this is quite amusing; Wharton is at her satirical best in much of this story. At the same time, she is calling the narrator's credibility into question. His attention to Mrs. Amyot's dimples, his general scorn of women intellectuals (and of women's intellects), and his eventual envy of Mrs. Amyot's success all suggest that he is a less than objective judge of her abilities.

Despite his biases, the narrator isn't necessarily wrong in his judgment of Mrs. Amyot: Wharton is not portraying, as she would in *The Touchstone,* a woman genius unappreciated by a dull male. On the contrary, two passages in the story suggest that, however biased the narrator's view, he is right to be skeptical of Mrs. Amyot's abilities. In the first instance, Mrs. Amyot demonstrates her tendency to "remember—wrongly" when she misquotes Emerson's "The Rhodora." Instead of "if eyes were made for seeing, / Then beauty is its own excuse for being," she blunders into inaccurate paraphrase: "she had remembered Emerson's line—wasn't it Emerson's?—that beauty is its own excuse for *seeing,* and that made her feel a little more confident, since she was sure that no one *saw* beauty more vividly than she" (89–90). Mrs. Amyot's memory is faulty: she has substantially altered the meaning of Emerson's line to justify her own inaccuracies, her own impressionistic approach to knowledge.

Yet more significantly, the ending of the story confirms the narrator's suspicions about the overall legitimacy of Mrs. Amyot's intellectual career. Throughout her thirty years of public lecturing, Mrs. Amyot's largely female audiences have waxed and waned. They seem from the outset to have seen her more as an object of charity than as a model of intellect: her constant refrain—and theirs in attending her lectures—is that she's doing it "for the baby." By the end of the story, ladies are, as ever, buying tickets for her lectures but sending their maids instead of going themselves. Yet more damningly, Mrs. Amyot is revealed as claiming still that she is lecturing "for her son"—who, self-supporting for a decade, at last realizes that his mother is continuing to use him to justify her lecturing. Regardless of the narrator's biases, Mrs. Amyot finally discredits herself. She is not only a mediocre lecturer but fundamentally a fraud as well.

"The Pelican" reflects several issues with which Wharton struggled as a woman writer trying to find her place in the literary world—and, as a necessary first step, trying to take herself seriously. The story parodies not only the conventions of the nineteenth-century lecture circuit but also the circumstances of much nineteenth-century women's intellectual activity. Women lecturers and writers—among them Fanny Fern, Louisa May Alcott, and Harriet Wilson—frequently took up their work to stave off insolvency and provide for their families. In an era that demanded modesty of women, this was one way for women to earn money and assert their intellect without risking their reputations.

In "The Pelican," however, Wharton looks at this tradition cynically, suggesting that "doing it for the baby" could, in fact, be little more than a successful commercial ploy. It gave a woman the appearance of noble self-sacrifice while also giving her a good chance of success. "The Pelican" reflects the fear that a woman could succeed *only* for that reason—only because others took pity, not because one really merited success. Realizing that his mother has used him as an excuse to lecture, her son says, "I thought she did it to amuse herself" (102)—and so, apparently, she has. But the implication is that selling one's meager talents for the goal of self-entertainment in the guise of charity is ridiculous. Mrs. Amyot's lecture career is thus stripped even of the dignity of necessary labor.

If Wharton mocks the convention of women exercising their intellect to support their families, she mocks even more the mental activity that has no excuse at all, not even a financial one. At the point in her life at which she wrote this story, Wharton herself had no financial excuse for authorship; the story suggests her fear of being in the ridiculous position of a woman who exercises her intellect as a mere hobby—a hobby justified neither by its financial necessity nor by its intellectual rigor. "The Pelican" may reflect Wharton's fears that even attempting an intellectual career could make her an object of scorn, and particularly of masculine scorn for feminine weaknesses. If "The Pelican" implicitly criticizes the narrator for his refusal to take Mrs. Amyot seriously, it also criticizes Mrs. Amyot for her own faults. She has learned to defer to the narrator's sense of masculine authority; she has also learned to exploit her good looks when her intellectual accomplishments fail to win admiration. She lacks self-confidence (or pretends to, perhaps to flatter the narrator); she avoids genuine scholarship and assumes that knowledge is not as important as sensibility. Mrs. Amyot is shaped by Wharton's own fears that her labors were financially unnecessary and intellectually unjustifiable—by the fear that the world of intellect was, in fact, a male world. As Candace Waid has written, "Realism and the real were associated with men; women in Wharton's view were protean and deceptive. Both the lives and the fiction of women were diffuse and formless, lacking the stable structure that would make them 'real.' . . . [Wharton] tend[s] to stress structure and plot as the formal requirements of the real by denouncing a feminine aesthetic . . . of decoration and ornamentation that substitutes description for structure" (8–9).

Mrs. Amyot's lectures reflect what the apprentice writer feared: the lack of both accurate content and reliable structure. Her lectures are a mere overlay of "decoration and ornamentation," and even these ornaments are ill-chosen: the narrator tells us that "[f]rom a large assortment of stock adjectives she chose . . . the one that taste and discrimination would most surely have rejected" (91). Moreover, Mrs. Amyot applies these verbal ornaments to a plagiarized base of knowledge: "the lecture was, of course, manufactured out of Lewes's book" (91). Mrs. Amyot's occasional success is derided because of its feminine, domestic quality: "[Her lecture] had the flavor of personal experience, of views sympathetically exchanged with her audience on the best way of knitting children's socks, or of putting up preserves for the winter. . . . It was her art of transposing secondhand ideas into firsthand emotions that so endeared her to her feminine listeners" (91). The lack of masculine ideas and the presence of feminine emotions account both for Mrs. Amyot's "prodigious . . . irrational success" and for the narrator's scorn of it: he chooses his adjectives really to condemn her popularity. Success for the wrong reasons, the story suggests, is no better than failure. In fact, it may be worse. Mrs. Amyot's intellectual efforts have made her an object of scorn, as Wharton may have feared that hers would.

As Wharton tells in her memoir, *A Backward Glance,* she cut her intellectual teeth on her father's "gentleman's library," admiring primarily male authors, with a few female exceptions (such as Fanny Burney, George Eliot, and Madame de Sévigné). She generally dismissed popular American women novelists, including Harriet Beecher Stowe and Louisa May Alcott. She remarks that even as a child "my ears, trained to the fresh racy English of 'Alice in Wonderland,' 'The Water Babies' and 'The Princess and the Goblin,' were exasperated by the laxities of the great Louisa" (*Backward Glance* 51). "Women's fiction," as Nina Baym has called it, neither attracted her nor earned her esteem—despite the fact that her juvenile novella, *Fast and Loose,* owes much to that genre.

As Wharton's youthful reading list suggests, her standard of success was masculine. Thus, even while the narrator in "The Pelican" is not fully credible, he has an important function. Whether university professor or amateur, he speaks with an authority that allows us to judge Mrs.

Amyot's intellectual limitations and her fraudulent practices. He provides an intellectual standard that is, within this story, the standard that must be met: and Mrs. Amyot fails to meet it.

In a briefer story, "April Showers" (1900), Wharton provides another example of the aspiring female intellectual—this time a fledgling author—whose inspiration comes from a female model and whose ambitions are corrected by two male guides. Like "The Pelican," "April Showers" speculates on the prospect of success for a woman intellectual—once again looking at that prospect with a skeptical eye.

Like the earlier story, "April Showers" both uses and mocks the conventional truths about nineteenth-century women authors. Theodora Dace's life circumstances differ substantially from Mrs. Amyot's—she is the oldest of four children, and both of her parents are alive. But because her mother is an invalid and her father a relatively poor physician, Theodora, like Mrs. Amyot, aspires to success for her family's benefit: "She meant to spend all her money on her family" (191). Theodora takes her inspiration not from intellectual female family members, but nevertheless from a female model. Her Uncle James tells her family the story of his new neighbor, the novelist Kathleen Kyd: "Ever hear how she began to write? She told me the whole story. It seems she was a saleswoman in a store, working on starvation wages, with a mother and a consumptive sister to support. Well, she wrote a story one day, just for fun, and sent it to the *Home Circle*. . . . They took her story and passed their plate for more. She became a regular contributor and eventually was known all over the country" (190). Hearing this tale, which makes literary success sound so easy, Theodora begins her own 500-page novel.

For all its simplicity and flatness of tone, "April Showers" is a vexing piece. While parodying the nineteenth-century I-wrote-it-for-my-family convention of female literary success, the story also mocks negative stereotypes of women authors—and the men who simultaneously envy and disdain successful women authors. For instance, Theodora's Uncle James, who unintentionally inspires Theodora with the tale of Kathleen Kyd's success, has a decidedly negative view of women authors, whom he seems to expect to be monsters of some sort: "She's a very pleasant, sociable kind of woman; you'd never think she was a writer," he says of Kyd (190). Despite the fact that he disdains the kind of "sentimental trash" she writes, comparing it to sewer gas ("[it] doesn't smell bad, and infects the system without your knowing it"), he envies her financial success, commenting to Theodora's father, "Now she tells me her books bring her in about ten thousand a year. Rather more than you and I can boast of, eh, John?" (190) In spite of her financial success (or perhaps because of it), in spite of her pleasant character and her surprising normality, Uncle James cannot condone Kyd, because he believes her writing to be morally corrupting.

Indeed, as with the criticisms leveled by the male narrator of "The Pelican," there is no reason to believe that Uncle James's judgments are entirely mistaken, regardless of his biases. William Dean Howells raised the issue of the morality of sentimental fiction more seriously in *The Rise of Silas Lapham*, questioning whether it did more moral harm than good in creating expectations of dramatic heroism and showy self-sacrifice. Wharton's rejection of sentimentalism suggests her leaning toward realism—not just as a genre but as a philosophy and perhaps even as a didactic tool. Certainly some women who turned toward journalism, humor, and sentimental fiction to earn their income succeeded; but as "April Showers" suggests, by far the greater number must have failed. The fact that this story was published in the magazine *Youth's Companion* suggests that its realism is tied to a certain moral earnestness: young people must not expect too much of themselves, and certainly most of those who set out to be rich and famous novelists must realize that they would never succeed.

In this context, it seems likely that "April Showers" is Wharton's response to Louisa May Alcott's *Little Women*, particularly to the chapter "Literary Lessons." As we have seen, Wharton had little respect for "the great Louisa"; curiously, in "Literary Lessons," Alcott seems to be mocking E.D.E.N. Southworth, *her* predecessor. In "Literary Lessons," Jo March reads an illustrated newspaper story by "Mrs. S.L.A.N.G. Northbury," recognizes the work as "trash" (347), but writes a story for the paper's fiction contest and wins first prize—a check for $100. With this money she sends her mother and ailing sister off to the seaside, despite her father's advice to "aim at the highest, and never mind the money" (348). Alcott tells us that Jo has no illusions of literary grandeur, but values her pen's earning power: "her 'rubbish' turned into comforts for them all. 'The Duke's Daughter' paid the butcher bill, 'A Phantom Hand' put down a new carpet, and 'The Curse of the Coventrys' proved the blessing of the Marches in the way of groceries and gowns" (350).

In her dismissal of E.D.E.N. Southworth, Alcott was arguing for a more realistic standard of fiction. She, too, was concerned about the moral effect of sensationalism, as readers find later in the novel when Jo sets herself to writing increasingly lurid tales and is finally set straight by a male mentor of her own, Professor Bhaer. Wharton, however, was clearly not satisfied with Alcott's standard of realism, and provides her own standard—the grimmer reality that most young ladies setting pen to paper were unlikely to pay for groceries, gowns, or butcher bills with their work.

Wharton further communicates the importance of realistic literary expectations in her portrayal of Theodora. Much of her portrayal is sympathetic; the girl genuinely devotes herself to her writing, is understandably thrilled when she receives an acceptance from *Home Circle,* and is excited by the prospect of financial solvency and literary success. But if Wharton captures something of the energy of youth, she also captures its overconfidence. Theodora is too sure of her own work, sure that she has outstripped the work of her own literary models. Theodora reflects that "if [her novel] lacked Kathleen Kyd's lightness of touch, it had an emotional intensity never achieved by that brilliant writer. Theodora did not care to amuse her readers; she left that to more frivolous talents. Her aim was to stir the depths of human nature, and she felt she had succeeded" (190). Theodora even compares herself favorably to George Eliot, looking condescendingly on that author's late success: "Theodora was only seventeen; and she remembered, with a touch of retrospective compassion, that George Eliot had not become famous till she was nearly forty" (190). Unlike "The Pelican," "April Showers" does not use a narrator to encourage the reader's skepticism about the young intellectual's abilities or about the ultimate uselessness of following female literary models, whether they be the sensationalistic (and fictional) Kathleen Kyd or the more philosophical (and historical) George Eliot. Rather, Wharton allows Theodora to lampoon herself.

Unlike Mrs. Amyot, who never realizes her own shortcomings or her essential fraudulence despite the narrator's guidance, Theodora abruptly learns through men that her novel is, in fact, a failure; the letter of acceptance was sent in error. When a novel resembling hers only in title comes out in *Home Circle* under the name of Kathleen Kyd, Theodora rushes to Boston to speak with the editor who sent her the letter of acceptance. This man tells her "in a flood of bland apology" that he has no intention of publishing her fiction: "An unfortunate accident— . . . Miss Dace's novel hardly suited to their purpose" (195). The editor is Theodora's first male guide out of the realm of fiction; her father is her second. Though she expects him to be furious with her ("She bent her head under the coming storm of his derision"), he is unexpectedly gentle (195). He explains, "Didn't I ever tell you? I wrote a novel once. I was just out of college, and didn't want to be a doctor. No; I wanted to be a genius, so I wrote a novel. . . . It took me a whole year—a whole year's hard work; and when I'd finished it the public wouldn't have it, either; not at any price. And that's why I came down to meet you, because I remembered my walk home" (196).

Thus the story ends. Aesthetically, it is a weak ending—a rare failing for a Wharton story. Thematically, it emphasizes the importance of the male guide, who gently leads his daughter away from wasting her life in the pursuit of fiction. The story implies that Theodora, moved by her father's example, will give up her literary aspirations and accede to a domestic career. She has already vowed that if the novel "was refused . . . she would admit the truth—she would ask her parents' pardon and settle down to an obscure existence of mending and combing" (192)—the future an unsuccessful Jo March might have faced as well.

Despite the story's endorsement of the father's realism and Theodora's apparent acceptance of her domestic fate, "April Showers" seems curiously unenthusiastic about that fate; there is not even a handsome young suitor waiting in the wings to provide Theodora with the "May flowers" that April showers proverbially bring. In this way, the story may be starkly realistic, or even pessimistic. Theodora seems to accept the prospect of settling down to a life of domestic drudgery rather than, say, setting her literary sights lower, working her way gradually and doggedly through the publication of shorter, less ambitious works, and gradually achieving some recognition (and perhaps earning some money) in the course of time. Certainly, the short snippet of Theodora's novel that is given suggests how far Theodora has succumbed to the school of sentimentalism, thus suggesting as well how little literary promise she has: "But Guy's heart slept under the violets on Muriel's grave" (189).

Those familiar with Wharton's juvenile novel *Fast and Loose,* however, will realize that Wharton is directly parodying her own work. The final sentence of *Fast and Loose* is "But Guy Hastings' heart is under the violets on Georgie's grave" (111). Wharton's own eventual success may hint that Theodora Dace, too, has literary talent. Perhaps it is too early for Theodora to settle entirely for mending and combing. Wharton herself, like the George Eliot whom Theodora pities, would not achieve fame until her late thirties and early forties. Yet on its own terms "April Showers" suggests only that Theodora should accede to the guidance of her father and give up her literary career: "want[ing] to be a genius," Dr. Dace teaches, is a waste of energy.

That Wharton saw aspiring female intellectuals differently from aspiring males is suggested by her treatment of a young male author in "That Good May Come" (1894). In this tale, young Maurice Birkton is in a situation analogous to that of Mrs. Amyot and Theodora Dace: his mother and sister are dependent on his intellectual output for family income. In Birkton's case, however, neither his economic need nor his intellectual abilities are mocked. On the contrary, his need is real: his father is apparently dead, his mother makes only a small and unreliable income from copying visiting lists and writing out ball invitations, and his sister is too young to work. Yet Birkton has resigned "his clerkship in a wholesale warehouse" so that he might "give more leisure to the writing of . . . literary reviews," and his mother approves this course—despite the fact that his vocational choice required that the family move from a "pleasant little flat uptown" to a tenement (25). Birkton's decision to support himself and his family by his pen is depicted as very serious indeed; he is thus unlike the amateurish Mrs. Amyot and the flighty Theodora, whose father is, after all, supporting the family without her help.

Further, the omniscient narrator explains that Birkton (unlike Mrs. Amyot and Theodora) is a true artist: his eyes are "the sensitive eyes of the seer whom Beauty has anointed with her mysterious unguent" (25). Even his choice of genre attests to his intellectual authenticity. He neither gives plagiarized lectures nor pens sentimental novels, but rather writes poems—often considered the highest and most demanding of literary genres. Even his failure to publish his poems can be construed as a measure of his literary ability: "Devil take it, why isn't there an audience for that sort of thing?" his friend Helfenridge asks after reading one of Birkton's poems aloud (22). Unlike Theodora and Mrs. Amyot, Birkton is not pandering to the vulgar multitudes in his work.

Birkton, moreover, stands on his own two feet literarily. As the story presents him, he neither follows any particular literary model nor needs any mentor to correct or encourage him. When Helfenridge advises him, it is as a friend, not as a superior; Helfenridge encourages Birkton's aspirations and articulates his conscience, but does not speak as a judge—a sharp contrast to the male figures in "The Pelican" and "April Showers."

Indeed, for Birkton the question is never whether or not he should write. Rather, he faces a moral and economic question about his writing: should he sell gossipy verse to the *Social Kite* for $150, a sum that would be more than enough to buy the white confirmation dress his sister so earnestly desires? He does sell the poem, but is then racked with scruples when he sees its target, Mrs. Tolquitt, in church with her daughter (who, with his sister, is about to be confirmed). In the end, though, even the choice to profit by his scandalous verse is exonerated: Helfenridge informs him that the adulterous relationship implied by his verse is a fact. Since it is factual, not slanderous, Birkton need agonize no further.

Thus the story ratifies the young male author's literary choices. It does not argue that salable gossipy verse is the aesthetic equivalent of unpublished great poems, but it does suggest that Birkton's decision to support his family through the occasional publication of society gossip is not wrong. Apparently, "sewer gas" is acceptable if it is accurate, if it is penned by a male, and if its proceeds are necessary. In the end his agony over moral niceties, though it speaks for his character, proves a kind of moral naiveté that Birkton is now mature enough to shrug off. He is financially and literarily independent, able to support his family, and beholden to no one for his success.

Wharton's only extended portrayal of a writer is the two-novel sequence *Hudson River Bracketed* and *The Gods Arrive.* There, as in "That Good May Come," the successful writer is a male—a fact that corroborates Candace Waid's remark that, for Wharton, "realism and the real were associated with men" (8). So, in some way, "real authors" were men, too. Yet there can be no doubt of how seriously Wharton took her own writing career. Perhaps it is more accurate to say that, for the Wharton who created fiction, it seemed more realistic to depict a successful male novelist than a successful female one. More precisely, many of the "successful" female authors Wharton mentions—Stowe and Alcott, for instance—seemed to her to have achieved popular and financial success, but not a high literary standard. By way of contrast, she respected "successful" male authors for their artistry and language use regardless of their financial success.

Nevertheless, little evidence suggests that in her personal life Wharton distrusted all female models or lacked good male mentors. In *A Backward Glance* Wharton notes that she found a trustworthy model in Vernon Lee, whom she called "the first highly cultivated and brilliant woman I had ever known" (132). And, by her own account, her experience of male mentors was quite positive—quite unlike the fictional experiences she created for her aspiring female intellectuals. She describes the beneficent influence of a number of men—Egerton Winthrop, Walter Berry, Edward Burlingame—and mentions "long and frequent" talks "on the subject of technique" with Paul Bourget and Henry James (199). Indeed, these men provided her with a standard of success represented by the narrator in "The Pelican," but provided something neither he nor Dr. Dace supplied: the encouragement and the belief in her abilities that Wharton needed to go on to finish her first novel, *The Valley of Decision,* and her succeeding works.

In the period of her apprenticeship, Wharton's portraits of struggling female intellectuals reflected not her own reality of supportive (and mostly male) mentors, but rather her fears of literary and intellectual failure—a failure assured, if not caused, by attractive but unreliable female literary models and correct but cold male guides. Women's intellectual work in these stories seems doomed to failure, not only because of their own inadequacies but because of the lack of support by those men who, in Wharton's view, both set the standards for and provided examples of real literary success. By the time of her 1907 letter to Robert Grant—with the successes of *The Valley of Decision* and *The House of Mirth* behind her, as well as the publication of *The Fruit of the Tree*—Wharton had apparently accepted that women as well as men could succeed in intellectual endeavors, and that perhaps women had had some hand in defining at least a portion of a standard of literary success: the "small incidental effects that women have always excelled in" have their value as well as the "architectonic" and "dramatic" subjects more typically chosen by men. The question of the relationship between an author's gender and his or her ability to write convincingly would reemerge for Wharton during the years of World War I, as evinced by a tale like "Writing a War Story." But by the time she wrote *A Backward Glance* in the early thirties, Wharton seems to have dropped the issue of gender from her mental plan, no longer labeling some elements of fiction masculine and others feminine. She had come to admire women of intellect like Vernon Lee and, by the same token, had achieved the artistic maturity she needed to resist sometimes the advice even of "the master" himself, Henry James. Female models and male mentors alike were internalized as she wrote that "the novelist's best safeguard is to put out of his mind the quality of praise or blame bestowed on him by reviewers and critics, and to write only for that dispassionate and ironic critic who dwells within the breast" (212).

Works Cited

Alcott, Louisa May. *Little Women*. 1868. New York: Grosset and Dunlap, 1947.

Baym, Nina. *Women's Fiction: A Guide to Novels by and about Women in America, 1820–1970*. Ithaca: Cornell University Press, 1978.

Howells, William Dean. *The Rise of Silas Lapham*. 1885. New York: Norton, 1982.

Waid, Candace. *Edith Wharton's Letters from the Underworld: Fictions of Women and Writing*. Chapel Hill: University of North Carolina Press, 1991.

Wharton, Edith. *A Backward Glance*. 1934. New York: Scribner's, 1964.

———. *The Collected Short Stories of Edith Wharton*. Volume 1. Ed. R. W. B. Lewis. New York: Scribner's, 1968.

———. *Fast and Loose* and *The Buccaneers*. Ed. Violet Hopkins Winner. Charlottesville: University Press of Virginia, 1993.

———. *The Letters of Edith Wharton*. Ed. R. W. B. Lewis and Nancy Lewis. New York: Scribner's, 1988.

Edith Wharton and Partnership

The House of Mirth, *The Decoration of Houses*, and "Copy"

Carol J. Singley

Successful partnerships—whether between women or between women and men—are rare in Edith Wharton's writing. But the very scarcity of such relationships can tell us a great deal about Wharton's view of herself as an author and as a woman. Indeed, Wharton's partnerships—imaginative and real—reflect one another, revealing her complex, often ambivalent attitudes toward mentorship and collaboration.[1]

As a writer Wharton seemed comfortable working alone. For example, she exercised as much control over her creative processes and professional life as possible. She habitually wrote in privacy, in the mornings in her boudoir before joining guests or friends for the rest of the day's activities. She meticulously revised and edited her own manuscripts. And she often imposed her wishes on publishers, monitoring every step of the production process and distrusting editors to select even the font size or jacket cover of her books. Despite this need for authorial autonomy, however, Wharton greatly valued relationship with others. Famous for her friendships, she nourished and maintained literary, romantic, and professional associations over great distances and periods of time. She coauthored one book and sought advice on the composition of many others. She believed passionately in mentorship, cherishing the intellectual awakeners who laid the foundation for her literary career and responding generously when she encountered others in similar need.

Wharton's interactions with others—whether based in travel, conversation, romance, or art—often demonstrate equality and reciprocity, those very qualities of give and take that characterize the best collaborations. Yet there often appears in Wharton's life and writing a hierarchy of relations in which one party falls vulnerable to another. At worst, differences in gender, age, education, or social standing destroy the opportunity for productive, pleasurable collaboration. At best, these differences are negotiated with care and delicacy, but the partnerships succeed only with such strain that one must ask whether collaboration is worth the effort. Wharton was drawn to collaboration in part as a solution for the anxiety she felt as a female writer determined to succeed in a masculine world of letters. However, although she profited from mentors and mentored others, she did not take full advantage of opportunities for collaboration; nor does she often allow her characters to enjoy its benefits. Wharton's ambivalence toward partnership becomes clear through a discussion of collaborative theory and practice, especially as related to women; an examination of ambivalence toward collaboration in Wharton's childhood experience; and an analysis of partnerships in three of her texts: *The House of Mirth, The Decoration of Houses,* and "Copy: A Dialogue." In these fictional and nonfictional accounts, Wharton portrays partnership with others as desirable but difficult.

In a society that privileges individualism, collaboration is often viewed skeptically. The traditional image of the author—an isolated genius toiling without conversation or encouragement until a creative product issues forth—pervades Western philosophy and has served since the Enlightenment as a model for insight and invention (Sullivan 12). In this model, the writer is often figured as male, and his distance from society becomes a hallmark—even a prerequisite—of his originality and greatness. Such masculine representations of authorship can be alienating to women. First, historically denied access to art and letters, women often suffer from isolation that the solitary model only exacerbates. Second, if it is true that women tend toward relational rather than discrete modes of knowing and being (Chodorow, Gilligan), then notions of singular creativity run counter to female experience. Women must write *against themselves* in order to conform to prevailing models of individual genius.

Collaborative theories of authorship, which are grounded in the fields of rhetoric and composition (in works by Kenneth Bruffee, Linda Brodkey, and Andrea Lunsford and Lisa Ede, for example); in narrative theory, especially Mikhail Bakhtin's dialogics; and in feminist studies (from the fiction of Sandra Cisneros and Amy Tan to the theoretical writings of Adrienne Rich, Hélène Cixous, and Luce Irigaray)—all offer an alternative to these traditional views. They emphasize the social rather than solitary dimensions of learning. They point to the power of conversation to break down authoritative structures of language, and they may posit communal rather than individual concepts of self. Such partnerships—whether in the form of mentorship or collaboration—can help women overcome historical prohibitions against speaking and writing. By expressing themselves in a united voice, women may resolve their ambivalence toward language—what Susan Elizabeth Sweeney and I describe elsewhere as "anxious power" (*Anxious*). Such joint labor may even reflect an alternative view of the world that Mary Belenky and her collaborators term "women's ways of knowing."

Collaboration is by no means a simple solution for women's anxieties about writing, however. Although it implies resistance to traditional concepts of authorship, its status as "other" or marginal aligns it with the feminine and implies weakness or an inability to succeed on one's own. With its emphasis on cooperation, it may reinscribe women in roles that emphasize their relations to others (Singley and Sweeney, "In League" 64). Mentorship, a specific kind of collaboration in which one party receives the knowledge, wisdom, and guidance of another, suggests an uneven distribution of power and may even involve coercion or indebtedness. And collaboration, which has the negative connotation of fraternizing with the enemy, suggests competition, betrayal, and violence as well as harmonious sharing.

For many female writers, then, collaboration is a process that defies definition or classification. Many people remain suspicious of it and may even insist that one partner actually wrote a given text. Others may be skeptical of feminist collaboration because cultural stereotypes of women as petty, bickering, and deceitful contradict the notion of productive, shared work. In practice, however, collaboration is often experienced as a pleasurable, even effortless, activity that "seems to complete itself, as if by magic—like the fairy tale about the shoemaker who wakes, each morning, to find that two elves have stitched together the separate parts of shoes that he laid out the night before" ("In League" 70). Such feminist collaboration produces a bond among partners, in part because of the experience of joint labor itself and in part because of the skepticism with which it is understood.

Feminist collaborators have proposed a variety of metaphors ranging from romance to sewing, music, and business to convey this elusive experience of working together. For example, Sweeney and I have described our collaboration as "simultaneously a romance, a sibling relationship, and a business partnership"—a "conversation" or "turning together" in which both writers are changed but neither is oppressed by the other ("In League" 75, 70). Coauthors Kaplan and Rose use the terms *lesbian erotics* and *jazz improvisation* to describe their method of writing together (550); Joyce Elbrecht and Lydia Fakundiny write of "an extension of oneself to the other" (249, 254); and Susan Leonardi and Rebecca Pope suggest a variety of metaphors, including "mosaic," "quilt," "part-singing," "stew," and erotic "intercourse" (262, 266, 267, 269). Whatever the metaphor, the process of collaboration—whether between mentor and mentee or between peers—involves subtle but constant negotiations that respect differences while moving toward consensus. It does not deny difference or rule out competition. On the contrary, collaboration depends upon frankness. As Evelyn Fox Keller and Helene Moglen note, such interaction may be alien to women, who are trained not to allow their disagreements to reach the point of confrontation and to develop strategies that disguise or avoid competition (22).

Wharton's life and fiction reveal her struggle with these multiple meanings of collaborative work. As an upper-class woman aspiring to be a writer, she faced a formidable challenge—namely, how to turn her energies from society to art, from capitalistic consumption to literary production. Her authorial ambitions set her apart from most women of her elite class, who conformed to convention by cultivating domestic rather than artistic and professional skills. Not surprisingly, Wharton's road to authorship was long and difficult. She lacked encouragement from her family and society, who considered serious pursuit of the arts a breach of good taste; she enjoyed few literary models; and she developed virtually no intellectual or artistic companions until adulthood. Her relations with women were especially problematic. She had no sisters, struggled with a disapproving mother, and describes only one girlhood friend in detail, Emelyn Washburn, whose suspected lesbianism she later describes as "degenerative" ("Life" 1085). In some sense, one's first mentors are one's parents. For Wharton, these formative associations were disappointing. Her cold, shallow mother was embarrassed by her daughter's social awkwardness and tried to dissuade her from the pen. Her father, although more literarily inclined, provided little support for Wharton's ambitions. Both parents thought formal education unnecessary, although they provided instruction for two older brothers. Wharton was forced to eavesdrop on the threshold of her father's library while her brothers were tutored, and to read surreptitiously the novels that her mother had forbidden. Although she aspired toward a literary career at an early age—"making up" was her grand obsession (*Backward* 42)—no one in her aristocratic society thought literature a proper pursuit for a lady. Her mother so effectively criticized her daughter's adolescent fictional efforts that Wharton virtually ceased writing.

When Wharton reflects on her childhood, she emphasizes its emotional and psychological loneliness. She notes that her friends "never had so much as a guess" of her literary aspirations and muses whether "any other child possessed of that 'other side' was ever so alone in it as I. . . . I never exchanged a word with a really intelligent human being until I was over twenty" ("Life" 1082–83). Wharton may exaggerate the extent of her deprivation; nevertheless, biographer Shari Benstock notes that, well into the 1890s, Wharton was still writing in isolation. "With no literary mentors to encourage and guide her," she was forced to rely on the evaluations of editors (*No Gifts* 70). Wharton's solitude produced a lifelong hunger for intellectual camaraderie, as well as a lingering sense that she was unfit for and undeserving of such support.

Gradually, Wharton found the mentors and colleagues she so desperately needed. She writes jubilantly about these intellectual "awakeners." First came family friend Egerton Winthrop, who nourished her love of art and literature and introduced her "to the wonder-world of nineteenth century science" (*Backward* 94). Next was Walter Berry, a lawyer and international diplomat whose friendship and critical advice benefited Wharton throughout her life. Writing reverently of their "communion of kindred intelligences," Wharton explains, "he found me when my mind and soul were hungry and thirsty, and he fed them till our last hour together" (*Backward* 107, 119). More than any of Wharton's mentorships, the one with Berry approached the ideal. He not only encouraged and guided her writing, he gave her the necessary confidence to think of herself as a writer. Wharton describes the harmony of mind and spirit that passed between them as a perfect collaboration in which two parties merge into one. "No words can say," she writes, "how the influence of his thought, his character, his deepest personality, were interwoven with mine" (*Backward* 115–16). Eventually, Wharton cultivated a close circle of artists, intellectuals, and critics that included Berry, Charles du Bos, Bernard Berenson, Paul Bourget, Henry James, Gaillard Lapsley, Robert Norton, and John Hugh Smith. These friends became travel and literary companions as well as sources of emotional support. Wharton also developed a close relationship with Rutger Bleecker Jewett, senior editor at Appleton, whom she frequently trusted to negotiate favorable contracts for her (*No Gifts* 371).

Wharton had a knack for developing friendships that combined personal and literary interests. The most famous of these was with novelist Henry James, but they also included her marriage to Edward (Teddy) Wharton and her romance with Morton Fullerton. Wharton sometimes drew on her husband's gift for storytelling, using his character sketches as the basis for some of her stories. Teddy's visit to the Riviera home of society painter Ralph Curtis provided Wharton with her story "The Pretext," and his trip to Hot Springs, Arkansas, with material for *The Custom of the Country* (*No Gifts* 187). She also gained inspiration from her love affair with Fullerton for her poetry and several novels, including *Ethan Frome* and *The Reef*, and she sought his advice about her writing. Dedicating her poem "Per Te, Sempre per Te" to Fullerton, Wharton even claimed him as coauthor (*No Gifts* 187, 209).

However, in most of Wharton's close relationships, we see a sense of limitation or disappointment as well as of possibility. Having married a man who little understood or appreciated her love of literature, Wharton endured a loneliness similar to that which she had suffered in childhood. There were rumors that the marriage was never consummated; this lack of marital experience further estranged her from her peers. As Benstock writes, "rather than bringing her into the magic circle of feminine self-knowledge, marriage isolated her from women" (*No Gifts* 60). She did experience the fullness of passion with Fullerton, but only to realize their romance was incompatible with friendship. As the affair waned, her letters to Fullerton pled for a return to the gender-neutral friendship they once knew. She desired "to be again the good comrade you once found me" and to be addressed in the masculine ("mon ami") rather than the feminine ("mon amie").[2] Although intimacy had fostered a felicitous collaboration, it ended in Wharton's reluctant reassertion of the boundaries of selfhood. Even within her circle of like-minded friends, Wharton remained somewhat of an outsider. As Susan Goodman notes, she was marginalized by her gender and often subjected to others' parody (*Wharton's Inner* 15).

The strain of collaboration is most evident in Wharton's relationship with James. Despite their high regard for one another, underlying tensions rubbed at the fabric of the friendship. Wharton's early lack of mentors had made her sensitive, sometimes defensive, about accepting others' help. She developed a fiercely independent nature and resisted relinquishing control of her affairs, especially of her writing. The popular assumption that she was James's disciple especially grated on her. James, on the other hand, freely gave advice during the early stages of her career. For example, admonishing her to write of "the *American Subject*," he stated the imperative that "she *must* be tethered in native pastures"; and he admitted that he wanted to "write" her work "over in my own way" (Edel 4:234–36). Benstock suggests that James's rhetoric betrays his "fear" of Wharton as a woman and artist and even his "hostility" toward her (*No Gifts* 188). It certainly reveals competition between the two and a license that the more experienced James felt free to take with the less experienced

Wharton. Eventually, Wharton redressed this imbalance in their relationship. Once confident of her literary powers, she made no secret of her distaste for James's later style of writing. And the power between them shifted whenever James visited. Their whirlwind journeys across Europe in her automobile left James "reduced to pulp, consumed utterly" (Edel 4:622–24), and his careful reserve was no match for her capacious energy and love of life.

Wharton's relationship with James reveals a quality that figures prominently in her life and writing: an intense interest in helping others less fortunate. Wharton's philanthropic tendency, established early on by her own feelings of indebtedness toward her mentors, bordered at times on obsession. While it demonstrates her magnanimity, it also suggests her competitiveness. Wharton enjoyed the sense of control that her expressions of generosity afforded. In many respects, she found it easier to be a benefactor than a collaborator. Her relationship with James became one-sided in this way when she tried to help him financially. For example, she underwrote costs of their trips, commissioned and probably paid for his portrait to be painted, and launched secret campaigns to increase his bank account. She lobbied for him to win the Nobel Prize, and she herself paid the $8000 advance that he received from Scribner's for *The Ivory Tower,* a novel he never completed. (She similarly convinced Scribner's to advance Fullerton a sum drawn from her account for a book that he never finished [*No Gifts* 268]). Most notoriously, she spearheaded an effort among James's American friends to give a gift of money, which he vehemently rejected. That James accepted a similar donation from his English friends suggests the fragile balance of power that existed between him and Wharton and the need each had for autonomy.

Wharton's relationships with women demonstrate a similar ambivalence toward collaboration. She did seek supportive, productive associations with women and enjoyed several female friendships, as recent studies by Goodman (*Edith Wharton's Women*) and others have shown. She was lifelong friends with Matilda Gay and Margaret (Daisy) Chanler. She socialized and traveled with Chanler and shared with her the deepest thoughts about her writing (Lewis and Lewis 483). She valued Sara Norton's emotional support, although she felt more intellectual affinity with Sara's father, Charles Eliot Norton. And she achieved a remarkably harmonious and productive collaboration with her friend Elisina Tyler, with whom she organized massive World War I relief efforts. It was Tyler who attended Wharton during her last weeks of life and kept a diary of their conversations. As both transcriber and interpreter during this time, Tyler served as Wharton's literary collaborator.

Despite satisfying relationships with women, an image that Wharton herself popularized is that of a regal, aloof aristocrat more at home in the company of men than women, a "self-made man," as Percy Lubbock described her (11). Wharton voiced disappointment in women, especially American women (*French* 98–121), and she sometimes distanced herself from them in striking ways. For example, she declared herself "entirely out of sympathy with woman-suffrage" (*No Gifts* 265) and never exercised her right to vote. She claimed that intelligent women always prefer the companionship of men to that of women (*French* 119), and she once hosted a tea for friend and former president, Theodore Roosevelt, to which she invited not one woman (*No Gifts* 236). Although Wharton expressed appreciation for English and European artists and intellectuals such as George Eliot, George Sand, Anna de Noailles, and Vernon Lee, she criticized her nineteenth-century American counterparts, decrying "the laxities" of the great Louisa and the "rose-and-lavender pages" of local colorists such as Sarah Orne Jewett and Mary Wilkins Freeman (*Backward* 51, 293–94). Literary collaborations of all kinds abounded in Paris in the early twentieth century, as Benstock notes in *Women of the Left Bank,* but Wharton seemed unaware of the cadre of female modernists living and working just blocks away (41). With the possible exception of Willa Cather, whose imaginative settings and plots differ markedly from hers, Wharton stands as a singular figure in her literary period, a lone female realist in the company of male writers William Dean Howells, Theodore Dreiser, and Henry James.

Wharton's fiction demonstrates longing for partnership at the same time that it reveals distrust of such alliances. Her female characters often lack supportive mothers and sisters, just as Wharton herself did. In novels as diverse as *The House of Mirth* and *Summer,* for example, heroines either make their way without female guidance or view women as competitors for scant resources such as husbands, money, and status. In other narratives, such as "Roman Fever," women who are purportedly friends are revealed as rivals. In this masterful tale of feigned collaboration, two women value the social positions afforded by their marriages more than their friendship. For years Grace Ansley and Alida Slade have collaborated against, not with, each other, and the disclosure at the end of the story that the father of Grace's child is Alida's husband only confirms the women's hidden antagonism.

Literary collaboration between women in Wharton's fiction is virtually nonexistent; indeed, Wharton depicts few female writers at all. For example, Margaret Aubyn in *The Touchstone* is a successful but deceased novelist, and Elsie Ashby in "Pomegranate Seed" writes from beyond the grave to undermine her successor's marriage. In a twentieth-century competitive environment, women who do write together—who labor joyfully and selflessly in keeping with nineteenth-century sentimental ideals of sisterhood—find the marketplace hostile to their endeavors. In "Writing a War Story," for example, Ivy Spang struggles futilely to write a short story to meet a publisher's deadline. Deserted by her muse, she accepts the help of her governess. Although Mademoiselle provides the heart of the story, Ivy Spang takes credit for authorship, in keeping with a class structure that erases the governess's identity—she is never even named in the story. The story is published, along with a photograph of the author. In a final irony, male readers ignore Ivy's writing and praise only her good looks. Wharton suggests that even when women do collaborate, they fall prey to social and economic hierarchies that they cannot change.

Indeed, Wharton's first bestseller, *The House of Mirth* (1905), serves as a paradigm of failed partnership. In Lily's story we can see Wharton's own desperate search for friends and mentors to accept her for herself rather than for her looks or social position.[3] No character in the novel fills this role, with the result that Lily's death at the novel's end is as much Wharton's indictment of failed communal love as it is a critique of individually squandered opportunity. Without the support of others, Lily is "rootless and ephemeral; mere spindrift of the whirling surface of existence" (319).

Lily's problems originate in her own home—as did Wharton's—with an extravagant, self-centered mother who attempts to "market" Lily's beauty as if it were a commodity. Her father, beleaguered but passive, fails to challenge her mother's greedy self-absorption; indeed, Lily feels that he "seemed always to blame her" for the family's monetary stress (30). When Lily's parents die, she is taken in by an aunt, as poor a maternal model as Lily's mother. Mrs. Peniston's charity is motivated not by concern for Lily, but by a desire for social approval: she could not have been "heroic on a desert island, but with the eyes of her little world upon her she took a certain pleasure in her act" (36). Weary of the hectic pace on the marriage circuit, Lily intuitively seeks relationships based on trust and reciprocity, not money or appearance. She turns down offers of marriage because they lack these essential qualities, explaining to Lawrence Selden, "What I want is a friend who won't be afraid to say disagreeable [things] . . . when I need them" (9). Selden, however, proves incapable of the love Lily needs; his republic of the spirit, ostensibly open, collaborative, and nonjudgmental, is no less hierarchical than society as a whole. Sisterly bonds prove as disappointing as maternal and romantic ones. For example, Lily's wealthy cousin refuses to grant her a much-needed loan; Bertha Dorset sacrifices Lily to her own social ambitions; and even sympathetic Judy Trenor levies a "tax" on her offers of hospitality (26).

Despite a competitive environment, Lily and her female associates do collaborate, and sometimes on Lily's behalf. Judy, for example, warns Lily to go slowly in pursuit of Percy Gryce, and she orchestrates social activities at Bellomont so that Lily becomes "the centre of that feminine solicitude which envelopes a young woman in mating season" (46). However, Judy's enthusiasm fades as Lily's prospects diminish. Lily herself internalizes competitive rather than cooperative ideals. For example, she compares herself with Judy, whose opulent rooms only "gave a sharper edge to the meagreness of her own opportunities." She is envious that rich, married women such as Bertha Dorset can afford to "take a man [such as Percy Gryce] up and toss him aside" (25), and she calculates that if she married Gryce, she "would have smarter gowns than Judy Trenor, and . . . more jewels than Bertha Dorset" (49).

As in "Roman Fever," friendship in *The House of Mirth* disguises animosity; indeed, when Lily first sees Bertha on the train to Bellomont, she is already her antagonist. Seating herself next to Lily, Bertha asks to borrow a cigarette, knowing that Percy Gryce considers smoking unladylike. Bertha uses intimacy as a weapon; caught off guard, Lily can only "wish there had been no vacant seat beside her own" (24). In true collaboration, conversation has the power to change the parties involved. In *The House of Mirth*, however, discourse between women is calculated to preserve each woman's place in the social scheme.

In a few scenes, women interact less selfishly; however, class differences prevent these collaborations from reaching their full potential. Feeling flush, Lily impulsively writes a check to Gerty Farish's charity, but she understands the meaning of such philanthropy only when she herself becomes poor. As Lily's hold on society becomes more tenuous, she becomes more sensitive to the needs of lower-class women. For example, at Bellomont, she decides not to ring for the maid because the hour is late and she "had been long enough in bondage to other people's pleasures to be considerate of those who depended on hers." It occurs to Lily that "she and her maid were in the same position, except that the latter received her wages more regularly" (28). Such empathy between women has no power to change social or economic structures, however. Lily and the maid remain dependent on these larger forces.

The most poignant scene of failed female collaboration occurs in the shop where Lily trims hats. Surrounded by twenty women facing similar economic hardship, Lily is nevertheless alone. She cannot benefit from the example of the other women's work or find meaning in the process of sewing itself, an activity that often serves as a metaphor for productive bonds between women. Her coworkers, who once counted her in the class of "fortunate womanhood" for whom their hats are designed, now find her "less interesting" and offer little assistance in her painful transition to manual labor. Her female supervisor evaluates her only in terms of a production quota dictated by the market. Lily's background and personality have ill prepared her for manual labor. Moreover, she has always thought of herself as a solitary worker rather than a member of a team. Her desire for "privacy and independence" and her habitual shrinking from "observation and sympathy" thus make her a poor candidate for mentorship or collaboration (287). One evening a coworker, Miss Kilroy, tentatively extends a hand as the two leave the shop, but Lily's reticence puts an end to their meeting. She continues on alone, filled with lassitude and despair.

Lily lives in a competitive, capitalistic culture that rewards individual rather than communal effort. To her credit, she refuses to use letters she possesses to blackmail her enemy; she maintains a collaborative rather than competitive relationship with Bertha Dorset even when it means her own destruction. Also to her credit, Lily refuses to mentor others as she has been mentored. For example, she refuses to advance an alliance between the socially established Freddie Van Osburgh and the outsider, Norma Hatch, because she views the relationship as manipulative self-aggrandizing. However, she—and to an extent Wharton herself—is unable to conceive of an alternative mode of behavior in which cooperation and trust replace competition and betrayal. Few alternatives exist within the world of the novel.

Wharton follows the pattern laid out in *The House of Mirth* in much of her fiction. Often female characters appear as doubles, and these pairings involve conflict rather than cooperation. Characters as diverse as Lily and Bertha, Zeena Frome and Mattie Silver (*Ethan Frome*), Delia Ralston and Charlotte Lovell (*The Old Maid*), Charity Royall and Annabel Balch (*Summer*), Anna Leath and Sophie Viner (*The Reef*), and Ellen Olenska and May Welland (*The Age of Innocence*) all compete with one another for romantic, financial, or social gain. Whether sisters, friends, mothers, or daughters, the characters follow social conventions that develop habits of rivalry rather than mutual support. However, in two pieces of writing, a memoir and a short story, Wharton demonstrates her interest in the reciprocal, empowering qualities of feminist collaboration and provides a glimpse of how such collaboration might be practiced.

Descriptions of collaborative authorship appear in Wharton's autobiography, *A Backward Glance,* in which she recounts the composition of her book on interior design, *The Decoration of Houses* (1897), and in her short story "Copy: A Dialogue" (1900). Both accounts describe a female writer's partnership with a man. In one, the relationship is based in friendship; in the other, in romance. In both cases, the writers' involvements with one another have potential to redefine the creative process as well as stereotypes about gender and authorial production. Both texts address what Whitney Chadwick and Isabelle de Courtivron pose as a central question for couples who share sexual and creative partnerships: how to reconcile the conflict between traditional views of authorship as individual and masculine with views of domesticity as social and feminine. "How," they ask, "do two creative people escape the constraints of this framework and construct an alternative story?" (7). Wharton shows with what difficulty such fluid and mutual relations are achieved.

One of Wharton's earliest publications, *The Decoration of Houses* (1897) was coauthored with Ogden Codman Jr., a Boston architect one year younger than she, who was a longtime friend of her husband's family and her neighbor on Park Avenue in New York. Wharton and Codman were united in their views of architecture and decoration and fell easily into conversation about this subject. Both believed that interior design should follow the balance and order of exterior architecture and that rooms should be light and spacious. Their partnership evolved both personally and professionally. Codman, for example, was familiar with the mental illness that afflicted Teddy Wharton's father and extended sympathy to Wharton when her husband began exhibiting similar symptoms. A trained architect, he also lent credibility to a project about which Wharton was knowledgeable but lacked credentials. He was young enough, however, not to have established his own professional connections or reputation. Wharton, at home in upper-class society, helped Codman win his first Newport commission to decorate bedrooms in the Cornelius Vanderbilt mansion, the Breakers. She herself hired him, first to renovate her New York townhouse and then her Newport cottage, Land's End. Toward the end of 1896, conversations about design inspired them to collaborate on a book on house decoration.

The early stages of their relationship were marked by affection and playful repartee. In a marital allusion that conveyed their closeness, Wharton called Ogden "Coddy" and referred to herself as "Mrs. Puss-cod." While in Europe conducting research for the book, she wrote Codman of her findings, urging him to adopt her view that eighteenth-century Italian architecture was superior to French. She even ran architectural and design-related errands for him. When a concern arose over Codman's having work at Land's End finished on time, she pleaded, "be an angel and have the rooms ready . . . when we arrive," and humorously added that should she find the paint wet, she would spread the rumor that he had inspired the hall and billiard room in Frederick Vanderbilt's Newport mansion, vulgar rooms that in her opinion "retard culture so very thoroughly" (qtd. in *No Gifts* 79–80). Wharton's early partnership with Codman, then, suggests an ease and ability to deal openly with differences, hallmarks of feminist collaboration.

As work on the book progressed, however, the relationship showed signs of strain. Interestingly, Wharton records none of this pettiness and rivalry in *A Backward Glance,* but biographers Benstock and Lewis note disagreements, including differing accounts about which of them wrote the first draft of the book.[4] In her memoir, Wharton describes only the creative joy with which *The Decoration of Houses* was conceived and written. She also suggests that true collaboration, by its very nature, breaks traditional epistemological and gender barriers. She notes that asking Codman to renovate the interior of her Newport home was itself unconventional because "architects of that day looked down on house-decoration as a branch of dress-making" (106). Architecture was deemed a masculine pursuit and interior design a feminine one, but Wharton adds that Codman willingly transgressed gender boundaries by agreeing to work with her. Wharton, in turn, violated gender norms by favoring the more masculine spareness of classicism over the feminine ornateness of Victoriana. Codman, she explains, "shared [my] dislike of Victorian clutter and preference for balanced, classic lines." With this common ground, their collaboration developed spontaneously. When she and the young architect examined Wharton's house and found that "we had the same views we drifted, I hardly know how, toward a notion of putting them into a book" (107). Her description of the project as mysterious and effortless ("we drifted, I hardly know how") and as mutually gratifying (reinforced by four repetitions of "we" in the sentences) suggests a harmony of minds described by practitioners of feminist collaboration.

According to Wharton's memoir, she and Codman developed ideas for the book in dialogue with one another, going "into every detail of our argument" so that the finished product was a seamless work that represented both writers collectively and neither individually. Indeed, Wharton demonstrates how the Bakhtinian notion of play of voices within a text functions to destabilize the idea of a single authority. The Codman-Wharton partnership evolved as a blending of mind and spirit, so much so that years after the book's appearance and the publication of many Wharton novels, an enthusiastic reader approached Wharton and congratulated both her and Codman on "every one of the wonderful novels he and you have written together!" (*Backward* 111).

Perhaps Wharton remembered her collaboration with Codman as more positive than it actually was, or she avoided mentioning difficulties in her memoir, which is circumspect about many personal and professional issues. In fact, *The Decoration of Houses* took two years to complete, with delays both parties regretted. From the start, Codman's commission to renovate Wharton's residences colored the partnership, placing Wharton in the role of Codman's employer rather than peer. At one point, Teddy Wharton threatened to sue Codman over his bill, and Edith herself complained about his high rates. Her disapproval extended to Codman's writing style: she even criticized the wording of advertisements he circulated for his business. When negotiations for a contract on *The Decoration of Houses* faltered at Scribner's, Wharton implicitly blamed Codman for failing to make a good impression at a meeting and made it a "condition that you leave the transactions entirely to me." An avid reviser, she "pursued" Codman with letters, begging him to respond to her rewrites and to choose photographs (*No Gifts* 84–85). Out of patience with his failure to respond—he was now overwhelmed with clients—she turned to Walter Berry for advice on revisions. She then oversaw every detail of the book's production.

Wharton's characteristic response to situations she perceived as threatening was to exercise more rather than less control. This was certainly true with respect to *The Decoration of Houses*. Her pursuit of perfection, coupled with Codman's busy schedule, strained the collaboration to the breaking point. Wharton took charge of the project, so much so that, toward the end, it must have seemed more her book than his. Indeed, Benstock declares that, "in its logical and direct manner of presentation, *The Decoration of Houses* is. . . . [s]tamped with Edith Wharton's signature" (*No Gifts* 87). The ordeal taxed their friendship, which entered a period of estrangement. However, the experience of joint labor also cemented a bond. After reading reviews of *The Decoration of Houses*, Wharton enthusiastically—perhaps impulsively—proposed that she and Codman write another book together, on garden architecture. She eventually authored this book, *Italian Villas and Their Gardens*, alone. However, Wharton and Codman remained friends. She visited him in the south of France just two months before she died, where they were planning a revision of *The Decoration of Houses*.

It would be tempting but incorrect, then, to think of Wharton's work with Ogden Codman merely in traditional terms, as that of a female novice seeking a male authority for a project about which she lacked confidence. Wharton initiated much of the work on *The Decoration of Houses* and took the lead whenever progress faltered. She had taken a risk when she persuaded Scribner's to publish the jointly authored text, since she was still relatively unknown as a writer. However, the risk was a calculated one: her standing with the editors was significantly enhanced with the book's commercial success. It would be equally misguided to think of Wharton's work with Codman in radically feminist terms, as a mutual and thoroughly satisfying collaboration that altered the way each thought about the production and control of knowledge. Wharton exercised a good deal of control over *The Decoration of Houses*—at times dominating it—and she never again engaged in collaborative writing. In sum, Wharton viewed collaboration as a positive departure from the norm. Her partnership with Codman suggests her sense of adventure and an uncommon ability to bridge gaps between herself and someone of different gender, training, and sensibility. Wharton demonstrated that she was capable both of flexibility and focus, of process and product, of clarity and fluidity. However, although her work with Codman yielded a book that was better than each might have produced separately, collaboration was difficult to achieve and impossible to sustain.

Although she went on to write and publish her fiction individually rather than jointly, Wharton remained interested in collaboration. In particular, she was intrigued by the effect that one writer could have on another, even when their texts remained technically distinct. Her short story "Copy: A Dialogue" provides another glimpse of a female novelist achieving both authorial independence and connection.

Wharton portrays few successful female writers in her fiction, as Mary Suzanne Schriber notes (166, 177–80). However, in "Copy," the story of a successful female novelist, Wharton explores both the economics and erotics of collaboration. She criticizes the commercial market's power to kill an author's enthusiasm for her art, but she applauds the power of love to inspire and sustain creativity. This fictional account of the evolving harmony of mind and spirit between two literary people alludes perhaps to her long-standing, satisfying relationship with Walter Berry. In the story, a best-selling novelist and an acclaimed poet who have not seen each other in years reminisce about their earlier romance. Through a series of clever linguistic maneuvers, which Wharton captures by writing the story in the form of a dialogue, each writer realizes not just the financial but the aesthetic and romantic value of the relationship they shared.

When the story opens, Helen Dale, described as forty, "slender," and "still young," receives an unexpected visit from her former lover, Paul Ventnor, who exhibits a "short-sighted stare" and "incipient stoutness buttoned into a masterly frock coat" (275, 277). The description of Ventnor as having aged more than Dale immediately suggests a competition between the couple. Ventnor purportedly visits Dale to renew ties, but his real motive—suggested by his name, derived from a Latin word meaning "to sell"—is to reclaim the love letters he wrote to Dale for his memoirs. Although he flatters Dale with references to past affections, he wants the letters not because of what they mean, but because of what they will earn. Dale, divining his purpose, refuses, and the story develops through a gentle repartee in which each writer tries to establish dominance over and at the same time reveal past and present feelings for the other. Wharton's view of the salutary effects of collaboration becomes evident when the writers read lines from their letters and realize the important role that each has played in the creation of the other's work.

Wharton writes the story in such a way as to suggest mutuality between the two writers. Ventnor, for example, recalls that his first book was dedicated to Dale. Although she never dedicated a book to him, he reminds her that, in fact, she "wrote for" him. The writers also praise each other's achievements. Whereas Ventnor says that he finds "little promise" in his first volumes, Dale claims, on the contrary, that she finds "distinct promise" in them (279). Dale compliments Ventnor when she discovers that letters he inspired her to write years ago have become the basis for her fiction. One letter in particular, composed after she and Ventnor went skating, describes the feelings of a woman falling in love. She finds that the "best phrase" in her fictional account is "simply plagiarized" from her letter (280–81). Ventnor also sees connections between his letters to Dale and his poetry. Rereading one letter, he discovers the material out of which he composed a sonnet, "one of his best" (282). Indeed, the influence of each writer on the other is so great that at one point Dale proclaims that "there's more of myself in [your letters] than of you" (283). In this statement Wharton conveys the idea that through collaboration, each writer's individual identity collapses and a new joint identity is forged.

"Copy" also describes the impact of the larger world on the craft of writing, especially women's writing. Wharton criticizes a capitalistic system that makes wealth the only measure of success, suggesting instead that a woman is fulfilled when she can combine critical acclaim with supportive personal relationships. Helen Dale's success is indicated by numerous requests she receives for autographs, royalties, new editions, translations, serial publications, and interviews; yet about all this "business" she exclaims, "The same old story! I'm so tired of it all" (276). Fame and money cannot substitute for the warmth of human relationship; indeed, capitalistic forces discourage such bonds by rewarding individuals who successfully compete rather than collaborate with each other. Dale's commercial success has meant emotional starvation.

Dale employs a young assistant, Hilda, who is thrilled to be in the presence "of the greatest novelist and the greatest poet of the age" (276). However, Hilda's attitude toward Dale does not suggest a protégée's unqualified enthusiasm for her mentor. Rather, Hilda admires Dale in part because she hopes to make a "fortune" on the diary she keeps about her work with her. At a young age, then, she is aligned with competitive and exploitative, rather than cooperative, forces. As she "modestly" admits, four publishers have already expressed interest in publishing her document (277). Hilda's mercenary notions combine with her romantic ones; in both, authorship is a solitary process. She tells Dale that it is "beautiful" to "sit here, watching, and listening, all alone in the night, and to feel that you're in there creating—" (276). Wharton suggests that traditional tributes to solitary genius are foolish and naive by associating them with a starry-eyed twenty-year-old with no real experience of life. The reality of individual authorship, demonstrated through the main character, is not nearly so romantic as Hilda believes. As Dale says, "living in the hearts of my readers" is not living at all but a depersonalizing process that turns author into artifact, a "classic" "bound in sets and kept on the top bookshelf" (283).

Wharton's choice of a title for her story is also provocative. "Copy" is a multivalent term whose meanings include writing, copying, publishing, plagiarism, repetition, and journalism. On the one hand, the title describes Dale's strategy once she discovers Ventnor's reason for visiting. She "copies" his method and tells him that she, too, wants to publish their love letters for financial gain. Dale has managed not to become a pale "copy" or disciple of male genius—what, according to popular opinion, Wharton herself was in relation to her literary friend Henry James. On the other hand, "copy" reflects the complex literary, romantic, and commercial relationship between the two writers. They are, in effect, equals or "copies" of one another, in that they were once lovers and are now famous writers who inspired each other and plan to exploit each other's letters for profit. "Copy," which echoes the word "copyright," also refers to the business of writing. Dale frequently refers to the fact that she has achieved fame but lost love. As she admits to Ventnor, "I died years ago. . . . A keen sense of copyright is *my* nearest approach to an emotion" (278). A copyright—that is, a legal protection of the right of sole authorship—is a poor substitute for a collaboration that can both warm the heart and inspire the pen.

By the end of the story, Wharton allows the more positive sense of "copy" to prevail. Dale and Ventnor decide not to publish their letters, which they now think of as the "key to our garden," rather than as a source of income. Unlike a man "who has sold the garden [and] . . . made a fortune that he doesn't know how to spend," they lay their letters next to each other, as if to suggest their sameness, and then toss them into the fire. This scene recalls a similar one in *The House of Mirth,* in which Lily Bart burns Bertha and Selden's love letters. The difference is that Lily acts alone and remains alone, whereas Dale and Ventnor act collaboratively and reaffirm their love. Just as they once created together, they now destroy together. In so doing, they create a "boundless" world that they "keep . . . to ourselves" (285–86). They are "in league" with each other in the sense that Susan Elizabeth Sweeney and I use this term to suggest the "intimacy, complicity, even exclusivity" of feminist collaboration ("In League" 76).

Wharton's description of the composition of *The Decoration of Houses* and her depiction of writers in "Copy" suggest her desire for a world where collaborative endeavors are more the norm than the exception. These texts demonstrate that Wharton, often thought of as a singular literary figure, understood the dynamics of feminist collaboration and found them congenial. However, in these two portrayals, women achieve feminist collaboration with men rather than with other women. Harmonious and effective partnerships between women are rare. Moreover, economic and social class differences, as well as traditional views of creativity as an individual process, frequently prevent women as well as men from experiencing the pleasures of partnership. However, although few characters openly defy the social conventions imposed upon them, some manage to question and even subvert these traditional terms of creativity, pointing the way toward revisionary, collaborative forms of knowledge and expression.

Notes

1. For the purposes of this essay, I define collaboration as a working relationship between peers or equals, and mentorship as an exchange between a more knowledgeable or experienced individual and a less knowledgeable or experienced one. I am grateful to my collaborator, Susan Elizabeth Sweeney, for helping me develop ideas for this essay. I acknowledge, in particular, the "Theories" section of our coauthored essay on feminist collaboration ("In League").

2. Both Gribben (35) and Lewis and Lewis (189) date this letter as "late summer 1909." Correcting them, Benstock dates it October 23, 1909 (*No Gifts* 503 n. 19).

3. See Showalter's discussion of the parallels between Lily Bart and Edith Wharton.

4. Lewis writes that the "authors' memories are at odds as to which of them wrote the first draft" (*Biography* 77), but according to Benstock, "records show" Wharton drafting the opening chapters and doing the bulk of the work on the book (*No Gifts* 83–84).

Works Cited

Bakhtin, Mikhail M. *The Dialogic Imagination: Four Essays.* Trans. Caryl Emerson and Michael Holquist. Ed. Michael Holquist. Austin: University of Texas Press, 1981.

Belenky, Mary Field, et al. *Women's Ways of Knowing: The Development of Self, Voice, and Mind.* New York: Basic Books, 1986.

Benstock, Shari. *No Gifts From Chance: A Biography of Edith Wharton.* New York: Scribner's, 1994.

———. *Women of the Left Bank: Paris, 1900–1940.* Austin: University of Texas Press, 1986.

Brodkey, Linda. *Academic Writing as Social Practice.* Philadelphia: Temple University Press, 1987.

Bruffee, Kenneth. "Collaborative Learning and the Conversation of Mankind." *College English* 46 (1984): 635–52.

Chadwick, Whitney and Isabelle de Courtivron, eds. Introduction. *Significant Others: Creativity and Intimate Partnership.* London: Thames and Hudson, 1993. 7–29.

Chodorow, Nancy. *The Reproduction of Mothering: Psychoanalysis and the Sociology of Gender.* Berkeley: University of California Press, 1978.

Cisneros, Sandra. *The House on Mango Street.* New York: Vintage-Random House, 1984.

Cixous, Hélène. "The Laugh of the Medusa." Trans. Keith Cohen and Paula Cohen. *New French Feminisms.* Ed. Elaine Marks and Isabelle de Courtivron. Amherst: University of Massachusetts Press, 1980. 254–64.

Ede, Lisa, and Andrea Lunsford. *Singular Texts/Plural Authors: Perspectives on Collaborative Writing.* Carbondale: Southern Illinois University Press, 1990.

Edel, Leon, ed. *The Letters of Henry James.* 4 vols. Cambridge: Harvard University Press, 1974–84.

Elbrecht, Joyce, and Lydia Fakundiny. "Scenes from a Collaboration: or Becoming Jael B. Juba." *Tulsa Studies in Women's Literature* 13, no. 2 (1994): 241–58.

Gilligan, Carol. *In a Different Voice: Psychological Theory and Women's Development.* Cambridge: Harvard University Press, 1982.

Goodman, Susan. *Edith Wharton's Inner Circle.* Austin: University of Texas Press, 1994.

———. *Edith Wharton's Women: Friends and Rivals.* Hanover, New Hampshire: University Press of New England, 1990.

Gribben, Alan. "'The Heart *Is* Insatiable': A Selection from Edith Wharton's Letters to Morton Fullerton, 1907–1915." *Library Chronicle.* n.s. 31. Austin: Harry Ransom Humanities Research Center, University of Texas, 1985. 7–71.

Irigaray, Luce. "When Our Lips Speak Together." *This Sex Which Is Not One.* Trans. Catherine Porter. Ithaca: Cornell University Press, 1985. 205–18.

Kaplan, Carey, and Ellen Cronan Rose. "Strange Bedfellows: Feminist Collaboration." *Signs* 18, no. 3 (1993): 547–61.

Keller, Evelyn Fox, and Helene Moglen. "Competition: A Problem for Academic Women." *Competition, A Feminist Taboo?* Ed. Valerie Miner and Helen E. Longino. New York: Feminist Press, 1987. 21–37.

Leonardi, Susan J., and Rebecca A. Pope. "Screaming Divas: Collaboration as Feminist Practice." *Tulsa Studies in Women's Literature* 13, no. 2 (1994): 259–70.

Lewis, R. W. B. *Edith Wharton: A Biography.* New York: Harper, 1975.

Lewis, R. W. B., and Nancy Lewis, eds. *The Letters of Edith Wharton.* New York: Scribner's, 1988.

Lubbock, Percy. *Portrait of Edith Wharton.* New York: Appleton, 1947.

Rich, Adrienne. "Compulsory Heterosexuality and Lesbian Existence." *Signs* 5, no. 4 (1980): 631–60.

Schriber, Mary Suzanne. *Gender and the Writer's Imagination: From Cooper to Wharton.* Lexington: University Press of Kentucky, 1987.

Showalter, Elaine. "The Death of the Lady (Novelist): Wharton's House of Mirth." *Representations* 9 (1985): 133–49.

Singley, Carol J., and Susan Elizabeth Sweeney, eds. *Anxious Power: Reading, Writing, and Ambivalence in Narrative by Women.* Albany: State University of New York Press, 1993.

———. "In League with Each Other: The Theory and Practice of Feminist Collaboration." *Common Ground: Feminist Collaboration in the Academy.* Ed. Elizabeth G. Peck and JoAnna Stephens Mink. Albany: State University of New York Press, 1998. 63–79.

Sullivan, Patricia A. "Revising the Myth of the Independent Scholar." *Writing With.* Ed. David Bleich, Thomas Fox, and Sally Reagan. Albany: State University of New York Press, 1994. 11–29.

Tan, Amy. *The Joy Luck Club.* New York: Ballantine, 1989.

Wharton, Edith. *The Age of Innocence.* 1920. Introduction by R. W. B. Lewis. New York: Scribner's, 1970.

———. *A Backward Glance.* New York: Scribner's, 1933.

———. *The Collected Short Stories of Edith Wharton.* Ed. R. W. B. Lewis. 2 vols. New York: Scribner's, 1968.

———. "Copy: A Dialogue." *Scribner's* 27 (June 1900): 657–63. Reprinted in *Crucial Instances.* New York: Scribner's (1901). And in *Collected Short Stories,* 1:275–86. Textual citations are from *Collected.*

———. *The Custom of the Country.* New York: Scribner's, 1913.

———. *Ethan Frome.* New York: Scribner's, 1911.

———. *French Ways and Their Meaning.* New York: Appleton, 1919.

———. *The House of Mirth*. New York: Scribner's, 1905.

———. "Life and I." *Edith Wharton: Novellas and Other Writings*. Ed. Cynthia Griffin Wolff. Library of America Series. New York: Literary Classics of the United States, 1990. 1071–96.

———. *Old New York: The Old Maid (The Fifties)*. New York: Appleton, 1924.

———. "Pomegranate Seed." *Collected* 2: 763–88.

———. *The Reef*. New York: Appleton, 1912.

———. "Roman Fever." *Collected* 2: 833–43.

———. *Summer*. New York: Appleton, 1917.

———. *The Touchstone*. New York: Scribner's, 1900.

———. "Writing a War Story." *Collected* 2: 359–70.

Wharton, Edith, and Ogden Codman, Jr. *The Decoration of Houses*. New York: Scribner's, 1897.

Meetings of Minds

Edith Wharton As Mentor and Guide

Helen Killoran

Since people rarely think of Edith Wharton as a mentor, they may be surprised at the extent to which she helped other writers—most younger, most American, some European or contemporaries. People may also be impressed by how much these writers gave back, sometimes in material terms, to Edith Wharton in the most valuable possible manner: the meeting and cross-fertilizing of intelligent, cultured minds. No evidence indicates that she maintained any motive other than to help, in two basic ways—through use of her friends and contacts and through personal advice to such writers as Howard Sturgis, Percy Lubbock, F. Scott Fitzgerald, Leon Edel, Sinclair Lewis, Zona Gale, Philomène de la Forest-Divonne, Morton Fullerton, Katherine Fullerton Gerould, and Vivienne de Watteville. Also intriguing are Wharton's letter to Victor Solberg, "a young poet," and her message to the audience of *The Writing of Fiction*.

As she guided and taught, Edith Wharton first insisted on practical matters such as determination to establish regular work habits; she scorned mental laziness, preferring to help productive, persistent people like Howard Sturgis, Sinclair Lewis, Zona Gale, Katherine Fullerton Gerould, and Vivienne de Watteville. She insisted on care with words, with language, avoiding clichés, jargon, and "dirt for dirt's sake" (*Writing* 65–66). because language is the tool of thought. Clichés, jargon, and dirt for its own sake represent lazy adoption of careless, infertile thinking, a concern underlying Wharton's letters to Morton Fullerton and to Bernard Berenson about keeping Philomène de la Forest-Divonne's attention away from Freud. She advocated that writers think deeply before they apply words to the result of their thought, that they avoid the swamps of jargon and the quicksand of intellectual fads by creating a solid cultural base for writing through reading great writers and studying "immortal" ideas, then "standing far enough aloof from them to see beyond. . . . Such an all-round view can be obtained only by mounting to a height" (*Writing* 15–16). Writers should absorb the influence of the greatest thinkers until it becomes part of something unique and personal, at which time, at intellectual maturity, they cast off direct influences.

Most of all Wharton insists to friends and protégés that a subject must "grow slowly in [the] mind" (*Writing* 57). For example, Goethe thought "a great deal about his art" (*Writing* 116). Finally, in her letter to Bernard Berenson about Philomène de la Forest-Divonne, Wharton used the word "brooding" (in the context of thinking and mulling over the work) for a specific purpose, since she mentions it more than once. "There is in the human intellect a power of expansion—I might almost call it a power of creation—which is brought into play by the simple brooding upon facts. . . . [T]his brooding is one of the most distinctive attributes of genius, is perhaps as near an approach as can be made to the definition of genius" (*Writing* 165–66).

The contemporaries Wharton hoped to help over the line to success, primarily by use of her contacts, included the charmingly eccentric Howard Sturgis, whom Edith Wharton had first met at Newport, becoming permanent friends with him after he accompanied Henry James on a visit to The Mount. At that time Sturgis had already demonstrated his work ethic, having published a children's book, *Tim: A Story of School Life* (1891), and a novel, *All That Was Possible,* about the "life of Mrs. Sibyl Croft, Comedian" (1895), books that Wharton described as "two charming, if slightly over-sentimental tales." However, at the time of his visit to The Mount, Sturgis had also published in England an autobiographical novel, *Belchamber,* which Wharton described as "very nearly in the first rank" (*Backward* 234). She worked zealously to convince William Crary Brownell of Scribner's to take the novel on the basis of Sturgis's past success and then tried to strengthen her argument by mentioning the approval of Henry James (*Letters* 87–88). However, when Brownell demurred in spite of her logic, she attempted to counter his objections that the novel contained "unpleasant" themes and was not "American enough." She agreed to the necessity of cutting but argued against "the objection on the score of *moeurs* in a book of such serious purpose and tragic import, and secondly the view that it isn't American enough to interest American readers. It isn't American at all, of course—it is an English novel, to all intents and purposes by an English novelist—but is that a reason why it shouldn't 'take' in America?" (Lewis, *Biog.* 141–42) Nevertheless, Brownell remained staunchly puritanical in his objections to Sturgis's subjects of an unconsummated marriage, adultery, and illegitimacy. Even so, in 1905, undoubtedly (but not provably) with Wharton's help, G. P. Putnam published *Belchamber* in New York to reserved critical admiration. Afterward, Sturgis wrote only a few book reviews and short stories, preferring to retire to needlework and entertaining the frequent meetings of minds of Wharton's "inner circle" at his home, "Qu'Acre" (Lewis, *Biog*. 167–68).[1]

The following excerpt from a letter to her close friend, John Hugh Smith, provides just one of a myriad of examples of Edith Wharton's love of intellectual conversation: "I always go with outstretched hands toward any opportunity for a free and frank exchange of ideas, and am too much given to omitting the preliminary forms where I find a fundamental likeness of mind! It was a great pleasure to wander over the cosmos with you in that easy fashion. . ." (Lewis, *Biog*. 246).

The importance of such intellectual exchanges provided Wharton with much of the fertile soil for her creativity. As Ruth Perry explains so perfectly in her Introduction to the collection, *Mothering the Mind:* "We all know what it feels like to be within the magic circle of good friends, among whom we feel more real, more unique, more vivid, more ourselves. With such friends we always discover the words to say what we mean; their receptivity helps us find a suitable voice; they seem to meet us on our own ground . . ."(9).

Wharton would strongly agree with Perry's comment that "the creative impulse, like any growing thing, needs to be cross-pollinated" (Perry and Brownley 11). At Howard Sturgis's home in May 1906, during one of these fruitful gatherings, Edith Wharton first met Percy Lubbock, a young man in his late twenties. A devoted apprentice to Henry James, Lubbock had recently published a fictional biography of Elizabeth Barrett Browning. At first he remained a quiet observer, learning what he could from the brilliant conversation around him, admiring Wharton so much that he could not help but absorb a great deal. So soon he, too, became a confirmed member of the "inner circle" (Lewis, *Biog*. 167–68). In 1916, after the death of Henry James, Wharton "felt strongly that someone was needed to decipher the vast number of letters to her and the other members of the old Queen's Acre constituency—'someone,' as she wrote to Edmund Gosse . . . familiar with the atmosphere in which Henry and our small group communed together" (Lewis, *Biog*. 426). She tried to convince the hostile James family—they wanted control of the letters—that Lubbock had "almost magical insight" into Henry James's point of view and an "extraordinary literary sense." He did eventually edit *The Letters of Henry James* (1920) and on November 28, 1921, Wharton asked Bain, her favorite bookseller, to send a copy of Lubbock's *The Craft of Fiction* to Sinclair Lewis, commenting that it "is full of interesting and suggestive things for people of our trade" (*Letters* 449, Benstock 383). Sadly, in 1934 the friendship between Lubbock and Wharton ended over Wharton's disapproval of his marriage to Sybil Cutting, which in turn seems to have led to the insidiously negative quality of Lubbock's *Portrait of Edith Wharton* (1947). Lubbock's 1955 edition of *The Letters of Henry James* fails even to acknowledge Edith Wharton's help. Unfortunately, it also appears that Wharton's appreciation of *The Craft of Fiction* disintegrated in proportion to her friendship with Lubbock, and although R. W. B. Lewis suggests that *The Writing of Fiction* (1925) might have been inspired by a desire to improve upon *The Craft of Fiction* (Lewis, *Biog.* 521), she may also have been motivated to distance her ideas from those of Henry James promoted by it.

The same year *The Craft of Fiction* appeared (1921), a representative of the younger generation, Sinclair Lewis, wrote Edith Wharton congratulating her on winning the Pulitzer Prize for *The Age of Innocence.* Although she certainly deserved the prize, Wharton became outraged to discover that she had received it because some members of the Pulitzer Prize committee had apparently objected to the "depressing, vengeful" attack on the small midwestern town portrayed in *Main Street* (a comment from Hamlin Garland's diary), which had been the preference of the rest, who felt that Wharton's novel represented a dead era (Benstock 364). Touched by Lewis's generous letter of congratulations, she remarked, "It is the first sign I have ever had—literally—that 'les jeunes' at home had ever read a word of me. . . . When I found the prize shd really have been yours, but was withdrawn because your book (I quote from memory) had 'offended a number of prominent persons in the Middle West,' disgust was added to despair" (*Letters* 445).

Afterward, Wharton was delighted to add Lewis and his first wife, Grace Hegger Lewis, to her list of friends, although, because of vagaries of Lewis's personality, their intellectually stimulating visits occurred less regularly than she would have liked. Even so, "Lewis's genuine respect for Edith Wharton can be traced to his undergraduate days at Yale in the early 1900s, when he read and studied her short stories. Her name appeared regularly thereafter on the little lists he used to compile of those whom he regarded as the most accomplished, and hence the most competitive, living American writers. Lewis seems even to have spoken of Edith Wharton's influence on him . . . " (Lewis, *Biog.* 434), an indicator of which is his dedication of *Babbitt* to her. Sinclair Lewis finally received recognition when he won the Nobel Prize in 1930, no doubt to the great pleasure of Edith Wharton (who herself had been nominated in 1927), in part because of the redress and in part because the award confirmed her opinion.

Among the examples of "les jeunes" to whom she offered more concrete personal guidance is Leon Edel, who recalls visiting Edith Wharton at Pavillon Colombe with the intention of securing her cooperation for a biography of Walter Berry, which of course would have involved substantial discussions of Wharton herself. In a friendly but professional manner, Wharton asked Edel why he wanted to write about Berry, adding that she had thought of writing a memorial essay but decided that there was nothing to say of public interest. Eventually, Edel confessed that focus on Berry had begun as a "footnote" to his primary interest in Henry James. After that, Edith Wharton kept the subject to James's playwriting. Edel recalls being "invited back to the Pavillon Colombe a number of times to talk about James" (Edel 522). The books Edith Wharton willed to Sir Kenneth Clark include a copy of Edel's *Henry James: Les Années dramatique* (Paris: Jouvé, 1931),[2] and, in *A Backward Glance,* Wharton remarks that "Mr. Leon Edel, in his suggestive essay on James's play-writing, has made out so good a case for him as a dramatist (if only circumstances had been more favourable) that I sometimes wonder if I was not wrong in thinking these theatrical experiments a mistake" (366). Though it is hardly surprising that Edith Wharton would encourage a talented young literary critic to write about her dear friend Henry James, the question becomes, if Wharton thought James's "theatrical experiments a mistake," why did she encourage Edel to write about them unless to keep his attention diverted from her still mysterious relationship with Walter Berry?

Like Edel, Zona Gale was a hardworking writer whom Edith Wharton indirectly linked with Sinclair Lewis. Some say informally that Gale habitually solicited helpful criticism from well-known authors by writing them flattering letters. Edith Wharton received one regarding *The Glimpses of the Moon,* but she rarely responded to praise unless it revealed that the adulator had engaged considerable intellect in the reading. Zona Gale had apparently done so, for when Wharton wrote to R. B. Jewett of D. Appleton in August 1922 thanking him for forwarding Miss Gale's letter, she commented that "I would give all the [favorable] reviews . . . for such a letter as Miss Gale's, not only because I admire her work so much, and consequently value her approval in proportion to my admiration, but also because she has put her finger on the very central nerve of my book. This does not happen more than once or twice, even in a long career."[3] Wharton's letter of September 1, 1922, thanking Zona Gale seems to indicate that "central nerve" as well as to reiterate what she said in the preface to *Ghosts*—that the reader and writer must meet halfway.[4] "[T]hat you should have felt the bracelet scene which nobody notices is balm to me."[5] She goes on to encourage and applaud Zona Gale: "How could you think

I hadn't felt the importance of Lulu, supposing you thought at all about my possible opinion of her? I'm always, watchfully and patiently, on the look-out for what the young people are doing, and exulting and triumphing when a Lulu or a Babbitt emerges."

A third among "les jeunes," Philomène de la Forest-Divonne (née de Lévis-Mirepoix) represents one of those talented but undisciplined writers whom Wharton attempted to retrain. Philomène was already an acquaintance of Edith Wharton's, having lived next door to her on the rue de Varenne, and she had written an autobiographical novel, *Cité des lampes* (1912). Meeting her again in 1920, Wharton undertook to reintroduce her into intellectual society but felt thwarted by "Phil's" attraction to literary fads. Prior to one of Philomène's visits to Bernard Berenson, Wharton wrote to him expressing her determination to guide and help:

> I want to give you a reminder. The pity is that, as you saw, her charming eager helpless intelligence has not been left empty, but filled with third-rate flashy rubbish, of the kind that most enervates the mental muscles—"occultism," the Sar Peladan, mediums ("after all there *is* something in it"), vital fluids, & all the lyre—or the lie! When R. Norton suggested her reading something about Egypt, she refused, on the ground that she wished to keep herself "uninfluenced," which means, that she's too lazy to fix her attention. In short, there is hardly a vicious sentimentalism, or a specious pretext for mental laziness, that doesn't run off her tongue. But something *can* be done—& is still, I'm sure, worth doing!—Above all, please ask Mary not to befuddle her with Freudianism & all its jargon. She'll take to it like a duck to—sewerage. (*Letters* 450–51)

While most commentators have puzzled over this remark in relation to Wharton's apparently ambivalent attitude toward Freud, it makes better sense considered in light of her exhortation to future authors in *The Writing of Fiction* to avoid "mental laziness" and "dirt-for-dirt's sake from which no real work of art has ever sprung" (*Writing* 65–66). Philomène apparently tended to fall into fads and fashions without thinking them through in relation to ideas of lasting value, and in her case, the temptation to use superficial Freudian jargon might have been too great. In January 1914 Wharton wrote, again to Berensen, that "Philomène continues her little train-train [humdrum activities], & we are trying to get her to read, in the hope that we may guide her toward writing. But I don't think she will ever do either!" (*Letters* 474–75) She felt that Philomène needed "to develop the *conscious*, and not grub after the sub-conscious. She wants to be taught first to see, to attend, to reflect" (Lewis, *Biog*. 438). The combined Wharton-Berenson assault eventually succeeded. Philomène emerged as one of the better-known writers and journalists in France under the nom de plume Claude Sylve. Robert Norton translated her prizewinning novel, *Benediction,* into English, and Edith Wharton provided one of her rare forewords (*Letters* 592). In the foreword, Wharton praises her protégée for the same quality she later commends in Proust—"the art of keeping us, from the first word of her tale to the last, in our daily world yet not of it" (2).

Another writer whom Wharton considered lazy and undisciplined was Morton Fullerton, her then-lover and correspondent to the London *Times.* Nevertheless, in 1909 she made an effort to further his career by suggesting to Macmillan that Fullerton be offered the opportunity to write a book on Paris because his attributes included an "intimate & varied acquaintance with the most complex of cities, in all its aspects, historical, architectural & sociological." Macmillan offered the book to Fullerton along with an advance arranged by Edith Wharton. He neither wrote the book nor returned the advance (Benstock 216). By October 1912, Wharton had become more clearly aware of Fullerton's weaknesses and less frightened of bringing them to his attention. After perusing a manuscript he had sent her, which she referred to as "Internationalities," and having praised the content, documentation, and organization, she went on to discuss his style in less positive terms, reiterating her objections to the third-rate influence of language that, of course, translates to ideas—or lack of them:

> I believe this style will be a serious obstacle to the success the book ought to have. Do, cher ami, in your own words, "adopt a franker idiom"! Such an argument ought to be as bare, as nervous, as manly & energetic as the young Sophocles of your poor sculptor; & you've hung it with all the heavy tin draperies of the Times jargon—that most prolix & pedantic of all the dead languages.—For the last years—I've said it before, I know!—you've read too much French & too much *Times.* I can't too strongly urge you to drop both tongues for a few weeks, & go back to English—to what Arnold called "prose of the centre." Read Emerson, read Tyndall, read Froud[e] even, read Arnold—get away from authors of your own métier, from all the scientific-politico-economic charabia of your own specialists into the clear air of the born writers—& then turn to "Science & Patriotism" . . . & see how capable you are of writing well, & how you've let yourself be smothered in the flabby *tentacularities* of "our own correspondent's" lingo. Drop 30 per cent of your Latinisms ("engen-

> dering a divergency" & so on), mow down every old cliché, uproot all the dragging circumlocutions, compress, diversify, clarify, vivify, & you'll make a book that will be read & talked of not only by the experts but by the big "intelligent public" you want to reach. (*Letters* 281–82)

Philomène de la Forest-Divonne and Morton Fullerton had in common a tendency to fall in with the trivial or the faddish in thought or language, but most frustrating for Wharton was their poor reading and work habits. Phil was "too lazy to fix her attention." Morton would promise anything, personal or professional, then abdicate. Over and over in *The Writing of Fiction* Wharton stresses the necessity of constant writing, reading, and study, for the successful author "usually keeps on [writing] with an indestructible persistency" (78). She deplores the "reluctance to look deeply enough into a subject [that] leads to the indolent habit of decorating its surface" (56).

While Morton Fullerton received the benefit of personal counsel, his cousin and adopted sister, Katherine Fullerton Gerould, benefited from Wharton's influence.[6] In 1909 Katherine sent Edith a copy of a poem written in the voice of Gemma, Dante's wife, who prays to "Madonna Beatrice." Edith praised its "terse, vigorous expression" and also mentioned it to Edward Burlingame. It appeared in the June 1910 issue of *Scribner's* (Benstock 211). In 1911 she wrote Morton that his "sister's story in Scribner is remarkable: far ahead of the Missionary Lady, & much more original in treatment" (*Letters* 243).[7] Later Katherine sent a collection of stories to Wharton for evaluation. Edith thought them promising enough to convince Scribner's to publish the book, which appeared in 1914 (Lewis *Biog*. 249–50). In 1922 Katherine Fullerton Gerould, astute and well read, wrote an intellectual and favorable review of *The Glimpses of the Moon* for the *New York Times Book Review* (Benstock 369) that pleased Edith Wharton, probably because Katherine shared Zona Gale's sharp perceptions. Appleton subsequently published the review as a promotional brochure.

Edith Wharton not only appreciated intelligent criticism, she tried always to provide it, even when she felt the need to be somewhat "frank." In October 1918 she replied to Victor Solberg, an American army private who had sent her some apparently mediocre verses:

> You ask me frankly what I think of your verses; & I will tell you in reply that I never give an opinion on literary questions unless I can give a frank one. You wish me to tell you 'whether these songs are simply the old songs of Wordsworth, Shelley, Moore, Tennyson, etc,

> [*sic*] resinging themselves because I have lived with them so much'; & you seem to think that the risk of being subject to the influence of great poets is one that young writers should fear.
>
> There cannot be a greater mistake than this, or one more destructive to any real poetic culture. Every dawning talent has to go through a phase of imitation & subjection to influence, & the great object of the young writer should be, not to fear these influences, but to seek only the greatest, & to assimilate them so that they become part of his stock-in-trade.
>
> I must tell you sincerely that in your own case I do not find the influences you suggest, but rather those of the poet's corner of a daily newspaper. . . . It takes a great deal of the deepest kind of culture to write one little poem, & if you will read the lives & letters of some of the poets you mention, you will see that they all had it. . . . (*Letters* 410–11)

Interestingly, Edith Wharton was entirely consistent in her advice to other anonymous writers such as those she addressed in *The Writing of Fiction* (unlike Percy Lubbock whose intended audience was critics). There she says again in a different way what she had written to the young poet: a "common symptom of immaturity [is] the dread of doing what has been done before; for though one of the instincts of youth is imitation, another, equally imperious, is that of fiercely guarding against it" (*Writing* 17). And her criticism of Morton Fullerton's jargon is also repeated in *The Writing of Fiction* where she comments: "Words are the exterior symbols of thought, and it is only by their exact use that the writer can keep on his subject the close and patient hold 'which fishes the murex up,' and steeps his creation in unfading colours" (24).

Another friend, a more determined young writer, Vivienne de Watteville (later Mrs. Gerard Goshen), had written *Out in the Blue* (1927), a travel memoir about East Africa, where the twenty-four-year-old woman had accompanied her father in 1923 for the purpose of hunting museum specimens. When a lion mauled and killed Bernard de Watteville, his youthful daughter took over the safari in a professional manner, writing about the event with great emotional restraint. Next, with Wharton's encouragement, Vivienne produced *Speak to the Earth* (1935), a travel adventure about her return to Africa, this time hunting with a camera. The book appeared with a rare foreword by Edith Wharton (Benstock 453). The tone of this preface is oddly sentimental for Edith Wharton: "When you gave me *Out in the Blue,* dear Vivienne, I remember exclaiming after I had read it: 'Oh please write another book as enchanting as this one, but in which nobody wants to kill an animal, and they all live happily ever afterward!' . . . And beautifully indeed you have proved [that you can do] it in these sunlit windswept pages. From the elephants romping with their friends, or twinkling at you ironically through the trees, to the least little bird hopping in at your hut door, they all had so much to tell that they had evidently been awaiting such a confidant for ages. . . . "

The mystery is that this saccharine tone is so unlike Edith Wharton. Certainly she was capable of being direct, even brutal, with aspiring authors, as in the letter to Victor Solberg above. As Lubbock comments, for Wharton "romance was not to lose touch with the practical" (*Portrait* 205). One possible explanation for Wharton's tone could be her love for animals in common with Vivienne's. Lubbock continues, "When the book, with her preface, subsequently appeared, [Wharton] took endless trouble to send it to England and America for review" (*Portrait* 203–5).

An alternate explanation for that sentimental approach may evolve from a sample of de Watteville's prose about the "twinkling" elephants "romping with their friends," which provides a point of analysis:

> They had finished their meal and stood quietly side by side under a tree facing me, and one of them toyed reflectively with a bunch of green-stuff in his trunk. I hesitated to film them, for they were in a beatific after-dinner mood, a little drowsy and at peace with the whole of creation. . . . [T]hey stiffened to attention and stood looking down at me with their enormous ears spread out. It was true that at any moment they might become dangerous, but just then I was struck only by their extraordinary lovableness. The way they stood there, puzzled and uneasy, blinking their eyes in a kind of huge, dumb patience, filled me with an insane longing to run up to them and try to explain. (116)

The prose is clear and direct, yet as a personal travel account, she uses the first person to create an intimate relationship with the reader. Sentimentality, represented by the phrase "being at peace with all creation" and the word "lovable," is present but well controlled. Consequently, one possible interpretation for Wharton's tone could be her wish to match the tone of *Speak to the Earth* while adding an expression of the affection that often springs from the rapport between teacher and pupil. For here Edith Wharton is acting exactly in the now traditional role of thesis or dissertation director. She has become, as Vivienne de Watteville refers to her in her memoir, "the master," successor in her elder years to Henry James's title of esteem and affection. Vivienne's account of Edith Wharton's mentorship for Percy Lubbock's *Portrait of Edith Wharton* does not explain Wharton's sentimental tone, but it does explain how Wharton worked with her:

> Most generous of all was her help to young writers. . . . I can yet hear Edith's voice saying as she picked up my book and turned to my husband: "But she's a born writer!" . . . [A]nd when the proofs came in I wondered for the hundredth time whether I should dare ask Edith to write a preface. . . . [I]t was her book, she had called it forth. When she told me to send her the proofs, I begged that she would glance through them with a red pencil. . . . [W]hen her letter came, her unexpected praise sent me reeling. . . . She had sent me a whole typed page of dry invaluable criticism, and granted me what every artist prays for, the opportunity to see the master at work, to be told not only "this is bad," but why it is bad, and how to put it right. For Edith had provided far more than a sheet of abstract criticism; she had done what no one writer in a thousand would have troubled to do, which was to go through the whole proof page by page, pencilling comments and suggestions, even correcting the punctuation.
>
> There could be no greater sense of companionship than this going forward almost hand in hand through the pages, and nothing could have so inspired confidence. It was as though she were at my elbow; and when she had written in the margin "rotten word" or "I don't like this" or "anticlimax," she presently uplifted my drooping spirits by a generous "good," and when the "good" came beside particular passages which I myself liked I could have shouted for joy. She never condemned without suggesting an alternative. . . . I now realise how gentle she was, how careful, while condemning till one squirmed with shame. . . . In one place she had even scribbled across the page "glorious chapter!" She was much amused in another by my perplexity over deciding which of two alternatives to keep, and wrote: "Do step into the next aeroplane and fly over with the alternatives wrapped up in cotton wool." (*Portrait* 203–6)

Evidence of Wharton's having earned similar affection from others, along with a sample of a personality now mellowed with the years, appears in two letters to Elisina Tyler, November 29 and December 9, 1935, in which she warmly expresses both empathy and sympathy for the novice writer: "Please thank Gioia [Tyler's daughter from her first marriage] for her messages, and tell her that I wish she would (in the way of fiction) read for the next few years none but the immortal things, and suspend her own writing for a time. If you think this is too severe, please *do not transmit* it; but my own experience goes to show that one or two sharp blows early in one's career are often useful. Tell her to begin by reading Santayana's novel, [*The Last Puritan*], which is the biggest I have read in many years." Her next letter returns to the subject: "Poor, dear Gioia—I hope she doesn't resent my brutality. I shouldn't have bothered if I hadn't thought she had real talent. What she wants now is high standards & soul stuff, which only the years can give—"[8]

As can be seen, Edith Wharton's guidance of writers consisted mostly of two major kinds: The first were authors who were actively writing and whom she simply encouraged and/or helped get published by using her contacts. That group included most of the people mentioned here. The second group, those she actively guided, tended to need discipline and direction, especially Morton Fullerton, Philomène de la Forest-Divonne, and Vivienne de Watteville. But, as even Lubbock admitted, however tough, scornful, or blunt Edith Wharton may seem in some of her letters to and about the writers she taught, she was far from self-seeking. Yet her advisees rewarded her materially, some with help in return, positive book reviews, or a dedication like Lewis's of *Babbitt*. Nevertheless, the "return" Edith Wharton valued most was the company of these writers who provided what she valued most—that cross-fertilization, that meeting of minds. For them she had only the highest hopes. As she wrote to Berenson about Philomène de la Forest-Divonne, she wanted writers to stand on the mountain, take in the world below and the world beyond, and "brood" until the intellect expands to reach that power of creation, which to her was the attribute of greatness. Further, Edith Wharton asked nothing of anyone that she did not ask of herself, and she wanted nothing less for "her" writers, and ultimately for America, than the genius and culture she felt it lacked.

Notes

1. The members of the "inner circle" were Edith Wharton, Henry James, Howard Sturgis, Robert Norton, John Hugh Smith, Percy Lubbock, and Gaillard Lapsley. See Goodman 1–2.

2. Maggs Brothers' booksellers list.

3. Laguardia 587 n. 1. The other occasion must have been when W. C. Brownell praised "the grand construction" of *The House of Mirth* and she rejoiced at his "seeing a certain amount of architecture in it."

4. Wharton, "Preface," *The Ghost Stories of Edith Wharton*. This more accessible volume is a slightly modified reprint of the original.

5. Killoran, *Edith Wharton: Art and Allusion.* Chapter 5 discusses the function of bracelet and wrist symbolism in *The Glimpses of the Moon.*

6. Morton Fullerton was formally engaged to his cousin as he carried on his affair with Wharton, matters he naturally kept from both of them. In 1910, after writing a final imploring letter to Fullerton, Katherine gave up and married Gordon Hall Gerould, a Chaucer scholar who eventually became chairman of the English department at Princeton. She bore him a daughter and a son and died of lung cancer in 1944.

7. The "missionary lady" story was Katherine Gerould's "Vain Oblations." Wharton's second reference probably meant Gerould's next published story, "The Wine of Violence." (Killoran, "The Influence of Edith Wharton on Katherine Fullerton Gerould," unpublished paper, 1998).

8. Unpublished letters, Wharton to Elisina Tyler, Lilly Library, Box 2, Indiana University, Bloomington, Indiana, quoted by permission of the library. At this time Edith Wharton was writing *The Gods Arrive,* in which "soul stuff" is an important theme. See Killoran, chapter 10.

Works Cited

Benstock, Shari. *No Gifts From Chance: A Biography of Edith Wharton.* New York: Scribner's, 1994.

Edel, Leon. "Walter Berry and the Novelists: Proust, James, and Edith Wharton." *Nineteenth Century Fiction* 38, no. 4 (1984): 514–28.

Gerould, Katherine. "Vain Oblations," *Scribner's* 49 (March 1911), 367–76.

———. "The Wine of Violence," *Scribner's* 50 (July 1911): 75–85.

Goodman, Susan. *Edith Wharton's Inner Circle.* Austin: University of Texas Press, 1994.

Killoran, Helen. *Edith Wharton: Art and Allusion.* Tuscaloosa: University of Alabama Press, 1996.

Laguardia, Eric. "Edith Wharton on Critics and Criticism." *Modern Language Notes* 78 (December 1958): 587–89.

Lewis, R. W. B. *Edith Wharton: A Biography.* New York: Fromm, 1985.

Lewis, R. W. B., and Nancy Lewis, eds. *The Letters of Edith Wharton.* New York: Scribner's, 1988.

Lubbock, Percy. *The Craft of Fiction.* New York: Jonathan Cape and Harrison Smith, 1921.

———. *The Letters of Henry James.* New York: Scribner's, 1920.

———. *Portrait of Edith Wharton.* New York: Appleton-Century, 1947.

Maggs' Bros. "Bookseller's List." Harry R. Ransom Research Center, University of Texas, Austin.

Perry, Ruth, and Martine Watson Brownley, eds. *Mothering the Mind: Twelve Studies of Writers and Their Silent Partners.* New York: Holmes and Meier, 1984.

Wegener, Frederick. "Edith Wharton and the Difficult Writing of 'The Writing of Fiction.'" *Modern Language Studies* 25, no. 2 (spring 1995): 60–79.

———, ed. *Edith Wharton: The Uncollected Critical Writings*. Princeton, New Jersey: Princeton University Press, 1996.

Wharton, Edith. *A Backward Glance*. 1934. New York: Scribner's, 1964.

———. Foreword to *Benediction,* by Claude Silve. Trans. Robert Norton. New York: Appleton, 1936.

———. *The Ghost Stories of Edith Wharton*. New York: Scribner's, 1973.

———. *The Gods Arrive*. New York: Appleton, 1935.

———. Preface to *Speak to the Earth,* by Vivienne de Watteville. New York: Harrison Smith and Robert Haas, 1935.

———. *The Writing of Fiction*. 1925. New York: Octagon, 1970.

———. Unpublished letters. To Elisina Tyler. Lilly Library, Box 2, Indiana University, Bloomington, Indiana. Excerpts reprinted with permission of the library.

"Someone young and teachable"

Dimensions of Mentoring in the Fiction of Willa Cather

Deborah Carlin

To raise the issue of mentoring in Cather's life and fiction is to call to mind the single story narrated by virtually all of Cather's biographers, the generosity of the established New England regionalist, Sarah Orne Jewett, to the aspiring young author and *McClure's* magazine editor, Willa Cather. Indeed, so legendary is this story in Cather circles that it requires only brief reiteration: after meeting Jewett at the home of Annie Fields in 1908, Cather exchanged letters with the elder writer for nearly a year and a half until Jewett's death in June of 1909. Jewett's letters are widely credited by critics to have had an enormous influence on the artistic direction of Cather's early career, particularly in their insistence that Cather abandon her pursuit of journalism to find what Jewett calls "your own quiet centre of life" (Jewett 249).[1] Jewett also counseled Cather to avoid the male persona in fiction (advice that Cather largely ignored), as well as to "be surer of your backgrounds" (Jewett 248), a suggestion that Cather took to heart as she searched for both a suitable subject and voice, locating them in 1913 with the publication of her second novel, *O Pioneers!*, which she dedicated to Jewett. In a 1921 interview with Latrobe Carroll, Cather directly attributed her confidence as a writer and her belief in the truthfulness of her subject matter to the advice she had been given by Jewett over a decade earlier:

> In *Alexander's Bridge* I was still more preoccupied with trying to write well than with anything else. It takes a great deal of experience to become natural. People grow in honesty as they grow in anything else. A painter or writer must learn to distinguish what is his own from that which he admires. I never abandoned trying to make a compromise between the kind of matter that my experience had given me and the manner of writing which I admired, until I began my second novel, *O Pioneers!* And from the first chapter, I decided

> not to "write" at all—simply to give myself up to the pleasure of recapturing in memory people and places I had believed forgotten. This was what my friend Sarah Orne Jewett had advised me to do. She said to me that if my life had lain in a part of the world that was without a literature, and I couldn't tell about it truthfully in the form I most admired, I'd have to make a kind of writing that would tell it, no matter what I lost in the process. (Bohlke 22)

What made Sarah Orne Jewett such a successful and compelling mentor for Willa Cather? One could easily cite Jewett's sympathetic engagement with the frustrations and insecurities of the younger writer, her generous praise of those qualities in Cather's prose that she sincerely admired, and her determination to speak the truth to Cather about the toll that Jewett believed a career in journalism would take on Cather's artistic inclinations. Perhaps most important, though, Jewett recognized something fine and promising in Cather's early stories and, putting aside her own artistic achievements, focused the intensity of her belief and her passion on the talents that she wished to help draw out of the younger woman. Her sympathetic engagement with the best in Willa Cather enabled Cather to locate it in herself and to draw upon it as the mainstay of her fiction until her death in 1947. As both guide and teacher, Jewett stands as one of the finest examples of mentoring in American literary history.

What comes as somewhat of a surprise, consequently, is that Cather herself never really effectively mentored anyone, never passed on the gift that Jewett bestowed on her to another writer. Her five-year high school teaching career in Pittsburgh (from 1901 to 1906) doubtless provided her with ample opportunities to foster the development of one or two special pupils, but no testimonies of any unique mentoring relationships exist. One of her students tellingly described her relationship to teaching as "natural and human, but without contagious sparks" (Brown 72). Nor did Cather seem particularly inclined to mentor later in her life, after she had achieved artistic and professional success. Truman Capote, in recalling Cather as "the person whose conversation has impressed me the most" (253), describes a rather impromptu friendship struck between the older woman and the eighteen-year-old fledgling writer in 1942, during which Cather read his work and "was always a fair and helpful judge" (255). Yet this liaison was apparently brief and neither Capote nor Cather biographers recount any further involvement between the two. Critic Patricia Yongue notes that, throughout the 1920s, Cather "especially avoided young, unknown authors who wrote to her asking for advice" (51). Even

Cather's twenty-year relationship with the flamboyantly queer Stephen Tennant cannot quite fall into the category of mentoring. Drawn as she was to Tennant's wealth, beauty, aristocratic pedigree, and European education, Cather nonetheless shied away from his request that she secure an American publisher for a volume of his drawings in the late 1930s. Their relationship appears to have been one based on mutual regard and delight; rather than mentoring the young man, Cather apparently basked in his wit, charm, social insouciance, and his openly expressed admiration for her work. Cather, it seems safe to say, learned from mentors, but never learned to mentor during the course of her life and career.

I raise this seeming disparity between Cather as the recipient of mentoring and her disinclination to serve as a mentor for another not to disparage her character as ungenerous or unsympathetic. Cather was clearly one of those writers who needed to engage exclusively with her own internal powers and concentration to produce the fiction she did. The necessarily narrowed scope of her artistic expression did not readily admit the needs, desires, and the relational complexities of giving oneself over to another's artistic aspirations. Rather, my purpose here is to highlight what I take to be the significant one-sidedness of Cather's relationship to mentoring, for I believe it to have important consequences for mentoring as a common trope in her fiction.

But it is not so much teachers as mentors that abound in Cather's oeuvre as it is willing, hungry, idealistic, and talented pupils. Jim Burden, of *My Ántonia* (1918), reads Virgil by lamplight in scenes of both homosocial and homoerotic bonding with his young tutor, Gaston Cleric,[2] whose untimely death propels Jim eastward toward the urban environment and social network that the novel will represent as arid and insubstantial compared to his nostalgic yearnings for the West of his childhood with Ántonia Shimerda. Claude Wheeler, the hypersensitive, desperately unhappy, and awkward young man of *One of Ours* (1922), longs for a man unlike his rugged and aggressive father who can teach him how to release the inchoate self he feels trapped inside. He finds such a guide in David Gerhardt, the soldier and violinist, who becomes for Claude "some one whom he could admire without reservations; some one he could envy, emulate, wish to be" (350). Niel Herbert, of *A Lost Lady* (1923), is obsessed with Marian Forrester throughout that novel as a figure who embodies the genteel, the luxurious, the privileged, and the feminine, and whose sexual mentoring of his rival, Ivy Peters, drives Niel to bitter and frustrated distraction. Tom Outland, whose rough manners and awkward social graces are softened by his inclusion into the family of Godfrey St. Peter in *The Professor's House* (1925), is effectively mentored both personally and academically by the "professor" of the novel's title. The naive and impressionable Nellie Birdseye of *My Mortal Enemy* (1926) becomes fixated on the mature Myra Henshawe as a model, ultimately, of how not to live one's life, despite the older woman's mesmerizing charm, élan, and social sophistication to which Nellie responds enthusiastically. Vickie Templeton, the eldest child of "Old Mrs. Harris" (1932), also seeks models of how and whom to become, spending numerous hours on the floor of the study at her neighbors the Rosens, consuming books and longing for an escape into college and education. All of these protagonists are represented by Cather as somehow exceptional: smart, sensitive, different, each of them longs for a guide who will teach them how to convert their pent-up yearnings, aspirations, and desires into some form of viable adulthood. Each of them longs, in other words, for someone to mentor them.

Aside from these glimpses of desire for mentoring in Cather's fiction, there remain only two novels in which a mentoring relationship is fully fleshed out, so to speak, in which the protagonist and the teacher/guide come into a significant and sustained relationship. *The Song of the Lark* (1915) and *Lucy Gayheart* (1935) both present young, female protagonists who are successfully mentored by older, established men. Both novels locate their evocation of the growth of the artist, or, in the case of *Lucy Gayheart*, the growth of an artistic sensibility, within the field of musical performance. And both novels spend significant time exploring the relationship between pupil and teacher; indeed, the dynamics, the rewards, the frustrations, and even, in *Lucy Gayheart*, the eros of mentoring are represented from the mentors' and recipients' consciousnesses alike.

Here, however, the similarities end. For there exists a yawning divide between the sensibility and outlook of the two novels that both readers and critics have felt.[3] This difference in these two texts, separated by some twenty years of artistic practice for Cather, centers mainly, I would argue, in their respective stances toward both the possibility of artistic achievement for their female protagonists, as well as—and perhaps most important—in their treatment of how each young woman is mentored. Andor Harsanyi, the aspiring concert pianist and music teacher of *The Song of the Lark*, is the linchpin of Thea Kronborg's career. Not only does he recognize that it is her voice, rather than his chosen instrument, the piano, in which her deepest gifts lie, but further it is his encouragement, persistence, and unwavering belief in Thea's person and talents that both enable and inspire her to become the recognized operatic artist "Kronborg" at the novel's end. He facilitates her development; her needs for a mentor and teacher predominate their relationship. Clement Sebastian, on the other hand, the baritone singer of *Lucy Gayheart*, displays none of the professional enthusiasm and personal rectitude that Harsanyi extends to Thea Kronborg. On the contrary, his mentoring of Lucy Gayheart is decidedly personal and physical, ambivalent, unboundaried, and full of both their needs for admiration, intimacy, and affection. Moreover, Lucy Gayheart never even comes close to fulfilling whatever artistic potential may exist within her; Cather's novel kills her off just as she is poised at the brink of discovering the "fugitive gleam" of life and art that she believes Clement Sebastian, as a self-actualized artist, to have possessed (183).

Cather has, in fact, provided us with two radically different views of mentoring in these vastly disparate novels, yet it is potentially illuminating, I believe, to compare their respective representations of what it means to be both teacher and pupil. Thea Kronborg's story, in *The Song of the Lark*, locates itself on a trajectory of artistic achievement, even as her personal life is subsumed within and, as the novel suggests, impoverished outside the context of her performing self. Harsanyi, within this framework, represents perhaps the most important of the many people who recognize and seek to cultivate Thea's talent. Thus, though Harsanyi's ruminations about Thea in his role as her mentor are frequent throughout the text, they nonetheless focus exclusively on the puzzle of her talent and temperament and on how he can best help her to unleash them. Their relationship remains organized first and last around this necessity. The relationship between mentor and student in *Lucy Gayheart*, conversely, centers upon precisely that—the relationship—and the novel spends much of its attention on the nuances, the interpretations, and the different desires each player brings to the dynamic. This is not to insist that Clement Sebastian is a failed or even harmful mentor. Rather, it seems to me important to note the qualitative difference between a representation of artistic achievement in *The Song of the Lark* and the related, though by no means parallel, representation of those qualities that draw teacher to student and vice versa in *Lucy Gayheart*. How these texts negotiate their frequently overt, and sometimes subtle, differences will be the subject of this essay.

Late in *The Song of the Lark*, just before Thea Kronborg emerges on stage to command the full power of her artistic talent and training, a conversation ensues between her former teacher, Harsanyi, and his wife about what can only be termed Thea's American exceptionalism:

> "She ought to be pleased that you are here," said Mrs. Harsanyi. "I wonder if she knows how much she owes to you."
>
> "She owes me nothing," replied her husband quickly. "She paid her way. She always gave something back, even then."

> "I remember you once said that she would do nothing common," said Mrs. Harsanyi thoughtfully.
>
> "Just so. She might fail, die, get lost in the pack. But if she achieved, it would be nothing common. There are people whom one can trust for that. There is one way in which they will never fail." (397)

Harsanyi's certainty that Thea Kronborg would do "nothing common" with her life reverberates from the novel's opening pages, for it seems that just about everyone in Moonstone, Colorado, the setting for *The Song of the Lark,* wants to mentor the young Thea Kronborg. Doctor Archie, the Kronborg's family physician, notices that "there was something very different about her" (9) in the novel's first chapter, and it is this ambiguous interpretation that characterizes Thea throughout her life. There is "something different" about this child. Her mother finds "her more interesting than her other children," though she cannot quite say why (57). Herr Wunsch, her first music teacher, similarly muses over a litany of imponderable questions about who and what Thea might be:

> What was it about the child that one believed in? Was it her dogged industry, so unusual in this free-and-easy country? Was it her imagination? More likely it was because she had both imagination and a stubborn will, curiously balancing and interpenetrating each other. There was something unconscious and unawakened about her, that tempted curiosity. She had a kind of seriousness that he had not met with in a pupil before. She hated difficult things, and yet she could not pass one by. They seemed to challenge her; she had no peace until she had mastered them. She had the power to make great effort, to lift a weight heavier than herself. . . . [Hers] was a face full of light and energy, of the unquestioning hopefulness of first youth. (85)

Even Thea herself recognizes that "there was something about her that was different" (70), this something, presumably, being the potential for great artistry that the novel will articulate and see embodied in her. Yet in her youth, what Thea feels but cannot express, what others sense but cannot find the words to utter, is precisely this potential for something extraordinary, something unique that will shape this young woman's destiny into the portrait of an assured and accomplished artist. Thea, in short, strikes everyone as exceptional, whether or not they can exactly put their finger on the qualities that contribute to making her so. Though her astounding gifts are, at this early point in her life, unrealized and inchoate, their presence seems to leave traces to which other people are drawn inexplicably and yet powerfully. Thus, Doctor Archie remains devoted to Thea throughout his life, shepherding her to Chicago to begin her musical training and reappearing at the end of the novel to confirm for the reader the realization of her musical genius. Fred Ottenburg, Thea's erstwhile lover and absent husband, is all too willing to use his economic resources to aid her developing talent, and it is he who is ultimately responsible for Thea's locating and embodying her voice by allowing her to discover herself in the stark and restorative environment of Panther Canyon. The rough, yet honest, Ray Kennedy also mentors Thea in a way, by providing her in his will with the money needed to begin her musical training in the East. Kennedy, in fact, is given the novel's most blatant statement about the allegedly predetermined "laws" that require others to help foster the growth of people like Thea, who possess such unabated and natural talents.

> [T]here are a lot of halfway people in this world who help the winners win, and the failers fail. If a man stumbles, there's plenty of people to push him down. But if he's like "the youth who bore," those same people are foreordained to help him along. They may hate to, worse than blazes, and they may do a lot of cussin' about it, but they have to help the winners and they can't dodge it. It's a natural law. (108)

Because Cather sets Thea up as such an unabashedly exceptional talent, the representation of Harsanyi as her mentor is a relatively uncomplicated one. Like virtually everyone else in the novel, Harsanyi responds immediately to Thea's talent. What singles him out, however, is his role as a teacher, especially the contrast between his responsible and engaged relationship with Thea compared to that of her first teacher, the depressed, frequently drunken, somewhat narcissistic, and finally peripatetic Herr Wunsch, who wanders away from Moonstone and out of Thea's life early and abruptly in the novel. Harsanyi, as the figure of responsible teaching in the text, exemplifies for Cather those qualities that engender growth in a pupil, inspire self-confidence, and encourage the fullest expansion of the student's self. The portrait she draws of him is really nothing less than a blueprint for successful mentoring, par excellence.

One of the qualities Harsanyi possesses as a successful mentor that his predecessor Wunsch did not is his attunement to the needs and the sensibilities of his student. Harsanyi, Cather notes pointedly, "noticed *at once*" (153, emphasis added) Thea's tenacity, focus, and determination, attributes essential in building the discipline required to transform oneself into an artist. His internally focalized narration in the passage below manifests that quality of attention to the other characteristic of good mentoring: Thea, as subject, dominates the centerpiece of this passage, emphasizing Harsanyi's ability to subordinate his self to the metaphorical exposition of her self.

> The best thing about her preparation was that she had developed an unusual power of work. He noticed at once her way of charging at difficulties. She ran to meet them as if they were foes she had long been seeking, seized them as if they were destined for her and she for them. Whatever she did well she took for granted. Her eagerness aroused all the young Hungarian's chivalry. Instinctively one went to the rescue of a creature who had so much to overcome and who struggled so hard. (153)

Despite the blatant romanticism of Harsanyi's "chivalric" desire to "rescue" Thea, as well as Cather's curious use of the verb "aroused," it is not so much sexual attraction that the passage reveals as it is Harsanyi's sympathetic imagination. Thea's drive to improve herself and Harsanyi's metaphor of her as a warrior render her into the androgynous "creature" of the passage. Harsanyi engages with her as a fellow "creature," I believe, rather than as a young and arousing woman. In the logic of Cather's text, it is Harsanyi's disengagement with Thea's sexuality that balances his imaginative penetration into and sympathetic identification with the essential qualities of her character. His sexual disinterest enables them both to pursue her agenda of artistic self-actualization.

Harsanyi's greatest gift to Thea, however, is his recognition that her voice is her true instrument of artistic expression. Cather accentuates the generosity of this gesture by including a brief scene between Harsanyi and his wife in which the latter muses "a little bitterly" (185) that the consequence of this action will be that Harsanyi loses the pupil who would have best dramatized his abilities as a talented teacher. The text, however, enacts a different, yet no less dramatic, scene between Harsanyi and Thea in which his gifts as a teacher—his prescience, his intuition, and his unselfishness—are fully revealed:

> "Oh, I have watched you very carefully, Miss Kronborg. Because you had so little and had yet done so much for yourself, I had a great wish to help you. I believe that the strongest need of your nature is to find yourself, to emerge as yourself. Until I heard you sing, I wondered how you were to do this, but it has grown clearer to me every day. . . . [A]ll the while you have been working with such good

> will, something has been struggling against me. See, here we were, you and I and this instrument"—he tapped the piano—"three good friends, working so hard. But all the while there was something fighting us: your gift, and the woman you were meant to be. When you find your way to that gift and to that woman, you will be at peace. In the beginning it was an artist that you wanted to be; well, you may be an artist always." (182–84)

Harsanyi's voice in this passage, like that of all responsible mentors, urges on the necessary transformations in his student. It resonates, too, with the advice Cather received from Jewett: to locate the true gifts of the self so that they may be released into artistic expression, to "emerge" as the fully realized, integrated woman both Cather, and her fictional counterpart, Thea, "were meant to be." Harsanyi's genius in the novel is to liberate Thea's genius, to guide her way to the gifts she has possessed all along, ones that are different from those he has so painstakingly been trying to teach her. His magnanimity and unselfish regard for her talent earns him her unequivocal trust in the novel, and, despite her misgivings, Thea does pursue voice studies with another teacher whom she likes far less than Harsanyi. Nevertheless, the text informs us, "She was, on the whole, happier since she had been studying with him than she had been before" (188). In the cadences of Harsanyi's wise and lovingly kind voice, Thea is at last able to discover her own.

Yet Harsanyi's role as Thea's mentor is not without its rewards, and the novel is careful to delineate the reciprocity inherent in such a relationship:

> He had never got so much back for himself from any pupil as he did from Miss Kronborg. From the first she had stimulated him; something in her personality invariably affected him. Now that he was feeling his way toward her voice, he found her more interesting than ever before. She lifted the tedium of winter for him, gave him curious fancies and reveries. Musically, she was sympathetic to him. Why all this was true, he never asked himself. He had learned that one must take where and when one can the mysterious mental irritant that rouses one's imagination; that it is not to be had by order. She often wearied him, but she never bored him. Under her crudeness and brusque hardness, he felt there was a nature quite different, of which he never got so much as a hint except when she was at the piano, or when she sang. It was toward this hidden creature that he was trying, for his own pleasure, to find his way. In short, Harsanyi looked forward to his hour with Thea for the same reason that poor

> Wunsch had sometimes dreaded his; because she stirred him more than anything she did could adequately explain. (166)

As a mentor, Harsanyi's temperament is necessarily attuned toward the pleasure he derives from making his way toward the heart, and the talent, of another. His engagement with her "stimulates" him; what she has yet to reveal "stirs" his imagination and creates "curious fancies and reveries." Again, Harsanyi's attachment to Thea is conveyed in a muted discourse of desire that signifies the erotic charge of unknown qualities that he pursues in Thea. Yet the desired object of this erotic energy is not Thea herself, but Thea's—and Harsanyi's—discovery of her self, the revelation of what she has heretofore kept private, hidden even from her own consciousness. The dynamic Cather describes here is nothing less than the delicate balancing act all great teachers master between the real erotic pleasure of knowing another who has opened to one in a gesture of trust, and maintaining the distance required to nurture, rather than merge with, those revealed qualities to which one is most drawn.

The exceptional quality of Thea's talent emphasizes and, according to the logic espoused by Ray Kennedy that guides the novel, attracts the responsiveness of someone who, like Harsanyi, experiences pleasure in and is temperamentally suited to "help the winners win." Thea remains, first and last, both the guiding force of their collective endeavors, as well as the novel's only subject. She, like Cather, occupies the position of talented artist who merits and receives what "the natural law" (108) Ray Kennedy alludes to bestows upon them as their birthright, their entitlement. Yet the loving portrait Cather draws of Harsanyi and his gifts suggests that even within the necessarily narcissistic sphere of the great artist, gratitude for a great teacher resonates and is not forgotten.

Clement Sebastian is the analogue of the mature Thea Kronborg. An accomplished and recognized artist, the mentoring he extends to the young and imminently "teachable" (34) Lucy Gayheart is something far different from what Harsanyi gives to Thea. Sebastian offers artistry instead of attunement, the transformative touch of greatness rather than the generous subordination of self to other. In a curious and almost paradoxical reversal, Lucy Gayheart occupies a position toward this exceptional artist remarkably similar to the one Harsanyi holds in relation to Thea. She is the one who possesses the sympathetic engagement, exceptional sensitivity and emotional permeability that makes the relationship possible. Like Harsanyi, she functions as a teacher in that what she ultimately learns from Clement Sebastian she has really taught herself. Sebastian is the medium through which Lucy's education takes place; as a mature adult and a seasoned artist he has much to teach Lucy, but only if she will take up the mantle of her own instruction.

Though it might at first seem as if the teacher/pupil role reversal and category-collapse in *Lucy Gayheart* renders suspect my claim that one of its primary preoccupations is with mentoring, I would suggest instead that Cather has revisited the subject in a less panegyrical, more complicated vein. For Lucy's awestruck devotion to Clement Sebastian exactly demonstrates the power dynamic inherent in the relationship between a charismatic artist/teacher and those who hope to learn simply by association with such a revered figure. Rather than expect that their teacher will actively seek to engage with them, students in this dynamic are seduced by the power of artistic performance inherent in the teacher's role, and they seek their enlightenment through proximity and the sublimation of self. What the artist/teacher receives from this dynamic is the confirmation of his own worthiness and attractiveness, and he responds as well to the revivifying "young ardour, [and] young fire" (88) of the worshipful youth by whom he is surrounded. Far from the parental model that characterizes Harsanyi's relationship to the developing artistic talent of Thea Kronborg, the teacher in this evocation is a powerful love object, and sometimes lover, for the student who desires intimacy, attention, and some kind of regard.

This different dynamic of teaching at work in *Lucy Gayheart* fosters a necessarily less boundaried relationship than that exhibited in *The Song of the Lark*. Yet one notes, too, that this relationship is consistently rendered in sympathetic terms throughout the novel, and Clement Sebastian is himself represented with such a degree of sexual indeterminacy that it obfuscates and de-emphasizes what the physical expression of his relationship with Lucy might be. The novel takes great pains, in fact, to present him in an engaging light. When he is first introduced to Lucy he looks at her "intently, with real kindness in his eyes" (36), and both recognizes her nervousness and attends to it with admirable grace and genuine solicitude. His initial interactions with her are distanced, cordial, and constructed. Lucy notes that Sebastian "kept well behind his courteous, half-playful, and rather professional manner,—a manner so perfected that it could go on representing him when he himself was either lethargic or altogether absent" (49). Sebastian's "perfected" role as artist is the magnet attracting the empathic and interpretive skills of Lucy Gayheart. It is she who seeks him out, she who attunes herself to the possibility of discovering something about his interior life.

That Lucy's reading is sophisticated—suggesting that she is necessarily conscious of the degree to which Sebastian's performative self functions to keep some part of him either hidden or absent—demonstrates both her appeal for the lonely Sebastian as well as her exceptional ability to intuit the gendered dynamics of power operating in their relationship. Lucy feels, for example, that Sebastian "liked her being young and ignorant and not too clever. [Theirs] was an accidental relationship, between someone who had everything and someone who had nothing at all" (61). One of the striking things about this passage is its reflection of Lucy's unconscious awareness of the qualities that have drawn them to one another. She responds to his power, artistic mastery, celebrity, wealth, education, and charm. He is, she mistakenly believes, someone who has "everything." He, in turn, responds to her lack of sophistication, to the unsullied potential of her youth to become something as yet undreamed and unrealized.

Cather makes explicit how the positions Lucy and Sebastian occupy in their relationship are constructed in part through their mutual, romanticized idealization of the other. In one of several melodramatic meditations, Lucy conjures up a genteelly shabby Sebastian framed "against the light in his heelless shoes and old velvet jacket" (46). Despite his appearance he would, in her imagination, "be equal to any situation in the world. He had a simplicity that must come from having lived a great deal and mastered a great deal" (46). While it seems likely that underneath Cather's gentle satire of her young protagonist lurks an implicit critique of a relationship constructed in part through romantic mythologizing, the text's next utterance legitimizes Lucy's relationship with Sebastian through an allusion to the power of creativity: "If you brushed against his life ever so lightly it was like tapping on a deep bell; you felt all that you could not hear" (46). This metaphor of resonance, and especially its belief in a quality of feeling that transcends the ability of the artistic medium to convey it, echoes Cather's famous passage in "The Novel Démeublé":

> Whatever is felt upon the page without being specifically named there—that, one might say, is created. It is the inexplicable presence of the thing not named, of the overtone divined by the ear but not heard by it, the verbal mood, the emotional aura of the fact or the thing or the deed, that gives high quality to the novel or the drama, as well as to poetry itself. (*On Writing* 41–42)

Though he is essentially as passive as the metaphor of the bell suggests, Sebastian nonetheless embodies the force of creativity that Cather extols in the passage above. An acolyte as responsive as Lucy merely has to brush up against the resonant depth of his artistry and she will feel its elusive power. It seems, then, that while Lucy's idealization of Sebastian may be called into question, the value of the artistic experience she receives from him is not.

Nor does the novel confine itself to an examination of Lucy's motivations to participate in this relational dynamic. Sebastian's deployment of Lucy as an object in his fantasies who addresses certain needs is also presented in the text with a significant degree of self-conscious irony. We learn, for instance, that Sebastian has "little for sweet reflection" (78) when he considers his relationships with women, so Lucy is a welcome anomaly. Part of Sebastian's problems with women he traces to his estrangement from his wife because of her inexplicable dislike for and jealousy of Marius, the "talented," "charming," and "sensitive" orphan boy who lives with the couple until Sebastian is forced to send him to boarding school (79). In the midst of his bitter musings, he yearns for "one lovely, unspoiled memory" (79) to lift him out of his despair, and it is Lucy whom he calls immediately to mind:

> He was thinking about Lucy; that perhaps he wouldn't have got so far down this morning if she had been there for an hour. It was dangerous to go for sympathy to a young girl who was in love with one, but Lucy was different. As he paced back and forth he told himself that hers was another kind of feeling than the one he had encountered under so many disguises. It seemed complete in itself, not putting out tentacles all the while. . . . When she gave him a quick shy look and the gold sparks flashed in her eyes, he read devotion there, and the fire of imagination; but no invitation, no appeal. In her companionship there was never the shadow of a claim. (80–81)

In his desire to console himself by substituting Lucy's disinterested devotion for his wife's unreasonable jealousy, Sebastian either purposefully ignores or is unaware of the reality, as Blanche Gelfant notes, that Lucy systematically "invades his privacy with a professional detective's persistence as she stalks the singer, following him through the streets and into church, listening to his telephone conversations, [and] spying upon him in order to ferret out his 'secret'" (136).[4] Sebastian's disinclination to take seriously Lucy's romantic attachment to him is one indicator of how little attention he has paid to her, how much the image that he has constructed of her serves his needs rather than hers.

Yet, rather than condemn him for such selfishness, the novel insists that Lucy has indeed been transformed through her relationship with Sebastian. One of the most profound and positive effects of their relationship mirrors the self-discovery and self-actualization that Harsanyi's kind attention awakens in Thea Kronborg. Like her predecessor, Lucy also notes that "she had changed so much in her thoughts, in her ways, even in her looks, that she might wonder she knew herself—except that the changes were all in the direction of becoming more and more herself. She was no longer afraid to like or to dislike anything too much. It was as if she had found some authority for taking what was hers and rejecting what seemed unimportant" (94).

As a mentor, Sebastian operates as a catalyst rather than as a guide for Lucy; in her association with him she reacts as the energized element. Their relationship, based though it is on mutual mythologizing, nonetheless provides Lucy with the medium through which she matures into a knowledge of what is most ephemeral, and therefore most valuable in her too-brief life—sensation, love, passion, and the ever-present consciousness of the inevitability of loss. When Lucy first hears Sebastian sing, it is the artistry of his voice that penetrates her; she experiences "a feeling that some protecting barrier was gone—a window had been broken that let in the cold and darkness of the night" (32). Her responsiveness to Sebastian's art is rendered in the passage in explicitly sexual terms; she falls into a consciousness of the connection between sexual desire and simultaneous loss that prefigures the literal death of Sebastian by drowning midway through the novel. Though nearly driven mad in her grief, Lucy recovers herself, ultimately, by imaginatively introjecting Sebastian as both a teacher and a mentor. What she has learned through their relationship is that the "flashes of promise" (183) and of joy registered in her emotional response to the artistry of his singing "could be the important things in one's life" (184). For Lucy, Sebastian represents "in his own person, the door and the way to that knowledge" (184). Rather than coaxing Lucy's talent to the surface, Sebastian's role as her mentor and teacher is figured by the text as an aperture through which she traverses. Her proximity to the art he embodies facilitates her growth and transformation. It is a different, though no less powerful, version of mentoring in Cather's fiction than the one offered by *The Song of the Lark.*

Like her mentor, Lucy Gayheart also meets an untimely death by drowning, her life extinguished before she can integrate what she has learned from Sebastian into her evolving sense of self. Despite the grim fates of Cather's protagonists, I would argue that she bravely explores in this text a much less sanguine and far more complicated depiction of mentoring than that presented in *The Song of the Lark.* I believe that Cather has significantly more affinity in *Lucy Gayheart* with Sebastian's character than she does with Lucy's, and part of the novel's argument, as a result, is organized around elucidating that which is valuable, life-enhancing, transformative, and liberating in the relationship between the established artist who has little desire to teach and the enthusiastic, exceptional student whose empathic affinity with what the artist has achieved ignites a mutually rewarding relationship. Though there is no moral to be drawn from a comparison between these two novels, one cannot help but be struck by the fact that while Thea lives and becomes the artist she was always meant to be, Lucy remains frozen in time, always on the brink of life, a ghostly promise of what could be and a haunting evocation of what will never be. In this way alone, *Lucy Gayheart* might suggest the failure of mentoring as an imaginative consolation for Cather late in her life. Unlike Harsanyi, she has no pupils whose genius she has helped to cultivate. Rather, like Thea Kronborg and Clement Sebastian, the talent of her artistry remains singular and exceptional, the cadence of her voice resonant and, finally, unteachable.

Notes

1. O'Brien offers a nuanced and illuminating analysis of Jewett's letters to Cather, 344–46. See Woodress, 197–207, for a record of the brief history of their relationship.

2. Woodress believes Gaston Cleric to be modeled after Herbert Bates, Cather's English instructor at the University of Nebraska, for whom she wrote "Peter," "the tale of the Bohemian immigrant who commits suicide on his Nebraska farm. Bates was so impressed that he sent the story off to a Boston magazine, *The Mahogany Tree*, which published it in May 1892" (76–77).

3. Cather critic Susan Rosowski, for example, argues that "*Lucy Gayheart* is [Cather's] nightmare of adolescence, as if she had returned to the idea of the early novel [*The Song of the Lark*] and explored it again, this time to probe its dark possibilities" (69).

4. Gelfant also persuasively argues that Lucy functions as a substitute for Marius in Sebastian's psychic economy: "Lucy allows him to recover the child of this strange triangle [his marriage], for when he conveniently defines her love for him as 'chivalrous loyalty' rather than 'passion,' he also redefines her sex: 'He had sometimes thought of her as rather boyish'" (132). Sebastian's disengagement from women generally and from his wife particularly, her unexplained, peculiar jealousy of a young boy, Sebastian's association with the "queer" and ultimately destructive Mockford, and his imaginative reformulation of Lucy's gender all serve to attenuate the impact of whatever physical relationship in which he engages with Lucy.

Works Cited

Bohlke, L. Brent. *Willa Cather in Person: Interviews, Speeches, and Letters.* Lincoln: University of Nebraska Press, 1986.

Brown, E. K., and Leon Edel. *Willa Cather: A Critical Biography.* 1953. New York: Avon, 1980.

Capote, Truman. *Music for Chameleons*. New York: Random House, 1980.
Cather, Willa. *Lucy Gayheart*. New York: Knopf, 1935.
———. *One of Ours*. New York: Knopf, 1922.
———. *The Song of the Lark*. 1915. New York: Signet, 1991.
———. *Willa Cather on Writing*. Lincoln: University of Nebraska Press, 1988.
Gelfant, Blanche H. *Women Writing in America: Voices in Collage*. Hanover, New Hampshire: University Press of New England, 1984.
Jewett, Sarah Orne. *The Letters of Sarah Orne Jewett*. Ed. Annie Fields. Boston: Houghton Mifflin, 1911.
O'Brien, Sharon. *Willa Cather: The Emerging Voice*. New York: Oxford University Press, 1987.
Rosowski, Susan J. "Writing Against Silences: Female Adolescent Development in the Novels of Willa Cather. *Studies in the Novel* 21, no. 1 (1989): 60–77.
Woodress, James. *Willa Cather: A Literary Life*. Lincoln: University of Nebraska Press, 1987.
Yongue, Patricia Lee. "Willa Cather's Aristocrats (Part 1)." *Southern Humanities Review* 14, no. 1 (winter 1980): 43–56.

"Efforts of Affection"

Mentorship and Friendship in Moore and Bishop

Margaret Wooster Freeman

The meeting took place at a specified bench outside the New York Public Library in March 1934. Elizabeth Bishop later learned that Marianne Moore would have chosen Grand Central Station, for easy escape, had she sensed less promise in the encounter.

Bishop, a senior at Vassar, had been gathering materials for a paper on Moore and was attempting to find a copy of Moore's *Observations*. Fannie Borden, librarian of Vassar, could not only provide it from her personal library, but knew Moore, and was willing to arrange a meeting with the poet. Bishop wrote to a friend, "I want very much to go see her. She can talk faster and use longer words than anyone in New York" (to F. Blough, March 2, 1934, *One Art* 17).

Moore was quite used to such overtures. Bishop was not; bold intellectually but shy and tending toward self-deprecation, she never before or after deliberately set out to meet a noted person. She regarded her own poems rather dubiously, although some had already been published, and, in fact, waited well beyond the first interview to confess her interest in becoming a poet. Just as well: her poetry was still experimental, unvoiced. Sometimes it was too sentimental, with shy, silver-antlered reindeer going about on dainty hoofs, and sometimes too directly influenced by the poets she was reading. Her fascination with Gerard Manley Hopkins could lead to "Ah! wouldst not, wax-faced, wooden-bodied one, have us to worship us-wise?" ("Hymn to the Virgin"). Yet at least two of her college essays strongly suggest the poet she would become. In particular, her 1934 essay on timing in Hopkins's poetry not only embodied her own later thoughts on rhythm but led her to find in his poetry and in her reading of the sermon-writers of the seventeenth century the attempt to portray "not a thought, but a mind thinking," a phrase she took from M. W. Croll's essay "The Baroque Style in Prose" (Bishop to D. Stanford, November 20, 1933, *One Art* 12). At first a deliberate approach, this became a signal trait of her poetry, from "The Map" onward, in a pattern very different from Moore's brilliant mosaics.

Moore, twenty-four years Bishop's senior, was by 1934 modestly well established as a poet and, through her years as editor of the *Dial*, a figure to be reckoned with in the literary world. Only two slim volumes of her poetry had been published, though, and most of her poetry was yet to come. As Bishop wrote to a friend, "Frani, she is simply amazing. She is poor, sick, and her work practically unread, I guess, but she seems completely undisturbed by it and goes right on producing perhaps one poem a year" (to F. Blough, April 1, 1934, *One Art* 24). Not until 1952 would Moore win the triple crown of the National Book Award, the Pulitzer Prize, and the Bollingen Prize, and only in her later years, when she virtually stopped writing poetry, did she become a true public figure. In 1934, as later, she deplored any rush to publish, and so advised the young poet.

From the beginning, Moore was a conscientious mentor, carefully reading Bishop's offerings and commenting in a straightforward and helpful way, encouraging but corrective as well. And from the beginning Bishop reacted both with gratitude and with an insistence on certain of her own poetic choices. Moore knew her to be the most gifted poet she had ever sought to guide, and for six years, as Bishop gradually came to discover and employ her own distinctive voice, the mentor-protégée relationship flourished. When the end of the first phase came, in important though courteous disagreements over Bishop's "Roosters," the friendship continued—continued, in fact, until the end of Moore's life, though never with the close attention of those early years.

The first meeting, with all its inevitable awkwardness, was a great success. Bishop quickly followed it with letters—"Are you interested in tattooing?" She was. "I am wondering if you have been to the circus yet this year?" Moore indeed always went, but enjoyed going with her new young friend. In fact, on this first excursion, Bishop was led to the animals and told to divert the adult elephants' attention so that Moore could clip a few hairs from the head of a baby elephant to repair an elephant-hair bracelet her brother had given her.

In the early days of their acquaintance, Bishop was shy about showing any of her work to Moore, waiting several months before confessing to writing poetry. When in 1936, full of self-doubt, she wrote to Moore that she was considering setting aside her writing ambitions and entering medical school, Moore wrote a bracing reply and asked, "Maybe you would care to show me what you have been writing? . . . I think I recall complaining of having to look at things which were sent to me for advice, but I never have complained of writing that I *asked* to see. In fact I have rather serious cause of complaint against you for stinginess in this matter" (August 29, 1936, *Selected Letters* 363).

Moore's comments on Bishop's poetry tended to be detailed, careful, and consistent with her own views on revisions. She disliked intensifiers; she corrected misspellings; she tended to subtract any words or phrases she deemed to be unnecessary. "Perhaps you would let me omit some words, the habit having fastened on me irremediably" (Costello 125). The exchanges were characterized by a certain courtesy and delicacy, balancing the directness of the content. "I fear to make suggestions," Moore wrote, "lest I hamper you." She encouraged, but not in broad flattery. And, early in their relationship, she made a public and discerning affirmation of Bishop's talent.

In 1935 thirty-two young poets, each with a sponsor, were introduced to the reading public in *Trial Balances.* Of the five poems of Bishop, one, "The Map," is recognizably in her voice and a startling advance over the earlier work. That she knew this is affirmed by her placing it first in her first book, *North and South.* While one may not go so far as her biographer Brett Millier in attributing its success to Moore, her comments do catch the focus of Moore's attempts to guide—"the example of meaning generated through contemplation of a single object, the familiar object re-seen, the commitment to accuracy, the reach of simile" (76). Moore, as sponsor, praises "the rational considering quality in her work . . . assisted by unwordiness, uncontorted intentionalness, the flicker of impudence, the natural unforced ending" (Bishop, *Trial Balances* 82–83).

These perceptive words already suggest differences between them, however much critics might speak of similarities. Moore and Bishop both loved precise, perhaps arcane words—"a priceless set of vocabularies"—but Bishop was far more apt to try for natural diction. Moore, who had first used syllabic verse in 1916, wrote her poems with "a musical inaudible abacus," a "soft uninvented music." Bishop was never attracted to syllabic experiments and spoke of herself as "an umpty-umpty-um sort of poet." Moore never liked working in set forms; some of Bishop's finest poems are in such preset patterns as the villanelle. Moore's poems are full of quotations, always carefully attributed in her notes; Bishop never did this, and she could say in a letter to a friend, "I think we might have fun—or 'fun,' as Miss Moore puts it" (to R. Lowell, December 22, 1949, *One Art* 196). And always, then and later, it was Moore who was attracted to "dynasties of negative constructions" and "grammar that suddenly turns and shines like flocks of sandpipers flying." All of the phrases are from Bishop's poem "Invitation to Miss Marianne Moore," written in 1948, after the mentorship period. Yet even at that late date Moore could scold Bishop gently for a misspelling. "Mackeral, Elizabeth? If they feel the way I do about the poem, presently everybody will be spelling it with an 'a'" (September 28, 1948, Millier 207).

A small group of examples shows the resistance Bishop developed, even in the early years of mentorship, culminating in the 1940 "Roosters" correspondence.

Bishop was particularly hesitant about sending Moore her prose experiments, sensing that Moore would disapprove. She wrote apologetically to Moore from Key West in early 1938 that she had sent a story off to *Partisan Review* for a contest, "and now of course regret it very much and hope they will send it back." Two weeks later she wrote that her story, "In Prison," had been accepted for immediate publication, but "I am so afraid you will not like it." She would send a copy, "if you will please not try to see a word of good in it or say a good word for it" (February 14, March 27, 1938, *One Art* 70, 71). Indeed, Moore replied, "It was very independent of you to submit your prize story without letting me see it. If it is returned with a printed slip, that will be why" (Millier 137). But later she paid Bishop an ambiguous compliment, writing that "never have I . . . seen a more insidiously innocent and artless artifice of innuendo." In the same letter she threw an important challenge to Bishop, to "risk some unprotected profundity of experience. . . . I do feel that tentativeness and interiorizing are your danger as well as your strength" (May 1, 1938, *Selected Letters* 390–91).

"Paris, 7 A.M.," a 1936 poem, occasioned some advice from Moore, and Bishop's reply is a good indication both of her gratitude for Moore's guidance and at the same time her willingness to assert her own voice. "I am enclosing a slightly corrected version. . . . I am sorry I am being so obstinate about 'apartments.' To me the word suggests so strongly the structure of the houses, later referred to, and suggests a 'cut-off' mode of existence so well—that I don't want to change it unless you feel it would mean a great improvement" (September 29, 1936, *One Art* 46). It stayed unchanged.

Similarly, a letter from Key West in January 1937 responds to Moore's suggestions for changes in "A Miracle for Breakfast": "You are no comfort to me, at all, Miss Moore, the way you inevitably light on just those things I knew I shouldn't have let go. . . . The boisterousness of 'gallons of coffee' I wanted to overlook because I liked 'gallons' being near 'galleries.' And the 'crumb' and 'sun' are of course its greatest fault. . . . It is probably just an excuse, but sometimes I think about certain things that without one particular fault they would be without the means of existence" (January 5,

1937, *One Art* 54). Amusingly, her mentor, too, claims the privilege a few years later of going her own unguided way. Moore writes "I am stubborn about my little crotchets too" (to Bishop, September 8, 1942, *Selected Letters* 430).

Bishop's abrupt emergence from Moore's close guidance came with the 1940 poem "Roosters." Moore and her mother had spent a whole evening with the poem and had then submitted their "improved" version. While Bishop politely (but rather pointedly) asks, "May I keep your poem? It's so interesting, what you have done . . . ," the pair had, in fact, gone too far. No doubt reflecting her unfamiliarity with slang, Moore changed the title to "The Cock." Bishop had chosen a demanding pattern of tight three-line rhyming stanzas, and this Moore had broken into a mixture of twos and threes. Bishop's deliberate repetitions were removed—the second "gunmetal blue" becomes "metal blue also." Aggressive words were altered or removed: "the roosters brace their cruel feet and glare / with stupid eyes" loses both "cruel" and "stupid"; in the Moores' version, the beds become "fastidious" and "the tin rooster" turns "golden." Bishop protests, "I know that esthetically you are quite right, but I can't bring myself to sacrifice what (I think) is a very important 'violence' of tone—which I feel to be helped by what *you* must feel to be just a bad case of the *Threes.*" While the Moores let the word "dung" remain, "water-closet" must disappear. Correspondence on this last point is revealing. Bishop writes, "I cherish my 'water-closet' and other sordidities because I want to emphasize the essential baseness of militarism" (October 17, 1940, *One Art* 96). Moore had written, "Regarding the water-closet. . . . Others feel that they are avoiding a duty if they balk at anything like unprudishness, but I say to them 'I can't care about all things equally, I have a major effort to produce, and the heroisms of abstinence are as great as the heroisms of courage, and so are the rewards'" (October 16, 1940, *Selected Letters* 404).[1] Actually Bishop, too, had a certain reticence in vocabulary, objecting to a friend about a coarse word in a movie, "I suppose I'm an old prude. No, I'm NOT!—but I don't like certain slang words for things" (to May Swenson, October 16, 1970, *One Art* 535). Always, however, in her poetry she used the word that seemed most exact. "Water-closet" remained.

After this exchange, Bishop withdrew from close mentorship. As she wrote, "After that I decided to write entirely on my own, because I realized how very different we were." If she wrote later for comment, it was to send along a work already accepted or published. Effectively, the mentorship period had ceased.

It would be misleading to imply that Bishop did not accept a great many of Moore's suggestions or grow in poetic skills as a result. And through this whole period, Moore was very active in Bishop's behalf.

Once Moore had learned of Bishop's wish to write poetry, she quickly assumed the obligations of helping to make Bishop known to publishers and editors. As she wrote to Edward Aswell of Harper and Brothers, "Taking an interest in her progress does not amount to having assumed a gigantic burden" (October 29, 1935, Millier 93).

In the summer of 1935, the year of Moore's *Selected Poems* and of Bishop's *Trial Balances* anthology, Bishop was preparing to travel in Europe, on a small inheritance from her father's estate. Moore suggested that, while there, she meet Winifred Ellerman Macpherson, known as Bryher, and offer some poems for the new journal *Life and Letters* that Bryher and friends had begun. And, indeed, "The Man-Moth" was accepted for its 1936 issue.

Partly through Moore's efforts, Bishop gradually began to be known and published. *New Democracy* accepted three of her poems for their April 1936 issue; as Moore reported to her, these caught William Carlos Williams's attention. Moore recommended she send work to Morton Zabel, editor of *Poetry,* and, when Zabel accepted three poems, Moore guided Bishop through his editorial requirements.

Bishop consulted with Moore when James Laughlin of New Directions Press asked if he could publish a book of her poems. "Don't you think," Bishop wrote, "that a publisher like Random House, if possible, would be better" (February 28, 1937, *One Art* 59).

As we know, Moore was uneasy with Bishop's sending her short prose piece "In Prison" directly to *Partisan Review,* even though it won publication and a $100 prize. In a way, Moore may have been right to scold her. Perhaps Bishop's misunderstandings with Harcourt Brace and later with Houghton Mifflin could have been avoided had she been more ready to take Moore's guidance. But as Bishop's poetry gained acceptance and as her acquaintance with writers of her own age increased, she grew more and more independent in her decisions. And her indecisions.

Moore continued to support Bishop in her reviews as well as in her efforts to help publication. Of *North and South,* Bishop's first book, Moore wrote, "At last we have a prize book that has no creditable mannerisms. At last we have someone who knows, who is not didactic" (*The Nation* 163). In reviewing Bishop's translation of *The Diary of "Helena Morley,"* a book Moore only partially liked, she wrote of Bishop's "gift for fantasy, her use of words and hyper-precise eye" (*Poetry* 247–49).

All her life Bishop resisted writing reviews and struggled with those she did undertake. She often told the story of an early sighting, at Moore's

Cumberland Street apartment, of a bushel basket stuffed with crumpled papers, some typed, some in Moore's handwriting. All were discarded drafts of a short review of a book by Wallace Stevens, finally published but not deemed by her worthy of inclusion in her *Collected Prose*. Yet, in fact, at various times in her life, Moore reviewed frequently and well, and she had simply been taking a vacation from the pressure-filled years on the *Dial* when they met. By contrast, Bishop's attempts always caused her trouble, and, if completed, tended to be very short. In 1970 she approached the *New Yorker* to see if she could take on the role of poetry critic, vacated by the death of Louise Bogan. At the end of three years, for all her self-scolding, she had not produced a single review.

In many ways Bishop misjudged Moore as a role model. The poet who must have seemed to Bishop able to live a life of pure poetry, free of writing reviews, giving readings, or teaching, had actually excelled in the first two at various times in her life. The poet who seemed to embody all the principles of modernist poetry that Bishop was struggling to understand was, in 1934, moving beyond them.

In one respect, at any rate, Bishop understood and absorbed Moore's teachings: one should never rush to publish. Bishop remembers leaving Cumberland Street each time "uplifted, even inspired, determined to be good, to work harder, not to worry about what other people thought, never to try to publish anything until I thought I'd done my best with it, no matter how many years it took—or never to publish at all" (*Collected Prose* 137). Her poems, stories, and memoirs almost always came slowly. The time between her writing to Moore about a Nova Scotia bus ride involving meeting a moose, and the publication of her poem about the moose, was twenty-six years. In her poem "North Haven," Nature herself repeats, "Or almost does: / repeat, repeat, repeat; revise, revise, revise." Lowell in 1973, in a group of poems about her, could ask, "Do you still hang your words in air, ten years unfinished, glued to your notice board, with gaps or empties for the unimaginable phrase?" ("For Elizabeth Bishop 4" 196).

Moore was indeed herself an inveterate reviser, tinkering, cutting, rearranging. Most dramatically, she reduced her famous poem "Poetry" from twenty-nine lines in her 1923 *Poems* to exactly three lines in her *Complete Poems*, a book that bears her cryptic note "Omissions are not accidents." Yet, still tinkering, she included the original version in the notes at the back of the book. "Complete" for Moore was never synonymous with "completed"; for Bishop, though she worked slowly and revised with agonizing care, at some point she deemed each poem indeed "complete," an artifact.

Twice in her life Bishop succeeded in writing about Moore for publication. The first time was for a special Marianne Moore issue of the *Quarterly Review of Literature,* in 1948. Many writers contributed, among them Wallace Stevens, Louise Bogan, and John Crowe Ransom. In this year, following Mrs. Moore's death, Moore needed and enjoyed the cheerful, affectionate, rather sassy tribute of Bishop's poem, "For M. M.," later called "Invitation." The Moore who had acted as mentor for Bishop was past, and so was the Bishop who had sought her help. In the accompanying article, Bishop named Moore "The World's Greatest Living Observer," a title one is tempted to say passed to Bishop on Moore's death. The comments are flattering, but not free of criticism: sometimes her "sense of duty shows through a little plainly"; sometimes Moore makes things "difficult for herself as a sort of *noblesse oblige*" ("As We Like It," 127).

For two years, from 1967 to 1969, Bishop planned and worked at a memoir of Moore, although it was not published until 1983, after Moore's death. Called "Efforts of Affection," after a poem of Moore's, the title catches the dual nature of their bond. The memoir is a warm tribute, full of favorite anecdotes and memories, though saying remarkably little about Moore's effect on her own poetry. She recounts with pleasure Moore's enjoyment of tennis, her interest in clothes and jewels, her flirtatiousness, her driving lessons, her learning the tango. At the end, in a Moore-like flourish, she fantasizes "a sort of subliminal glimpse of the capital letter M multiplying . . . Marianne's monogram: mother; manners; morals; and I catch myself murmuring, 'Manners and morals; manners *as* morals, or is it morals *as* manners?" And, after all, "it doesn't much matter which way I put it; it *seems* to be making sense" (*Collected Prose* 156). Indeed it does. A look at the maternal or nurturing side of the relationship and at the conflation of morals and manners in Moore goes a long way to fill out an understanding of the mentorship and friendship.

A few weeks after the two poets met, Bishop's mother died. Essentially, Bishop had always been parentless. Her father had died when she was an infant; and, except for a few troubling memories from her first four years, Bishop never knew her mother, not even being quite sure of the location of the insane asylum where, after many decades, her mother had finally died. Moore, too, had grown up never knowing her father, as her parents had separated when she was very young, but her strong, capable, God-fearing mother was the anchor of her life, with her Presbyterian-minister grandfather a staunch model and her brother Warner a close and supportive guide. With this brilliant, essentially homeless new protégée, Moore often in the early years found herself playing a maternal role. It was one that came naturally to her. "I'm inclined to worry about people," she said in a 1967 interview. "I keep thinking have they enough money? are they happy?" (Howard 40). She kept a bowl of change for subway tokens on hand for her visitors, most easy with those who, without comment, took what was needed. She comforted a distressed Bishop when an automobile accident in which Bishop was involved caused a passenger friend to lose an arm. She kept Bishop's spirits up during long dry spells, insisting that poetry cannot be rushed. Bishop could appropriately refer to her "very generous and protective apron."

Bishop, too, had a strong maternal and nurturing instinct, present all her life but most easily traced during her happy years living with Lota de Macedo Soares in Brazil. Her life, her letters, and in time her poems are full of domestic events and concerns. She was a fine cook, often taking over that responsibility for the large household. She was at ease with the many children who so often filled that house, including the maid's baby daughter, named "Betchy" in her honor. As she writes about Brazilians in her book on Brazil, "Everyone seems to know how to talk to infants or dandle them, and unselfconsciously" (*Brazil* 10). She continued through Moore's life to worry about her, and her letters are full of friendly pleading: "Happy New Year, Marianne, and please please take care of yourself—eat proteins, vitamins, carbohydrates, and everything else they discover" (January 13, 1958, *One Art* 354). When she was in New York, she found it painful to attend readings by Moore or Lowell, because she so worried over whether they would do well.

For an earlier strong maternal figure we need go no further than Marianne Moore's mother. Early in their acquaintance, Bishop became a regular visitor to the Moores' Brooklyn apartment. Here, indeed, was Moore's principal mentor, and the pattern for her mentorship. Mrs. Moore was "very serious—solemn, rather—although capable of irony, and very devout. . . . Her manner toward Marianne was that of a kindly, self-controlled parent who felt that she had to take a firm line, that her daughter might be given to flightiness or—an equal sin, in her eyes—mistakes in grammar" (*Collected Prose* 129). Mrs. Moore and Moore had much the same attraction to unusual animals and objects. David Kalstone cites "the Moores' habit of scrutiny, appropriating the exotic to their self-contained world" (10). It was Mrs. Moore who most shared not only her daughter's thoughts but her words. In a postscript to her *Selected Poems* Moore writes: "Dedications imply giving, and we do not care to make a gift of what is insufficient; but in my immediate family there is one 'who thinks in a particular way'; and I should like to add that where there is an effect of thought or pith in these pages, the thinking and often the actual phrases are hers" (*Selected Poems* 108).

When Bishop balked at Moore's guidance, as she began to know and to listen to poets her own age, Moore could have remembered her own very similar rebellion and (her word) her "misdemeanors."

In her charming "Invitation to Miss Marianne Moore," Bishop writes "Manhattan is all awash with morals this fine morning." Moore's life was firmly underpinned with good Presbyterian morals, and, while she never proselytized, they permeated her writing. W. H. Auden wrote that her poems "delight, not only because they are intelligent, sensitive and beautifully written, but also because they convince the reader that they have been written by someone who is personally good" (305). The morals that guided Moore's life guided her poetry, too. However brilliant, observant, and intellectually intense the play of her mind may be, however microscopically she may study animals or objects, throwing off sparks of metaphor or digression, the poem resolves into a moral statement. This may be unexpected and unpretentious, but it will be there. Like Horace, she instinctively believed that literature should delight *and* instruct. As she wrote in a 1937 letter to Bishop, "a thing should make one feel after reading it, that one's life has been altered or added to" (March 7, 1937, *Selected Letters* 384).

Certain keywords surface repeatedly in Moore's writings. "Humility, Concentration, and Gusto." Fortitude. Courage. Integrity. Spontaneity, too, although Bishop refers in her notes to "the absolutely wild contrast between [Moore's] form and her admiration of 'spontaneity'" but does find that quality in "her wit, and in the laugh with which she greets other's witticisms" (Goldensohn 152).

Bishop sensed early and often that she must protect Moore from the knowledge of some of the deepest wells of her own experience. She could confess to sloth and often did. Typical of her letters to Moore is her comment "I am afraid you may be *displeased* with me because of my recent laziness and miscalculations" (September 1, 1940, *One Art* 92). She was more hesitant to communicate her growing pleasure in knowing literary and artistic contemporaries, her yearnings, her waywardness. But she adamantly guarded from Moore all information about her lesbianism and her desperate bouts with alcoholism. (Moore, in "Camellia Sabina," writes "The wine cellar? No, / it accomplishes nothing and makes the / soul heavy" [*Complete Poems* 17]. In her letters to Bishop, the only allusion to homosexuality is one of deep distaste.) The sympathetic relation of the two, however, could let Moore sense when Bishop was most distressed, and Moore sent what comfort she could.

Manners for Moore were indeed inextricably mixed up with morals. Even her habitual grace before meals can be seen as a type of polite "thank you." Her idiosyncratic way of enmeshing quotations into her poetry, as she often explained, was to give full credit to the original writer of the phrase she seized, a nod to the ability of the writer to say something better than she could, a nod to manners.

As we approach a new century, the permission to use first names seems a bygone courtesy. But for Bishop, to whom Moore granted this permission in 1938, four years after their first meeting, it was a signal event, and her next letter starts DEAR MARIANNE in large capitals decorated to look like electric lights. In her poem "Manners," Bishop recalls her Nova Scotia grandfather's training her in polite behavior, training that must have found fertile ground.

Bishop's reaction to meeting Moore resulted first in a series of invitations, received with pleasure: an excursion to Coney Island; trips to the zoo, where Bishop received lessons in meticulous observation. Bishop's sensitivity to Moore's enjoyment extended through Bishop's life, in imaginative offerings. Her travels resulted in gifts to Moore, full of affectionate attention—swan feathers, postcards, leaves, a book on Erasmus, the seeds from a Saboteira tree, the "sting" of a stingray fish. And over the years Moore responded, not only with thanks but also with replies so discerning that Bishop could write, "Your careful appreciation of my post-cards always shames me—I'm afraid I won't really have made this trip at all until I have lured you into commenting on every bit of pictorial evidence I can produce" (Keller 412). Moore's "Paper Nautilus" came as a response to a gift from her prize protégée.

Knowing Moore's love of detail, Bishop would share her observations of the way swans turn their eggs, or a puff adder mimes death. Bishop would also send gifts of vivid descriptions of places Moore would never see. From Brazil, she writes, "Last week was the week when all the grass goes to seed and turns red—drifts of rubies all over the mountains—at sunset the sun shines through grass-tops, like pink snow-fields. It would be a lovely week to have you as a visitor" (Keller 429).

Yet she frequently felt uncertain about her offerings. "I often become slightly confused at the very point of bestowal, and feel that perhaps, after all, it is inadequate or unwanted" (February 14, 1948, *One Art* 69). Her awareness of the uncertain fate of acquiring even the most desired objects is clearly evident in her piece of prose fiction "In the Village," drawn, she insists, with accuracy from her troubling childhood memories of her mother and the home in Great Village, Nova Scotia. There were things of her mother's that she craved—"a thick white teacup with a small red-and-blue butterfly on it, painfully desirable"; she absconded, she remembers, with a little ivory stick from a case of embroidery tools, but hid it near a crab-apple tree and never found it again. She's given a five-cent piece, but in carrying it home swallows it. The blacksmith makes her a ring, but it is too big and hot. In "Gwendolyn," another story based on her childhood, she remembers an early present of a strawberry basket of marbles. But when she finds it again, "they were covered with dirt and dust, nails were lying mixed in with them, bits of string, cobwebs, old horse chestnuts blue with mildew, their polish gone" (*Collected Prose* 225). In one of her last poems, "Santarem," about a river trip, she sees on a pharmacist's shelf an empty wasps' nest, "small, exquisite, clean matte white, and hard as stucco." He gives it to her. Back on board a fellow passenger asks, "What's that ugly thing?" (*Complete Poems* 186–87).

Some of Bishop's concern about the acceptability of her gifts might even have been warranted, although Moore assured her that *her* gifts were always perfect. Or almost always. Even Bishop's sensitive instinct could err, as in a gift of a coral snake that Moore apparently hated, but could not bring herself to throw away until Bishop herself suggested it. In a *New Yorker* "Profile," Moore did protest, "I never want to own anything any more. . . . No more shells and feathers! People present you with things they think may suggest an idea for a poem, but there simply aren't enough alcoves and embrasures to put them all in" (Sargeant 44).

In speaking of Moore and Bishop, it has been difficult at times to separate details of mentoring from those of friendship, but at least we can write of the first six years when Moore's guidance was strongest as a period of mentorship. We need to remember, though, that both Moore and Bishop knew and respected certain of their own contemporaries and, with them, too, mixed literary guidance and practical help with acts and attitudes of friendship. In Bishop's case, this was most strikingly true of her friendship with Robert Lowell, who thought of her, at least for a while, in terms stronger than friendship, and could write of her as "*the* might-have-been" (Lowell to Bishop, August 15, 1957, Millier 203). Lowell was attracted to Bishop's poetry before he came to know her. In his 1947 review of her newly published *North and South* he pointed out that, while Bishop undoubtedly borrowed some elements of tone and style from her mentor, she was always present in her poems in a way that Moore was not. When newly appointed to the position of Library of Congress poetry consultant, he quickly asked her to do a reading, and later recommended her for the same position. Over the years their friendship deepened, weathering periods of crisis and absence. In an unpublished poem to her he writes, "our old fellowship / Resumes its old transcendence like a star." He steered her toward possible grants and awards, often garnering them first as the more prominent poet. She feared his influence on her poetry but responded warmly to his, questioning and correcting as well as praising. He credited her with his freeing himself from his elaborate earlier verse to "the spacious relaxation of free verse" and, in dedicating "Skunk Hour" to her, said he was directly influenced by her poem "The Armadillo." In other words, elements that we can call mentoring were certainly a part of this friendship. And this was true of her relation to other poet friends. The give and take of suggestion, practical help, and consolation were part of the everyday life of Bishop as of Moore and their contemporaries.

Unavoidably, from the beginning of her own career, Bishop's work was perceived in terms of Moore's mentorship, and this must often have been an irritant. For all their superficial resemblances, the differences are major. Bishop is present in her poems in a way Moore is not; she has a strong narrative sense; her poetry, especially after *North and South,* is full of believable people. There is a linear quality—"everything connected by 'and' and 'and.'" Her poetic procedure, harking back to her college essay on Hopkins, is based on "the releasing, checking, timing, and repeating of the movement of the mind" (Kalstone 37). Her poetry questions, circles, may conclude tentatively.

In 1954, Moore wrote to Bishop, "I was dumbfounded and gratified to read in *Les Journal des Poêtes* [*sic*] that your work showed traces of my influence." Bishop replied in part:

> In my own case, I know . . . that when I began to read your poetry at college I think it immediately opened up my eyes to the possibility of the subject-matter I could use and might never have thought of using if it hadn't been for you.—(I might not have written any poems at all, I suppose.) I think my approach is much vaguer and less-defined and certainly more old-fashioned—sometimes I'm amazed at people's comparing me to you when all I'm doing is some kind of blank-verse—can't they *see* how different it is?
> (October 24, 1954, Millier 68)

Different or not, Bishop's poetry was certainly, especially in the early years, prodded and to an extent shaped by Moore. The intensity of the first six years and the components of effort and affection that filled the remainder make Moore's and Bishop's an affecting example of both mentorship and friendship.

Note

1. The full Marianne and Mary Moore version of the poem is in Kalstone, appendix, pp. 265–69.

Works Cited

Auden, W. H. "Marianne Moore," *The Dyer's Hand*. New York: Random House, 1962.

Bishop, Elizabeth. "As We Like It," *Quarterly Review of Literature* 4 (1948): 127–35.

———. *Brazil* (with the editors of *Life*) New York: Time-Life Books, 1962.

———. *The Collected Prose*. Ed. Robert Giroux. New York: Noonday, 1991.

———.*The Complete Poems. 1927–1979*. New York: Farrar, Straus and Giroux, 1986.

———. *One Art: Selected Letters*. Comp. and ed. Robert Giroux. New York: Farrar, Straus and Giroux, 1994.

———. *Trial Balances*. Ed. Ann Winslow. New York: Macmillan, 1935.

Costello, Bonnie. "Marianne Moore and Elizabeth Bishop: Friendship and Influence," *Twentieth Century Literature* 30 (summer/fall 1984): 130–50.

Goldensohn, Lorrie. *Elizabeth Bishop: The Biography of Poetry*. New York: Columbia University Press, 1992.

Howard, Jane. "Leading Lady of U.S. Verse." *Life* 62 (January 13, 1967): 37–44.

Kalstone, David. *Becoming a Poet: Elizabeth Bishop with Marianne Moore and Robert Lowell*. Ed. Robert Hemenway. New York: Noonday, 1989.

Keller, Lynn. "Words Worth a Thousand Postcards: The Bishop/Moore Correspondence," *American Literature* 55 (October 1983): 405–29.

Lowell, Robert. "For Elizabeth Bishop 4," *History*. New York: Farrar, Straus and Giroux, 1973: 198.

Millier, Brett C. *Elizabeth Bishop: Life and the Memory of It*. Los Angeles: University of California Press, 1993.

Moore, Marianne. *The Complete Poems of Marianne Moore*. New York: Macmillan, 1967.

———. Review of *The Diary of "Helena Morley." Poetry* 94 (July 1959): 247–49.

———. Review of *North and South. The Nation* 28 (September 1946): 163.

———. *The Selected Letters of Marianne Moore*. Ed. Bonnie Costello, Celeste Goodridge, and Cristanne Miller. New York: Knopf, 1997.

———. *Selected Poems*. New York: Macmillan, 1935.

Sargeant, Winthrop. "Humility, Concentration, and Gusto," *The New Yorker*. (February 16, 1957): 38–77.

Eudora Welty

The Silent Mentors

Jean Frantz Blackall

I don't think any ideas come to you from other people's minds, when you're writing, as directives. . . . That all has to come from within. It doesn't mean that you haven't read things and understood things through reading and come to think things through reading that don't filter down and apply.

Eudora Welty, *Conversations*

From the very beginning of her writing career, Eudora Welty won both respect and moral and practical support from editors, her agent, and more established writers, among them John Rood, John Woodburn, Albert Erskine, Robert Penn Warren, Cleanth Brooks, Katherine Anne Porter, and Ford Madox Ford (see, for example, *Conversations* 40–42); above all, from Diarmuid Russell, who was her literary agent for more than thirty years. "It has helped me so much in all my work to think that at the other end there are people who are interested" (*Conversations* 340). It is the idea of the presence of a sympathetic listener there "at the other end" that sustains her: "After he [Diarmuid Russell] finished reading it [*The Golden Apples*] he said, 'I think this is a very, very good book.' That meant a lot to me—the reader, you know, speaking from the other end" (*Conversations* 193). No writer has been more richly blessed with mentors and guides.

Yet Welty's own conviction is that the writer must find her own way (Porter, Intro., *Curtain* xiv–xv). In conversations with interviewers she pictures herself as a very conscious writer, a maker (*Conversations* 256, 297), someone working in isolation—there beside the window, at the typewriter—to solve a problem: "It's just you, out there by yourself" (63; cf. 199). She occasionally acknowledges her indebtedness to William Faulkner in learning how to express the relationship between locale and character (220) and to both Faulkner and Chekhov in the creation of the effect of authentic speech (208, 280). There are other writers whom she singles out as the subjects of appreciative essays and reviews. But, generally speaking, Welty is consistent in the conviction that she does not consciously turn to other writers for guidance or for models when trying to work out a problem in her own fiction. "I think in the act of writing, 'how I am going to handle something,' and *not* 'how would so-and-so have done it'" (220). She has been a voracious and appreciative reader since childhood, and, no doubt, she has been influenced by others, but not directly, not explicitly, nor in ways that she can readily account for. Analysis follows on delight, and seems more frequently prompted by the queries of interviewers or by her response to specific assignments such as the symposium in honor of Willa Cather held at Red Cloud, Nebraska, in 1973, than by any inner imperative (209; *More* 27–28). In answer to an interviewer's question, "Early in your career, who influenced you among the female writers across America?" she replies, "I don't know. . . . I never can put my finger on these things for sure. Of course I was influenced. I love to read, and I adore what I read. You know that it's worked on me, but not in any specific way I can think of, not in any immediate ways when I work. . . . I must have learned this or that from this or that person, but not consciously" (*Conversations* 324).

What I should like to suggest here is that some of Welty's convictions about her stance and objectives, perhaps, too, certain strategies that she devises in the practice of her craft, may owe something to the presence of Jane Austen and Willa Cather, looming there, subliminally, in her imaginative landscape. In a sense they are her silent mentors, showing the way and, at some level, giving Welty confidence in her enterprise and in the value of the kind of fiction that she was writing. For instance, in Jane Austen, Welty perceived that the domestic matrix and the comic voice are worthy grounds for enduring fiction and that scope may reside in a breadth of knowledge of human nature. Judging by her essay on Cather, Welty discovered that scope may be attained by leaving out the middle distance; by placing a finite, concrete, palpable foreground against a historical, legendary, or mythical horizon so that the mind's eye travels from the near to the far in time and space. In both she perceived the validity of place in defining the form of a work and that the invigorating passion that vitalizes a work may be the artist's devotion to her art rather than erotic love. Such insights emerge when one ponders Welty's own reflective remarks about these two writers, her sentiments about the writing of fiction, and her own circumstances and practices as a writer.

Craftsmanship is a bond between Welty and Austen, an overt delight in the painstaking fashioning of the work. Jane Austen's familiar remark the "little bit (two Inches wide) of Ivory on which I work with so fine a Brush" (*Austen's Letters* 469) is not only a modest acknowledgment of limited scope; she is also celebrating the care with which she fashions her work. Ivory is a precious material, and she draws with ever so fine a brush. Austen's metaphor intimates a sense of form, quality, nuance, detail, and precision. Welty likewise reflects upon her craftsmanship in numerous passages in the interviews. But there is in *The Optimist's Daughter* a counterpart to Austen's square of ivory in Eudora Welty's "breadboard" passage. There, in her final showdown with her stepmother, Laurel Hand cherishes and celebrates the beauty of fine craftsmanship. "'Do you know what a labor of love is? My husband made it [the breadboard] for my mother, so she'd have a good one. Phil had the gift—the gift of his hands. And he planed—fitted—glued—clamped—it's made on the true, look and see, it's still as straight as his T-square. Tongued and grooved tight-fitted, every edge—. . . . My mother blessed him when she saw this. She said it was sound and beautiful and exactly suited her long-felt needs, and she welcomed it into her kitchen'" (*Optimist's* 203–4). Here the character within the work is articulating her author's own regard for fine craftsmanship. Welty sees herself, outside the fiction, as just such a painstaking artisan: "When you're writing a story, you're constructing something. You really are making something using dialogue, and using what the ear tells you to help you out. . . . I have to get a thing as well made as I can do it before I let anyone see it. . . . I don't want anyone to see it if it's not the best I can do" (*Conversations* 256–57). Meticulous like Austen in her metaphor of the miniaturist, Welty is attentive to every detail. Names must be authentic to locale (50–51; *More* 94). Every comma must be in the right place. Punctuation determines the rhythm of a piece (*Conversations* 150). "To me the detail tells everything. One detail can tell more than any descriptive passage in general" (162).

The liability associated with this painstaking and perfectionist approach to fiction-making is that the writer's scope may be limited, her attention directed to the particular and local rather than to larger social movements and events. Austen avows that "3 or 4 Families in a Country Village is the very thing to work on" (*Austen's Letters* 401). Welty "find[s] even a town like Jackson too big for me to manage. I have to have a small enough stage, a small enough arena, to confine it and to be able to manipulate what I am doing" (*Conversations* 217). But this choice of smallness, be it circumstantial or elective, is metamorphosed in Welty's understanding of Jane Austen's work into a resource and a virtue. In her essay on Austen she juxtaposes the eighteenth-century ambiance with that of her own time: "We have nothing in our own best that corresponds to the orderliness, the composure, of that life, or that meets its requirements of the small scale, the lovely proportions, the intimacy, the sense of personal security. . . . [O]urs is the century of unreason, the stamp of our behavior is violence or isolation; non-meaning is looked upon with some solemnity; and for the purpose of writing novels, most human behavior is looked at through the frame, or the knothole, of alienation" (*Eye* 10).[1] Implicit here is a counterdefinition of smallness: narrowness, a knothole view of life that authenticates alienation, violence, and isolation over just proportion, order, and composure.

Viewed against these definitions, Welty's own perspective is nearer to that of Jane Austen than to that of her own time, and for a reason they share: stability, their sense of personal security within a loving and nurturing household and within a defined community of which each one has an intimate knowledge, together with their conviction in a sympathetic audience. Welty believes that Austen "must have enjoyed absolute confidence in an understanding reception of her work" by her own "lively, vocative family," to whom she read her chapters aloud (*Eye* 6). Welty herself rejoices in the felt presence of that audience of admiring friends, colleagues, and editors there, "at the other end."

Welty goes on to speculate that out of such stable circumstances comedy may emerge. Austen "wrote from a perfectly solid and firm foundation, and her work is wholly affirmative. There is probably some connection between this confidence, this positivity, and the flow of comedy" (*Eye* 6). Comedy, which Welty regards as interactive with, not opposed to, tragedy (*Conversations* 54, 189; *More* 241), grows out of stability. Moreover, comedy thrives on smallness. Austen's "stage was small because such were her circumstances and . . . she was perfectly equipped to recognize in its very dimensions the first virtue and principle of comedy" (*Eye* 7). Comedy requires a close focus: "A clear ray of light strikes full upon the scene, resulting in the prism of comedy" (7). A comic vision also requires a balanced perspective, Austen's "seeing both sides of her own subject" rather than being limited to a partisan or proselytizing point of view (7–8).

"But it cannot be allowed," Welty maintains, "that there is any less emotional feeling contained in the novels of Jane Austen because they are not tragedies. . . . They are profound in emotion. . . . There is passion, the stronger for being concealed until it can be concealed no longer" (*Eye* 8). And Austen's novels will endure, she believes, "because [her themes] pertain not to the outside world but to the interior, to what goes on perpetually in the mind and heart" (11). These things are constants in human experience. "I don't see how anyone could have a greater scope in knowledge of human nature and reveal more of human nature than Jane Austen" (*Conversations* 54). This is Welty's resounding answer to those purblind readers who would judge Austen by her circumstances rather than her vision. Welty is proposing an answer to the question she had posed near the beginning of her essay on Austen: "Will the future treat her as blindly as we have been known to treat her and take her down because she was a spinster who—having never lived anywhere outside her father's rectory and the later family homes, . . . whose notion of travel was an excursion to Lyme Regis—could never have got to know very much about life?" (*Eye* 5)

Welty's vindication and affirmation of Jane Austen could be read as a personal apologia and manifesto. The "radiance" (*Eye* 3) of her precursor's example authorizes and enables Welty to believe in her own kind of fiction. Austen's achievement affirms Welty's conviction that rootedness in place is a resource and that limitations are a challenge. "[P]lace is a definer and a confiner of what I'm doing" (*Conversations* 87; cf. 158–59). Like Austen's, Welty's fiction combines painstaking craftsmanship with depth of insight into human behavior and motivation contained within a comic vehicle. Challenged by an interviewer as to what "important piece of knowledge" she may have left out of her fiction, she can therefore reply with conviction that "you can't live without having limitations that you're aware of, but . . . the limitations themselves are the, well, shall I say springboard?" (235) Thus, like Jane Austen before her, Welty transcends the bounds of a sheltered life and a self-contained community by delving within, imaginatively probing into the constants in human character and motivation, which are recurrent and universal. The great leap, she tells us, is the imaginative leap into another person: "To live inside *any* other person is the jump" (54).

The presence of good and evil, of sexual passion, of violence, these things are not overtly treated or labeled in their fictions, but they are motivating forces for their characters, who themselves are the agents of revelation in the choices they make, the way they behave, the symbolic gestures through which they communicate. Jane Austen uses social matrons as agents of violence—Lady de Burgh (*Pride*), Mrs. Elton (*Emma*), Emma herself when she humiliates Miss Bates. Welty says of *The Optimist's Daughter,* "I do feel there is 'evil' in the world and in people. . . . I thought there was 'evil' in Fay" (*Conversations* 227; cf. *More* 96–97). A cruel abuse of a helpless human being is the occasion for "Keela, the Outcast Indian Maiden." Miss Eckhart's mother is evil when she goads her daughter in "June Recital," and Miss Eckhart's responsive slap is the eruption of violence into an overt gesture—just as Emma Woodhouse's cruel remark to Miss Bates is a verbal slap. What does William Wallace mean when he spanks Hazel at the end of "The Wide Net" (*Wide* 72)? Or Livvie when she dances with Cash (*Wide* 177)? Or King MacLain when he leers at Virgie at her mother's funeral and cracks a marrow bone in his teeth (*Golden* 257)? Think of Loch Morrison's brutal revival of Easter in "Moon Lake" (*Golden* 144–52). Such gestures epitomize and express unnamed emotions. An interviewer comments, "It is astonishing to me in this day and age of explicit sex, violence, and so forth, how Austen can keep you hanging, waiting for the hero to call the heroine by her first name." Welty: "Absolutely. Exactly. Well, it's symbols either way—the whole thing means coming intimacy or intimacy arrived. Today's explicit sex and Jane Austen's calling by the first name speak of human beings reaching the same thing, within the dramatic possibilities of the day" (*Conversations* 195)—and, one might add, within the dramatic possibilities elected by the writer.

Darker, passionate, and violent, emotions are held in check in both Austen and Welty because of the comic vehicle. (See Welty on Austen, *Eye* 8.) In her remarks to interviewers Welty is ever mindful that comedy must be written from the outside. The symbolic gesture suggests, and leaves the reader to discover its meaning. Asked "What actually happened in 'The Wide Net'? Did [William Wallace] think that his wife was really at the bottom of the river?" Welty replies: "I didn't go into him, did I? That was on purpose. I was trying to write about it from the outside as well as I could because I wanted it to be a comic episode. The point I really wanted to make was that the whole thing was an adventure; they enjoyed dragging the river. I don't think he thought she was down there. But she could have been" (*Conversations* 24). William Wallace's adventure can elicit laughter because the reader does not experience his anxiety or his pain from within. Like Miss Bates he is an object of laughter because the reader is distanced from his inner life.

Jane Austen goes on to invoke Mr. Knightley to chastise and to instruct Emma within the work, but here Welty moves in a different direction. She eschews Austen's eighteenth-century didacticism (*Eye* 9) and prefers (like Chekhov) to represent rather than to judge (*Conversations* 27, 151, 182; cf. *More* 135). It is Miss Bates in her superficial garrulity and conversational disjointedness, above all in her capacity to advance the narrative through her unbridled gossipy meanderings (*Conversations* 279), that is suggestive to Welty. Sister in "Why I Live at the P.O.," Leota in "Petrified Man," Mrs. Faith Rainey in "Shower of Gold," Edna Earle in *The Ponder Heart*, perhaps intimate an evolution in Welty's fiction of Austen's secondary character to the center of the fictional stage (more feasible in a shorter form). Welty's tale becomes the story of their telling the story (*Conversations* 56). "Edna Earle has captured an audience," Welty says, "and that's her character. I mean, she's got to tell you this story" (284; cf. *More* 132). In both Austen's and Welty's localized, isolated, self-contained social groups, conversation becomes an art and an entertainment. Of Southerners Welty explains, "All they have to talk about is each other, and what they've seen during the day, and what happened to so-and-so. It also encourages our sense of exaggeration and the comic, I think, because tales get taller as they go along" (*Conversations* 164–65; cf. 19, 94). Welty is overtly concerned with Southerners, not with Jane Austen, but are we so very far here from Catherine Morland's Gothic fantasies or Emma Woodhouse's fabrications of romantic entanglements among her friends?

In both Austen and Cather there is a domestic center to the fictions, the representation of ordinary people performing the rituals and routines of daily living. Austen's fiction is more cerebral, concerned with abstract values as these are expressed or abused in the interaction of characters. Cather more explicitly details the processes of living, as for example the preparations for a prairie Christmas in *My Ántonia,* the detailed description of Mr. Shimerda's death and funeral. Welty alludes to this domestic matrix in naming her essay on Cather "The House of Willa Cather." The house, both literal and figurative, is a central focus in Cather's fiction. But, contrasting with Austen, there is a spacious landscape beyond the domestic foreground. Welty is very mindful of the vistas and horizons, of the great spaces, and the vitality of the living earth against which Cather's characters are placed. She is mindful, too, of what she calls Cather's "technique of juxtaposition" (*Eye* 47). "She worked out some of her most significant effects by bringing widely separated lives, times, experiences together—placing them side by side or one within the other, opening out of it almost like a vision—like Tom Outland's story from *The Professor's House*—or existing along with it, waiting in its path, like the mirage [that Thea Kronborg comes upon in the desert]" (*Eye* 47). Welty quotes this passage: "'a shallow silver lake that spread for many miles, a little misty in the sunlight. Here and there one saw reflected the image of a heifer, turned loose to live upon the sparse sand grass. They were magnified to a preposterous height and looked like mammoths, prehistoric beasts standing solitary in the waters that for many thousands of years actually washed over that desert: the mirage itself may be the ghost of that long-vanished sea'" (from Cather, *Lark,* I:7).

Welty, like Cather, has a breadth of vision. From early on she has a tendency toward juxtaposing the familiar with the exotic and remote. She moves freely from the present into the mythic past, from waking into reverie or dream, from history into legend and folklore. *The Robber Bridegroom,* she explains, is not "a *historical* historical novel. . . . [I]nstead of burying itself deep in historical fact, it flew up, like a cuckoo, and alighted in the borrowed nest of fantasy" (*Eye* 311). But Welty's techniques for juxtaposing the near and the far differ from Cather's. Cather paints vast landscapes in which past and present, the mirage and the Sunday picnickers, confront one another. "The past can be seen—[Cather] lets us see it in physical form. It can be touched—Thea can flake off with her thumb the carbon from the rock roof that came from the cooking stove of the Ancient People" (43). Welty juxtaposes the near and the far through allusion, by suggestive naming, by sleight-of-hand transitions from concrete descriptions into symbolic ones. These transitions are often facilitated by the introduction of suggestive words—such as *mystery, magic, wonder, dream, radiance, vision, phantasm*—that transmute the finite character or moment or event (cf. *Conversations* 307). Welty employs heightened rhetoric and poetic rhythms to transform simple description into the exotic, as when a snake in the river is metamorphosed into a dragon in "The Wide Net": "In the center of three light-gold rings across the water was lifted first an old hoary head ('It has whiskers!' a voice cried) and then in an undulation loop after loop and hump after hump of a long dark body, until there were a dozen rings of ripples, one behind the other, stretching all across the river, like a necklace. 'The King of the Snakes!' cried all" (*Wide* 59–60). Is William Wallace's river-dragging a frolic or a quest? Of course it is both. The comical outing superficially enacted is at once the vehicle for a journey into greater understanding, into the "dark clear world of deepness, and he must have believed this was the deepest place in the whole Pearl River, and if she was not here she would not be anywhere. . . . So far down and all alone, had he found Hazel?" (56)

An interviewer comments that in reading the stories in *A Curtain of Green,* "you feel that you are in the objective world of ordinary human experience, but in all of the stories in *The Wide Net,* there is a dream-like quality" (*Conversations* 24). Welty answers by speculating that the stories in her first volume were written over a period of six years and those in *The Wide Net* within a year. In fact, there are visionary moments even in the very early tales, as when the salesman in her first published story drives down a Mississippi back road toward his own death in an allegorical landscape: "The cloud floated there to one side like the bolster on his grandmother's bed. . . . He drove through a heap of dead oak leaves. . . . Then he saw that he was on the edge of a ravine that fell away, a red erosion, and that this was indeed the road's end" (*Curtain* 324). Phoenix Jackson's name yokes the local with the mythic. Her journey to Natchez is through a familiar landscape, and the character originated in a woman Eudora Welty saw: "I was reading under a tree, and just looking up saw this small, distant figure come out of the woods and move across the whole breadth of my vision and disappear into the woods on the other side" (*Conversations* 167). "I wouldn't have used the word 'phoenix' in 'A Worn Path' if it hadn't first come to me as an appropriate Mississippi name. I'd heard of old people named Phoenix; there's a Phoenix town" (188, cf. 51). "White owners often gave their slaves mythological names" (*More* 84). Yet the connotations of phoenix are inescapable in a tale about endurance and survival.

Was Welty's own breadth of vision nurtured by Cather's great vistas in time and space? Asked to name books or authors that "changed [her] life," Welty responded that, among others, "Willa Cather did, but I was kind of slow finding her. I wish I had had the sense to read her sooner. One time I just sat down and read it all through" (*Conversations* 324). Hence we do not know whether the technique of juxtaposing the near and the far that Welty scrutinizes in her essay on Cather confirmed certain tendencies, ways of seeing, that Welty had already discovered for herself or whether Welty's immersion in Cather's fiction may have assisted her to develop her own attitudes and technique. In any event, Cather's "technique of juxtaposition" affirms that impulse in Welty, her yoking of the finite and the phantasmal.

By the time she wrote *The Golden Apples*, Welty was surely susceptible to an imaginative charge from Willa Cather, for where do the vaunting heroes and heroines come from, the nonconformists, those characters who break away from the closed community or ignore its boundaries? (See *Conversations* 307.) Welty in *The Golden Apples* is, in effect, rewriting Cather's fairy tale of Thea Kronborg in *The Song of the Lark* into the more realistic tale of Virgie Rainey. Cather regretted that she had not ended Thea's tale with "the girl's escape" (Preface, *Song* ii–iii). Welty does just that, leaving it to chance whether Virgie will succeed or fail in her breakaway from, in Cather's words, "a smug, domestic, self-satisfied provincial world" (Preface, *Song* ii). *The Golden Apples* is populated with rebels and runaways: King MacLain, his sons Ran and Eugene, Easter, Loch—above all, Miss Eckhart, counterpart to Cather's Wunch, expatriates both, passionate people whose social ostracism, penury, and devotion to their art in an uncomprehending community bring them to symbolic acts of self-destruction. Wunch chops down the dovecote, symbol of his transient peace (*Song* I: 7), and Miss Eckhart, deranged, burns the piano that has been her life (*Golden* 30–34, 78–86). Both Wunch, whose very name is "desire," and Lotte Eckhart fix upon their most promising pupil and seek to nurture in her the same ambition, the same passionate devotion to music, that animates themselves. (See *Conversations* 304–5, *More* 138.) But Cather writes a fairy tale in which every obstacle falls before Thea, a series of mentors teaching, financing, escorting Thea to Chicago, New York, and Europe, and thence to a career as a Wagnerian soprano. Welty is more responsive to Cather's humbler characters, to the host of déclassé immigrant hired girls in *My Ántonia,* who leave the farm for Black Hawk, Lincoln, San Francisco, Seattle, and Alaska; especially to Lena Lingard, whose coexistent voluptuous lifestyle and commitment to her mother resemble Virgie's own. Is Lena's vocation as a dressmaker subliminally echoed in Virgie Rainey's satisfaction in tackling a "hard-to-match-up plaid" (*Golden* 234–35)?

For Eudora Welty all things are double. As early as *The Robber Bridegroom* she articulates this theme in the reflections of Clement Musgrove (*Robber* 126). Readers have identified love *and* separateness as a motif throughout her works. For Welty, comedy and tragedy shake hands. She sees Miss Eckhart as a tragic character (*Conversations* 207), but the spectacle of Miss Eckhart setting afire the piano, symbol of her life's work, is a burlesque episode. Miss Eckhart's picture of Perseus slaying Medusa is an emblem of doubleness: "She had absorbed the hero and the victim and then, stoutly, could sit down to the piano with all Beethoven ahead of her. With her hate, with her love, and with the small gnawing feelings that ate them, she offered Virgie her Beethoven" (*Golden* 276). Virgie's response is double: "Miss Eckhart, whom Virgie had not, after all, hated—had come near to loving, for she had taken Miss Eckhart's hate, and then her love, extracted them, the thorn and then the overflow—had hung the picture on the wall for herself" (276).

Welty's appreciative response to the fictions of both Jane Austen and Willa Cather, writers so dissimilar in all but craftsmanship and the passion that informs their art (*Eye* 8, 46, 55), illuminates the doubleness in Welty's own vision. Like Austen, she needed and required a firm foundation in place and in the support of a nurturing community of family and devoted friends. Place, total mastery of the local environment, became her material for fiction. Welty's evolution is an inversion of Cather's. Willa Cather had to stop fleeing the Midwest and turn back in spirit to her homeplace in order to find her fictional vein. Welty, for her part, found in her inner life—in her omnivorous reading and, it would seem, in Cather's great vistas and venturesome heroines—an instigation to venture further afield. This she does in earlier works through uninterpreted gestures of vaunting, such as that frozen moment when Cash stands at the foot of Solomon's bed, his arm raised, but cannot strike Solomon ("Livvie," *Wide* 174–75). Others set out on journeys literal and metaphoric: the salesman, William Wallace when he dives into the Pearl River, Jenny in "At the Landing." In mid-career Welty populates *The Golden Apples* with restive characters, who are ever breaking away and leaving town or being broken because they remain. These are Welty's "wanderers." "I use the term rather loosely," she explains, "because it also means planets, and I have got a number of characters that I try to suggest can move outside this tiny little town in the Delta. . . . I wanted to suggest . . . [t]hat there was a larger world" (*Conversations* 307). In *The Optimist's Daughter* Laurel at last relinquishes the breadboard, symbol for her of the "'whole solid past'" (206), of all she has assimilated and now distances herself from. (See *Conversations* 237–41.) "Virgie and Laurel were such different people, backgrounds and everything, but they were doing the same thing" (*Conversations* 335). Like Cather's Thea Kronborg, Laurel leaves home twice, in fact and then in spirit, in a willing reaffirmation of her professional life as a designer of fabrics in Chicago (*Optimist's* 25) and of the world outside Mount Salus, Mississippi. Finally, at the end of her autobiographical volume, Eudora Welty identifies herself with the adventurers: "As you have seen, I am a writer who came of a sheltered life. A sheltered life can be a daring life as well. For all serious daring starts from within" (*Beginnings* 104).

Notes

This is a general note of indebtedness to the host of scholars and critics whose views have surely influenced my own during years of teaching these three great writers. The present essay was written, however, with recourse only to what Eudora Welty herself says about writers and her own practices and sentiments as a writer of fiction. All admirers of Eudora Welty are deeply indebted to Peggy Whitman Prenshaw for making available the two volumes of Welty interviews, on which I have drawn heavily. Initial and terminal ellipses have been omitted in quotations.

1. From *The Eye of the Story* by Eudora Welty. Copyright 1978 by Eudora Welty. Reprinted by permission of Random House.

Works Cited

Austen, Jane. *Jane Austen's Letters*. Ed. R. W. Chapman. Oxford: Oxford University Press, 1952. Reprint 1979.

Cather, Willa. *My Ántonia*. 1918. Boston: Houghton Mifflin, 1961.

———. *The Song of the Lark*. 1915. Boston: Houghton Mifflin, 1983.

Welty, Eudora. *Conversations with Eudora Welty*. Ed. Peggy Whitman Prenshaw. Jackson: University Press of Mississippi, c. 1984.

———. *The Eye of the Story: Selected Essays and Reviews.* New York: Random House, 1978.

———. *The Golden Apples.* New York: Harcourt, Brace, and World, c. 1949.

———. *More Conversations with Eudora Welty.* Ed. Peggy Whitman Prenshaw. Jackson: University Press of Mississippi, c. 1996.

———. *One Writer's Beginnings.* Cambridge: Harvard University Press, 1984.

———. *The Optimist's Daughter.* New York: Vintage Books, 1978.

———. *The Ponder Heart.* London: Virago, c. 1983.

———. *The Robber Bridegroom.* New York: Harcourt, Brace, 1942.

———. *Selected Stories of Eudora Welty: A Curtain of Green and The Wide Net.* New York: Modern Library, 1966.

CONTRIBUTORS

Jean Frantz Blackall, professor emerita, Cornell University, has published numerous essays on Henry James, Edith Wharton, and others, as well as *Jamesian Ambiguity and the Sacred Fount.*

Deborah Carlin is associate professor of American Literary and Cultural Studies; director of Graduate Studies, University of Massachusetts at Amherst; lecturer, School of Social Work, Smith College; and the author of *Cather, Canon, and the Politics of Reading.*

Margaret Wooster Freeman is professor emerita of the College of William and Mary and senior member, Robinson College, Cambridge University.

Irene C. Goldman-Price is lecturer in English and women's studies at the Pennsylvania State University–Hazleton and former associate professor and director of women and gender studies at Ball State University. She publishes on American realist fiction.

Helen Killoran, associate professor of English at Ohio State University Lancaster, has published extensively on Edith Wharton, including *Edith Wharton: Art and Illusion.*

Esther F. Lanigan is an independent scholar living in Colorado. She is author of *Mary Austin: Song of a Maverick* and *American Political Women,* coauthor of *Women's Studies, A Recommended Core Bibliography,* and editor of *The Mary Austin Reader.*

Julie Olin-Ammentorp, professor of English at LeMoyne College, has published on Edith Wharton, Henry James, and Adrienne Rich.

Melissa McFarland Pennell is professor of English at the University of Massachusetts Lowell. She specializes in nineteenth-century American literature and is the author of the *Student Companion to Nathaniel Hawthorne* (1999).

Robert J. Scholnick, professor of English and American Studies, College of William and Mary, and former dean of their graduate school, publishes on nineteenth-century writers and culture, including *Edmund Clarence Stedman* in the Twayne series and a profile of Lizette Woodworth Reese in *Legacy*.

Carol J. Singley is associate professor of English at Rutgers University at Camden, coeditor of *Anxious Power: Reading, Writing, and Ambivalence in Narratives by Women*, and author of *Edith Wharton: Matters of Mind and Spirit*.

Cheryl B. Torsney, professor of English at West Virginia University, has published numerous articles on major American writers. She is the author of *Constance Fenimore Woolson: The Grief of Artistry* and editor of *Critical Essays on Constance Fenimore Woolson*, *Quilt Culture: Tracing the Pattern*, and the Dent edition of *Wings of the Dove*.

INDEX